A Brotherhood
of Memory

A Brotherhood of Memory

Jewish Landsmanshaftn in the New World

MICHAEL R. WEISSER

Basic Books, Inc., Publishers

NEW YORK

Library of Congress Cataloging-in-Publication Data

Weisser, Michael R.
    A brotherhood of memory.

    Includes index.
    1. Jews, East European — New York (N.Y.)—Societies,
etc.   2.   Jews—New York (N.Y.)—Societies, etc.
3.   Friendly societies—New York (N.Y.)   4.   Jews—Europe,
Eastern—Social conditions.   5.   New York (N.Y.)—Social
conditions.   6.   Europe, Eastern—Ethnic relations.
I.   Title.   II.   Title: Jewish landsmanshaftn.
III.   Title: Landsmanshaftn.
F128.9.J5W45   1985   974.7'1004924006   83-46077
ISBN 0-465-00779-1

To our treasure,

Mary Savetsky,

and to the beloved memory of

Joseph Savetsky

CONTENTS

PREFACE

THIS BOOK incorporates a unique methodology that I choose to call *bubbe mayse* history, or history as recounted by our grandparents. It is a mixture of facts, anecdotes, fairy tales, fables, innuendos, truths, half-truths, memories, experiences, and even some outright lies. It can be culled from the memory of any older person who, in living his or her life, has constantly shaped and reshaped a view of the world. It is also the stuff of which real history has always been made, serving as an explanation, a rationalization, and a justification of the present and the past.

When I set out to write this book, I knew intuitively that its success or failure would ultimately depend on my success in making use of this methodology. Not that a *bubbe mayse* replaces facts, nor can one ignore the obligation to search for truth. But if I were not attentive to *bubbe mayses*, their content and form, how could I produce a work that would accurately capture the identity of a group of people lodged deep within the consciousness of each of its members?

For the real purpose of this book is to tell a story about people—a true story, an accurate story, but most of all, a story, a *mayse*. The stories of these immigrants form part of a great historical drama, which has real meaning only if it portrays the hopes, dreams, disappointments, and delights of its participants. So the reader should be forewarned that while this book is a historical narrative, it does not use history to prove a point or render a judgment. It utilizes history and historical techniques to provide a context in which *bubbe mayses* can be readily understood.

The reader should understand that a *bubbe mayse* is a particular type of story told only to a particular type of audience: it is told only to those who understand it even before it is told. When Jewish immigrants get together, nobody lets anyone else finish a sentence because everyone knows what is about to be said. What might appear as rudeness in a different context here becomes a profound and intuitive sharing of culture, emotions, and ideas. This book invites the reader as well to share in that endless variety and vitality.

To rely on *bubbe mayses* requires the strength and sensitivity best provided by the resources of others. How can I thank my devoted parents, Saul and Jean Weisser, and my lovely and loving wife, Susan, for their parts in all this? How can I ever express my love to the great-grandparents and grandparents whose lives flow through me and on into the lives of my children and their children? These are the questions this book can hope to answer.

ACKNOWLEDGMENTS

THE FOLLOWING persons deserve special mention: David and Jonathan Leff, for providing documentary and personal evidence about their father; Joseph Masliansky and Norman Gilmovsky of the United Jewish Appeal; Rose Klepfisz, archivist of the Joint Distribution Committee; Samuel Norich, executive director, and Rosaline Schwartz, director of the Landsmanshaft Project, of the YIVO Institute for Jewish Research; Steve Fraser, senior editor at Basic Books, for his unfailing encouragement, support, and advice; Madeleine Santella for the use of the archive at Washington Cemetery; Paula Schaap for her research assistance; Mark Stempa, President of Mt. Zion Cemetery, for sharing his knowledge of and insights into Jewish burial practices and places in New York; Professor Seymour Spilerman for a critical reading of the text; James P. Lewis and Beth H. Israel for their numerous kindnesses; and Rabbis Jonathan Galef and Peter Knitzer for their profound commentaries on the state of all things.

ACKNOWLEDGMENTS

THE PEOPLE I wish to thank...

NOTE ON TRANSLATION
AND TRANSLITERATION

THE READER will notice that some of the quotations from English and Yiddish sources, both oral and written, depart from standard spelling and usage. They are directly transcribed from the actual source material, and are intended to maintain the style, flavor, and idiom of immigrant expression. In addition, the spelling of geographical terms and place names reflects variations in the immigrants' own Yiddish transliteration.

A Brotherhood
of Memory

Introduction

AROUND the year 1880, the first of several million East European Jews began leaving the cities, towns, and villages of their homeland in the Russian Pale. Crammed into oceangoing steamers, they ultimately disembarked at the port of New York. This enormous movement of people, which ended in 1923, would change forever the history of the Jews and indelibly alter the societies from where they came and where they settled. This "Great Migration" has been the subject of countless books, essays, dramas, poems, and songs. As with all historical events of this magnitude, however, looking beyond the obvious reveals whole areas yet to be explored and crucial questions yet to be answered.

The focus of this book is that part of the immigrant population which, after arriving in America, made the decision to avoid most of the paths and mechanisms open to all immigrants who desired to achieve some degree of assimilation within the New World culture. These were people who did not learn good English, rarely went to school, never had more than minimal contact with non-immigrants—in short, people who chose to remain fundamentally unassimilated by creating a social and economic environment that mirrored the environment out of which they had come. Of necessity, certain compromises were made between the old and the new; a certain degree of acculturation naturally took place. English was never a primary language, but its rudiments had to be learned or at least understood. Public education was irrelevant to their own lives but was a central element in the lives and development of their children. Indeed, comparing the experiences of unassimilated Jewish immigrants with the experiences of their totally assimilated descendants clarifies the extent to which American culture replaced traditional habits and beliefs in the passage from one generation to the next.

The process that allowed certain immigrants to remain outside the mainstream entailed more than a continuous rejection of the American way of life. More importantly, the process involved the conscious recreation of Old World activities, relationships, and patterns. The chief vehicle for accomplishing this task was the immigrant benevolent society, known in immigrant circles as a *landsmanshaft*. From the moment they came down the gangplank, most East European Jewish immigrants became involved in a landsmanshaft consisting of individuals from the same village *(shtetl)* or region in the Pale. The landsmanshaftn provided the initial point of contact with the New World and the initial point of departure from the Old. Its social and benevolent activities were a crucial means of supplying the basic psychic and cultural stability that was largely absent from the American experience.

Just as the immigrant population comprised an enormous diversity of groups, so there were many different types of landsmanshaftn. There were religious societies, which were adjuncts of synagogues and performed many of the ritual functions surrounding orthodox belief. There were vocational societies whose members were affiliated not only through geographical origin but also by participation in a certain occupation or trade. There were also many societies that did not require a specific geographical or *landsleit* connection among their members; these voluntary associations were in some instances nothing more than local social clubs.

Nearly every immigrant who came to America from the Pale was involved in one sort of voluntary association or another. But the independent landsmanshaftn, those organizations whose membership consisted only of persons from a particular place and were unaffiliated with any outside agency or institution, represented the largest single category of voluntary associations within the immigrant milieu. Of the more than 2 million Jewish immigrants who arrived in New York between 1880 and 1923, it is estimated that perhaps 1 million of them belonged to an independent landsmanshaft at some time in their lives.

Many—indeed, a majority—of the immigrants who joined these societies either quickly left them behind or did not actively participate in their affairs. The societies were viewed as relics of the Old World. They were considered politically conservative and culturally backward. If they helped an immigrant to retain his sense of the past, they did very little to prepare him for the challenges of the future. Active participation was anathema to those immigrants who were prepared to meet head-on the demands of the new society around them.

On the other hand, people who joined a landsmanshaft and kept it at the psychic core of their existence were at the same time rejecting the larger society and resisting its opportunities for assimilation. The landsmanshaftn offered the possibility of continuing the cultural and social traditions of the Old World in such an undiluted form that there was little ambiguity about cultural identity once a member decided to retain an active interest.

The problem of cultural ambiguity appears again and again in the history and mentality of American Jews. The contemporary debate over the Jewish-American stance toward Israel strongly echoes the debate that erupted among immigrant Jews over the entry of the United States into World War I. But the question of whether one is first a Jew or an American has never really involved the landsmanshaft population. They have stood outside the debate, just as they have remained beyond the pressures and tendencies of American society that pull most Jews in many different and sometimes conflicting directions.

This book deals with the questions and implications of assimilation through the medium of the landsmanshaftn. Chapter 1 establishes a social and historical definition of the landsmanshaftn in New York. Through the perceptions of the members of a single society, it illustrates the reasons why these organizations came into existence and why they are now on the verge of dying out. The century 1880–1980 spans the history of the New York landsmanshaftn, as well as the lifetimes of their membership.

Chapter 2 examines the social and historical roots of the landsmanshaftn in the villages, or shtetlach, of the East European Pale. Jewish life in Eastern Europe has been the subject of many works. What is new and different about the present book is that it attempts to analyze the shtetl from the perspective of those former residents who tried to maintain its basic qualities in a New World context.

Chapter 3 explores the beginnings of the landsmanshaftn after 1880 and traces their activities up to World War I. The chapter considers the societies within the wider context of the growth and development of New York. The world's

6

greatest city has yet to receive a comprehensive history, although specific periods and aspects of the topic have been examined. Perhaps the lack of an overall synthesis reflects the magnitude of the events themselves. Certainly the new immigrants could not fully comprehend the turmoil and chaos around them, a self-evident motivation for the organi- zation of social groupings like the landsmanshaftn.

Chapter 4 recounts the attempts by the landsmanshaftn to rescue relatives and friends from the war-torn and po- grom-wracked regions of the Pale. It illustrates why this heroic effort could only have been accomplished by groups in America that maintained intimate links with the Old World. To the extent that the landsmanshaftn were a con- scious recreation of the shtetl, they were also the primary vehicle for maintaining the connection back to the Pale.

Chapter 5 brings to a close the immigration period and shows how the ending of European immigration began to affect the Jewish (but no longer immigrant) community in New York. This chapter examines the failure of American Jews to recreate the communal organization of the Old World, a reflection of the extent to which the Jewish com- munity in New York was beginning to lose its European roots. The chapter also shows how the landsmanshaft popu- lation retained its own sense of communalism through the maintenance of certain customs and activities, most notably funerals and cemeteries, which no other part of the immi- grant community was equally able to provide.

Chapter 6 recounts the heroic attempts by the landsman- shaftn to rescue the remnants of their homeland following the devastations of the Holocaust and World War II. But the story in this chapter has a different twist from the analogous events in chapter 4. The landsmanshaftn were no longer a major force in the immigrant community, and the Europe of

1945 was not the Europe of 1918. The rescue effort after World War II took a form much different from the earlier episode and had decidedly different results.

Chapter 7 moves the reader back to the 1920s and picks up the themes discussed in chapter 5. It examines how changes in the urban economy and society widened the cleavage between the landsmanshaftn and the rest of the Jewish community, as well as between the original immigrants and their own descendants. Just as the book begins with a discussion of the reasons for the birth of the landsmanshaftn during the Great Migration, so this chapter ends with a discussion of the demise of the landsmanshaftn during the past several years.

Chapter 8 brings the book full circle, returning to the benevolent society that occupies the central portion of chapter 1. We left that society in the midst of a great problem, and this chapter shows how it will be resolved. The intervening chapters have provided the reader with a historical context in which the resolution of the problem can now be fully understood.

This book tells why a certain group of people chose to live their lives in a way we probably cannot fully comprehend. The lack of comprehension is reflected in the fact that the voluminous writings about immigrants hardly mention these people at all. Most sociological and historical analyses of ethnicity deal primarily with the pace of assimilation from the perspective of those who assimilated. We argue about how fast different immigrant groups moved up the socioeconomic ladder, but with few exceptions, we largely ignore those groups that, consciously or unconsciously, remained on the first rung. But there is much to be said about those who acculturated at a slower pace; their responses to the opportunities of American life are usually explained by saying either that they did not possess the necessary social and cultural equipment or that realistic opportunities did not present themselves.

Yet just as Jewish immigrants who formed landsman-shaftn have remained outside the debate on Jewish-American identity, so they have remained outside the boundaries of the debate on assimilation. This is because, from their point of view, the ladder never existed at all. Consequently, this book can avoid making judgments about the "success" or "failure" of their lives, just as these immigrants never seriously entertained such judgments about themselves. We can examine their strengths and weaknesses on their own terms.

We live in an age that celebrates self-reliance and self-sufficiency. As we shall see, the landsmanshaftn members were paragons of these ideals. But they did not necessarily arrive at these values in positive fashion. A large part of their resistance to the society around them grew not out of hope but out of fear. In placing limits on their degree of involvement with the larger society, they placed severe limits on themselves. These limitations flowed out of the experiences of their pre-migration existence. They came to a free land, but they did not arrive free of their past experiences. As a result, America could never offer them the freedom to choose.

I

Face the Future,
Face the Past

> The name of this organization shall be "First
> Przemysler Sick Benefit Society," which name
> shall never be altered as long as seven members
> in good standing shall insist on retaining same.
> —Article 1 of the Przemysler Society
> Constitution

ON A SUNDAY in March 1980, the officers and members of the Boyerker Benevolent Society came together for their monthly meeting at the United Jewish Appeal building on 59th Street in New York City. While their daughters shopped in Bloomingdale's and their sons tended suburban lawns, this small group of elderly Jews met as they had been meeting for sixty years, and as they would continue to meet until the life of their society came to an end.

When the Boyerker Society was first organized, there were nearly 150 members and their families. Today the active members number only a handful, but they press on with the society's business as usual. The agenda of the meetings of the Boyerker Society is always the same: first old business (as we shall see, there is always *something* that can never be settled to everyone's satisfaction), then new business, which means who is sick, who has moved to Florida, who has returned from Florida, and who (God forbid) has died. The meeting always begins with a spirited, if off-key, rendition of "Hatikvah" and the "Star-Spangled Banner" (the latter anthem is hummed, since nobody knows the words) and ends with an announcement about the next meeting.

The Boyerker Benevolent Society consists of the former residents (landsleit) and descendants of the little shtetl of Boyerke, a village of fewer than 300 families located somewhere near Kiev in the Russian Ukraine. A member of the society was once asked whether the shtetl was east or west of Kiev. He answered with a characteristically indifferent shrug, "East or west, what's the difference?" Actually, there was no difference. If the shtetl of Boyerke lay east of Kiev, no doubt another forlorn little shtetl of similar size lay to the west. The Russian Ukraine was part of the Pale of Settlement, which stretched from the Baltic provinces in the north to the Black Sea ports in the south and enclosed the endlessly contested borders of Russia and Poland. The shtetl of Boyerke was just another tiny dot on the map of Jewish existence in the Pale that would not survive the Cossack and Nazi onslaughts of the twentieth century.

Beginning around 1900 (as near as anyone still alive can remember or figure out), a few people left the village year by year to make the great journey to America. There is an unverified allegation that one resident of the shtetl, a certain Stavisky, did not go to America but traveled instead to Switzerland, thence to Paris, and ultimately became involved in the infamous political scandal that bears his name. Another of the village's former residents, so it is said, was a rabbi and freethinker who was expelled from the territory by the local rabbinical hierarchy. Eventually he found his way to Buenos

Aires, where he supposedly became chief rabbi of Argentina or perhaps only chief rabbi of Buenos Aires (but what's the difference?). These two individuals, in fancy or fact, were the exceptions. Most of the residents of Boyerke stayed put until the shtetl was pillaged during a pogrom in 1919, whereupon many of the survivors escaped to America and reconstituted their Old World ties through the medium of the Boyerker Benevolent Society.

The Boyerker Society, known as a landsmanshaft, was a small but fairly typical example of the thousands of immigrant benevolent societies organized by East European Jews in the aftermath of their arrival and settlement in America. Beginning with the formation of the Bialystok Mutual Aid Society in 1864, East European immigrant Jews organized landsmanshaftn representing nearly every city, town, and village that sent residents to America between 1870 and 1923. A few of these landsmanshaftn, like the Pruskurower Society, blossomed into huge, umbrella-like organizations. The Pruskurower Society embraced several thousand members and was divided into sixteen distinct organizations with specific social and benevolent functions. The Pruskurower Society even had a number of branch societies in other cities. The United Brisker Relief Society, comprising at one time eight affiliated organizations, had branches in Newark, Detroit, Chicago, Cleveland, and Los Angeles. The former residents of Bialystok eventually constituted eleven separate organizations, including three societies for members who were bricklayers, cutters, or cloakmakers, as well as distinct societies for landsleit who lived in Brooklyn and the Bronx.

Within the immigrant community there were hundreds of benevolent organizations and groups that carried out many of the selfsame activities as the landsmanshaftn but whose membership was not based on any strict landsleit connec-

12

tion. Most of the Jewish labor unions had benevolent societies, as did the various fraternal orders. Individuals engaged in the same trade or profession similarly formed benevolent associations and social clubs. But the independent landsmanshaftn, whose criteria for membership and participation flowed nearly exclusively from the landsleit connection, were different from all these other groups.

The overwhelming majority of landsmanshaftn were on the scale of the Boyerker Benevolent Society or even smaller. They were loose-knit organizations whose formal structures (constitutions, bylaws, officers, and so forth) belied a friendly informality. Their membership was drawn nearly exclusively from the former residents of a particular shtetl or group of shtetlach, and their chief aim consisted of maintaining the traditional and comfortable social relations of the Old World milieu. In the words of a member of the Storonitzer Society, the organization was a "home away from home."[1]

Most of the smaller landsmanshaftn were amalgams of the many voluntary associations in the shtetl, known as *chevras.* Every village had a burial society, the *chevra kadisha,* which was affiliated with the synagogue. If there was more than one synagogue, which was usually the case except in the poorest and most woebegone shtetl, there was also more than one burial society. In the larger and more prosperous villages or towns, the burial society was sometimes a wealthy organization, and it was a mark of social prominence as well as a reflection of great piety to belong to it. The members of the *chevra kadisha* were responsible for arranging the funeral, gathering a *minyan* (group of ten males) to recite the *Kaddish* (prayer for the deceased), and supervising the *shivah* (mourning period) which followed the funeral itself. The shtetl also had a chevra that collected and dispensed charity, a chevra

13

that enforced dietary laws, and possibly a chevra that arranged matrimonials. Shtetl society was bound together by a series of communal functions, and each function had its own chevra. In the New World, many landsmanshaftn began as adjuncts of the small orthodox synagogues that sprang up in every immigrant neighborhood. But just as quickly as they were formed, many of these chevras split, with the "independent" faction forming its own landsmanshaft to carry on benevolent and social activities.

The Landsmanshaft Impulse

The phenomenon of people reconstituting their traditional social groupings and relationships when thrust into an alien environment far from home is not limited to the experience of immigrants in America. When the young Karl Marx first enrolled at the University of Bonn in 1835, he immediately joined the student landsmanshaft of his native town of Trier. Soldiers in the Russian army during World War I formed village societies and utilized contacts within these organizations to circumvent official censorship and keep abreast of news from the home front. The need to form such organizations was exemplified by a Russian peasant proverb: "When your son goes into the army, bid him goodbye, because you will never see him again."

Every East European (and Southern European) immigrant population that came to America during the nineteenth century formed benevolent and social organizations in order to maintain cultural and physical ties to its land of origin. The Italians, the Greeks, the Poles, and the Ukrainians all utilized their social and benevolent associations as a "hedge" against

14

the vagaries of immigrant life in New York. But no ethnic group became so completely involved in landsleit-type activities as did the Jews from Eastern Europe. By 1923, at the tail end of the Great Migration, more than a million persons, or one of every two Jewish immigrants, had been enrolled at one time or another in a New York landsmanshaft.

What was it about the character of these Jewish landsleit organizations that allowed them to embrace such a large proportion of the East European immigrant population? The most essential component, of course, was the cultural affinity of the membership, expressed most directly through the instrument of a common language. For many elderly immigrants today, the earliest recollections of life in America involve the frustration of being unable to surmount the language barrier. One man, now in his eighties, who has still not completely mastered his adopted tongue, remembers entering a restaurant but being unable to order anything until the counterman asked him if he would like "coffee and apple pie." For days thereafter, desperate to disguise his linguistic shortcomings, he subsisted on a regimen of coffee and apple pie, an experience which became a stock-in-trade joke on the early Yiddish vaudeville circuit. The language problem meant that a newly arrived immigrant, a "greenhorn," could not travel through the city, could not secure a place to live by himself, and could not look for a job outside his immediate circle of immigrant friends.

Today it is difficult for us to comprehend the trauma of culture shock initially experienced by Jewish and other European immigrants who arrived at the turn of the century. We live in an age when government at all levels provides social welfare services to a degree totally unknown before the 1930s. Most of these welfare services, to the extent they were provided at all for the immigrant population, grew out of private, voluntary charitable activities that were largely undertaken by the immigrants themselves; such private programs were woefully inadequate. It should also be recalled that immigration is now a "normal" phenomenon within the context of American history, but this was not the case when East European immigrants began arriving in massive numbers several decades before the end of the nineteenth century. New York City contained a majority of German and Anglo-Saxon residents in 1880, despite the significant influx of Irish immigrants since 1840. The pattern of German and Anglo-Saxon predominance was then entirely upset by successive waves of new immigrants, a phenomenon that continues up to the present day.

At the time of their arrival, Jews and other immigrants from Eastern and Southern Europe found little official acceptance of their presence or recognition of their problems. Consequently, they were forced to rely on their own ingenuity and on a fragile network of relatives and friends who had faced and solved similar problems alongside or shortly before them. Jewish immigrants often secured their first employment by means of a landsmanshaft, either directly, through a society member who offered work and utilized the landsmanshaft as an informal employment agency, or indirectly, through information gleaned at a society meeting about where to look for a job. Similarly, the landsmanshaftn were social clearinghouses, providing the essential contact point between families who were looking for a place to live and those who needed to take in boarders in order to "make" the rent.

Perhaps even more important than providing social and economic contacts during the crucial period immediately after arrival, the landsmanshaftn maintained the bonds between new immigrants and their families who had been left behind in the shtetl. By making the arrangements for the arduous journey to America and by providing a temporary refuge for the immigrant once the trip was completed, a landsmanshaft formed a necessary conduit for the physical and psychic transition from one culture to another. One elderly immigrant recalls how his steamer arrived in New York harbor and he was transferred to a small launch for the trip to Ellis Island. He was literally herded into a large building where he sat on a bench for several hours until his name, William Post, was called out. As he walked toward the desk where an official sat who had called his name, he recognized two landsleit from his village who had come to America before him. They were waiting for him behind a fence on the other side of the desk. Within an hour, he was standing outside Castle Garden at the Battery with his two friends, who then took him by subway to Grand Central Station and gave him a railroad ticket with instructions to join his brother in a small town in Vermont(!). "My brother had gone to Vermont to get a job," Post recalled many years later, "and he didn't have time to write to me in the Ukraine before I left. He was supposed to meet me at the boat, but he sent these two landsleit in his place. If they hadn't come, I would still be sitting on Ellis Island."

Even allowing for a bit of hyperbole, this immigrant's comment exemplifies the extent to which the landsman-shaftn and the landsleit network were crucial ingredients in the initial transition and resettlement experience of Jewish immigrants. Before, during, and after the immigrants' arrival, the landsmanshaftn formed a base, a cultural and psychic refuge in which the daily events, successes, frustrations, and failures of the immigrant experience could be evaluated and understood. The landsmanshaftn were collective data banks, so to speak, which allowed immigrants a margin of safety and security in a world that hardly any immigrant was equipped to comprehend.

Another elderly immigrant related the following story. Within a week after coming to New York, he went with a cousin to the meeting of his landsmanshaft. After the meeting was over, he followed his cousin onto the subway for the ride home. He did not yet have a job or a permanent place to live. In fact, he had been sleeping in a cot in the hallway outside his cousin's apartment. After the train had passed two stations, it pulled into a third stop, the doors opened, and a policeman stepped onto the car. The newly arrived immigrant, a "greenhorn," cowered behind his cousin-protector at the rear of the car, fearful that the police officer might ask him to produce identity papers which he, of course, did not possess. After a moment, the cousin became conscious of the newcomer's sense of panic, and speaking to him in a voice loud enough to be heard throughout the car, said, "What are you worried about? This is America. You left the tsarist police behind." Much to the embarrassment of the new arrival, the anecdote was retold amid much laughter and derision at the meeting of the landsmanshaft the following week.

Although many immigrants considered the landsmanshaft to be a refuge and salvation, for others the societies were a brief and sometimes bothersome experience. Before being transplanted to America, the East European Jewish population was divided between small-town and large-city dwellers. Although initially unfamiliar with the language and customs of their new society, those who came from the urban ghettos of Poland, Rumania, and Russia had already been exposed to the rigors and rhythms of city life and city work. They were, in general, much more sophisticated than their "country cousins," usually better educated, more secular in outlook, and better prepared to confront the modern American experience on its own terms. In many instances, Jewish immigrants from European urban ghettos were politically advanced—radicalized through trade union and Zionist affiliations in Eastern Europe, activities they continued after their arrival in New York.

A precise chronology of the successive waves of immigration from the various regions of the Pale would be impossible to construct, but interviews with surviving immigrants provide some clues as to the geographic and social backgrounds of those who came during different stages of the Great Migration. It appears that a majority of those who came to America from the Pale before 1900 had lived in the cities or in the larger towns and villages. They might have started life in a small shtetl, but generally they had lived and worked in a more sophisticated urban environment before making the crossing to America. Consequently, many of these earlier arrivals had already discarded some of the more obvious manifestations of shtetl culture before they got off the boat. This is an irony of sorts, because East European Jews who began arriving in New York after 1880 were regarded as backward, vulgar, and barely civilized by the old-line German Jews who had settled in New York in previous decades.

The real hard-core shtetl population, particularly from the smallest villages, did not begin arriving in large numbers until the first decades of the twentieth century, culminating in a massive wave of shtetl dwellers who managed to escape after the pogroms of 1919–21. While Jews from the larger cities and towns often made conscious decisions to migrate to America, or had experienced at least a taste of "modern" life before their departure, residents of the small, more isolated shtetlach often ran from their homes on a moment's notice with the dreaded Cossacks at their rear. They had not made preparations to leave the old way of life behind them, nor were they prepared to face the new way of life that lay ahead.

The immigrants from urban backgrounds, on the other hand, regarded the shtetl and its residents with a mixture of disdain and contempt, and they manifested similar attitudes toward the landsmanshaftn that represented the survival of the shtetl in the New World. It was a common belief, not without substance, that the landsmanshaftn were utilized by Jewish employers as a means of exploiting workers and breaking or retarding the growth of class consciousness and unionism in the shops. Entrepreneurs openly appealed to a worker's landsmanshaft loyalties and expected that such sentiments would win out over claims to labor solidarity.[2] In reaction to these attitudes, immigrants arriving in America with a background in shops and factories quickly developed other organizations, such as labor unions, to defend their interests.

Thus, the landsmanshaftn were not the only—or even the most important—institutions serving the vital needs of the immigrant Jews. An evaluation of the role played by the landsmanshaftn within the immigrant community must ultimately hinge on a consideration of the needs of the landsmanshaft constituency. For just as the landsmanshaftn have remained outside the scrutiny of scholars, so the population that formed the bulwark of landsmanshaft membership has also been largely ignored in the literature dealing with Jewish immigrants and their experiences in American society.

Our image of immigrant Jews and their history consists primarily of those immigrant "types" who successfully acculturated themselves into the mainstream of American life.

The American social ethos has been predicated on success, achievement, and mobility, and many Jewish immigrants have typified this pattern over the course of their lives. Consequently, experiences of immigrants who were unable or unwilling to adapt to a new way of life have been obscured by a literature that celebrates the opposite pattern.[3] For immigrants who genuinely regarded the New World not as a place of unbounded opportunity but simply as a place where they might survive, few organizations offered a degree of support to equal the landsmanshaft. The majority of landsmanshaft members, especially members of smaller groups like the Boyerker Society, were too unprepared—culturally and psychically—to develop social contacts in America beyond the circle of safe and secure relationships that were extensions of their lives in the shtetl.

Many of the social attitudes and customs of the shtetl reappeared and were retained within the landsmanshaftn, long after they had been stripped of any possible rationale within the context of American life. For example, one small landsmanshaft was run for years by a cantankerous elderly widower whose bookkeeping and secretarial skills left much to be desired. Despite the fact that his petty mistakes and innocent errors had incurred heavy liabilities for the society in federal tax court on more than one occasion, nobody dared suggest that he vacate his position of leadership. Along with making a shambles of the books and correspondence, this landsmanshaft "general" had also proved to be an incorrigible gossip and meddler in the personal affairs of other members, to the point of provoking severe annoyance and outright distress on many occasions over his long years of tenured leadership. In the face of defections from the ranks of the society by younger, more modern-minded members who could not abide the heavy-handed tactics of the President-Secretary (his official title), the original members of this organization persisted in according their chief an almost universal, if somewhat grudging, respect. When old age finally robbed him of his faculties and he was placed in a "home," the surviving members of the society went to inordinate lengths to avoid naming a permanent successor, leaving the presidency officially vacant until he passed away. Asked to explain the situation, one of the members said (with several other old-timers nodding vigorously in the background): "His father was the *melamed* (teacher) in the village. To remove him from his position would have been a great insult. How could we dishonor the memory of the man who educated us all?"

The landsmanshaft recreated the world and values of the shtetl. For those shtetl dwellers who had not left their native villages willingly, and were thus totally unprepared for the trauma of immigration and resettlement, the landsmanshaftn became the fundamental mechanism for retaining their social and psychic equilibrium. This reconstitution of village life was manifested through a variety of primitive welfare activities. There was a sick or provident fund, which carried on functions similar to the welfare chevras in the shtetl. Each society purchased and administered a cemetery, whose importance was like that of the shtetl cemetery described by the Yiddish storyteller Sholom Aleichem as "a treasure, a rare gem, a piece of wealth,"[4] even though it was usually an unkempt, overcrowded, and overgrown patch of ground on the edge of town. The society brought people together for marriage in a manner very similar to that of the traditional marriage broker, and it arranged for employment and a place to live with the same degree of paternal concern that had characterized these activities in the shtetl. But the essential function of a landsmanshaft was much less obvious, and could only be discerned through a sensitivity to the habits and consciousness of its members. The society became a means for prolonging the attitudes and beliefs that had shaped the culture of the shtetl, beliefs that were the fundamental signposts for the survival of its inhabitants in the New World. "We all got together," says one landsmanshaft member, explaining the origins of his society in typically self-effacing style, "because that's all we knew how to do anyhow."

For Jews It Was Different

To the extent that the benevolent societies of other immigrant groups were responsible for maintaining and continually reasserting the traditional culture, there were few immediate differences between the roles played by Slavic or Greek benevolent societies and the role played by the landsmanshaftn in Jewish immigrant life. Old World patterns of thought and behavior were as important to one ethnic group as to another; family and kinship relations were the bedrock upon which all alien groups relied when forced to confront the demands of a new society to which they were at first only marginal elements.

By the end of the Great Migration, however, one crucial difference had emerged between the landsmanshaftn and the other immigrant benevolent societies. For the Poles, Italians, Greeks, and other ethnic European populations, the initial voyage to America was often just the first of many such trips that they and their families would undertake between Old and New worlds over the course of their lifetimes. To be an Italian, Polish, or Greek immigrant frequently meant taking a deliberate but temporary absence from one's native village, coming over to the new country but never losing contact with one's roots. During the 1920s, for example, the Polish National Alliance enrolled thousands of Polish-Americans in yearly trips back to Poland. After World War II, the Christian-Democratic Party in Italy utilized campaign literature which featured an appeal for votes by none other than Joe DiMaggio.

For most European immigrants, America may have been a "land of opportunity," but the opportunity existed only in a relative sense. One might make more money in America, but the ultimate mark of success was to save enough money to retire in one's native land. The connection to the original village in Cephalonia or Sicily was never broken, nor was the initial departure conceived of as permanent. Natives of a village in Italy or Greece came over to work in America, went back to the other side to take a bride, returned to America to raise a family, then went home again to live out their final years, a pattern that persists up to the present day. The benevolent societies formed by most Central and East European immigrant populations were simply a mechanism to ensure the survival of the Old World–New World connection, rather than a mechanism for ensuring survival in the New World itself.

For Jewish immigrants from Eastern Europe, particularly in the aftermath of World War I, the situation was entirely different. Up to the eve of World War I, the Pale remained a homeland for most Jewish immigrants to America, and there was continuous contact between those who still lived in the shtetl and those who had made the journey to America. Not every shtetl family could claim kin in the New World prior to 1914, but the population of every shtetl knew about America, knew some relative, neighbor, or friend with relations in America, and possessed some vague (if not entirely realistic) idea about what life was like on the other side. Letters, photos, and packages were exchanged between the village and America, and on occasion a transplanted resident might return to get married or aid some relatives who were trying to get out.

The pogroms of 1919–21 definitively altered that state of affairs. When the massacres came to an end, the Pale was no longer a homeland for Jewish emigrants in the way that Greece and Italy were still homelands for their former residents now living in New York. Many of the smaller shtetlach had disappeared entirely, and many of those that remained were now enclosed within the domains of a Russian Bolshevik regime which shut down the borders and discouraged movement either in or out of its territories. Consequently, of all the immigrant groups that came to America during the Great Migration, the Jews of Eastern Europe were the one population that finally could not contact or go back to its native land. Every immigrant group came to America hungry and impoverished, and most immigrants viewed America as the place of escape from a life of deprivation. But along with the economic and social pressures that led other ethnic populations to migrate to America, the Jews of Eastern Europe carried with them an additional burden. For they constituted the one group of immigrants whose movement away from their homeland resulted from a conscious policy of extermination and expulsion. They were the one immigrant population in America that could never return home.

It has been estimated that approximately 6 million Jews inhabited the Pale between 1880 and 1920. By the end of the Great Migration, 2 million were crammed into the urban ghettos or survived in the ravaged countryside of the Pale; 2 million had perished from hunger, disease, and pogroms;

and 2 million had made the journey to a new life in America.[5] An interesting statistic culled from immigration records underscores the unique circumstances surrounding the Jewish migration. From 1889 to 1910, the proportion of males to females among Jewish immigrants arriving in New York was 58–42, and nearly 25 percent of all Jewish immigrants were under the age of 14.[6] These figures clearly indicate that Jewish immigrants arrived overwhelmingly as family units. No other immigrant population exhibited such a high proportion of females or brought so many children along with them. Other immigrant groups could afford to leave women and children behind until minimal requirements for food and shelter had been met. The Jews from Eastern Europe did not enjoy the "luxury" of beginning life in New York as single people, free of immediate family responsibilities until work and residence had been established. Jews arrived as family units and were forced to seek permanent settlement from the moment they stepped off the boat. This only served to increase the difficulties inherent in the immigrant experience.

There were still many shtetlach and many shtetl Jews in the Pale after World War I and the pogroms, but economic, social, and political conditions in the Pale effectively eradicated this zone as a base from which immigrants could freely leave or a haven to which they could return. The Jews who came to America from Eastern Europe knew from the moment they arrived that the Old World was no longer a safety valve in case things did not work out as planned. As the shtetl began to disappear in a physical sense, the landsmanshaftn became replacements for the Old World community, as well as repositories for an entire social and cultural tradition. Living in an alien environment, totally cut off from their origins, the Jews of Eastern Europe had a special need to recreate the psychic bonds that had defined a traditional way of life. For other immigrant populations, benevolent societies functioned as conduits between New World and Old World communities. The landsmanshaftn, on the other hand, functioned as the Old World community *within* the New World.

Not only were the landsmanshaftn distinct from other ethnic societies, but they also operated in contrast to and sometimes open conflict with Jewish organizations established to hasten the process of acculturation and assimilation. When large numbers of unkempt, impoverished, and totally alien Jewish immigrants first stepped onto the piers of New York harbor, the established (and Establishment) German-Jewish community overcame its antipathy toward these new arrivals and began the process of educating the "inferior" masses. Out of this approach arose the movement to establish settlement houses, of which the earliest was the Educational Alliance, formed as a "downtown" branch of the Young Men's Hebrew Association in 1893.[7] The staff of the Educational Alliance, which had earlier included Emma Lazarus ("Give me your tired, your poor, . . ."), was imbued with a mission to Americanize the immigrants through linguistic education and vocational training. Success in this enterprise was gauged by the extent to which the overt customs and habits of the shtetl could be made to disappear. Jewish labor organizations such as the International Ladies' Garment Workers Union (ILGWU), the Fur Workers' Union, and the Amalgamated Clothing Workers Union also sought to indoctrinate modern ideas and progressive attitudes into the minds of their newest members.

The landsmanshaftn chose a different route. Most societies ignored the obvious manifestations of Americanization, although some degree of accommodation with the realities of the situation could not be ignored. The lands-manshaftn usually avoided the organized political activities that characterized other immigrant organizations, such as the national confederation of unions that allied under the banner of the socialist Workmen's Circle. The landsman-shaftn manifested no desire to deal with the present except in terms that continuously reaffirmed a collective memory of the past. To the extent that the landsmanshaftn helped their members acclimate to the demands of a new society, they contributed to their members' survival, but survival was not the same thing as success. If anything, adherence to the ideals of the landsmanshaft became an obstacle to the pro-cess of learning how to define and cope with a new way of life.

The values of the landsmanshaftn were the values of the shtetl. Maintenance of tradition and a generalized fear of change were the premises of shtetl existence, acted out within a context in which self-denial, minimum expecta-tions, avoidance of risk, and a conviction that life would never be different from one generation to the next were self-fulfilling prophecies. Life in America, as future genera-tions discovered, offered a profound contrast to these values, since it was based largely on materialism, self-gain, and the denial of attitudes that might limit aspirations for advance-ment from one generation to the next. Membership in a landsmanshaft, on the other hand, not only prolonged the attachment to friends and relatives who represented the Old World society, but it also sustained an emotional and cul-tural world view that created a barrier against adapting to the new culture.

To a certain extent, landsmanshaft members did make compromises with the realities of American life and style, but they picked and chose the areas of compromise according to the narrow perceptions of their previous existence. In their own lives, landsmanshaft members had to choose between different sets of values; they could not retain the warm and secure sense of the Old World if they wanted to participate fully in the New. The structures of life, work, and thought in America were simply too different from those of the shtetl, too distinct and too alien for any real degree of accommodation. So the immigrants had to make a choice, and those who chose a landsmanshaft as their basic social milieu usually turned their backs on the alternative.

A salient example of the refusal to relinquish Old World attitudes except at great personal cost is provided by the life of Harold Benjamin, a member of a small landsmanshaft formed by immigrants from a little town in Galicia. Born at the turn of the century, Benjamin came to America in 1912. Having been apprenticed in the shtetl to an eyeglass maker, he soon found work grinding lenses in a small shop in midtown New York City. Over the next four decades he worked for a succession of petty entrepreneurs, all of whom were either fellow landsleit or natives from adjacent villages in the Pale. During this entire period, he never worked in a shop without being able to carry on all conversation with his fellow employees in Yiddish. Furthermore, he several times turned his back on opportunities to make more money in larger concerns because the prospective employers were either Americanized Jews or, what was worse, gentiles. In 1961, Benjamin's more assimilated and more successful older brother, who had formed a partnership with several non-Jews, managed to convince Harold to come to work in his enterprise. Acting against the advice of all his landsmanshaft friends, Benjamin accepted the offer. The arrangement lasted for less than a year, and when it ended, the relationship with his brother broke off in bitterness and rancor. Benjamin was able to find another job in the shop of a former employer. There he worked until he retired in 1969, earning a maximum salary in his last year of $280 a week.

Sitting on the veranda of a rundown but homey little hotel in Miami Beach some years later, Benjamin summed up the whole experience: "My friends told me it wouldn't work out, and they were right. My brother and I were different, that's all. He made money and I didn't, he knew how to talk in English and I still talked in Yiddish. He couldn't take me downstairs to meet his *goyishe* friends. I had the choice to go with my brother and learn a new way or stay put and do things the way they had always been done. Thank God I still have my health."

This is not to say that Benjamin's choice was necessarily made in a positive fashion. Many immigrants like him remained within the landsmanshaft milieu as a negative defense against the challenges of a new society. The primary impulse that often kept people within their landsmanshaft circle was fear: fear of the outside world, fear of the unknown, fear of doing anything that might leave them vulnerable to another wave of violence, dislocation, and decimation.

The daughter of immigrant parents tells a typical story about how her parents' fears shaped their perceptions of life and limited her own: "My parents arrived in New York from Rumania in 1910, and I was born in 1917. I went to Hunter College and received a master's degree, which was rare for a woman in those days. In 1942 the war was on and I was offered a government job in Washington. Why didn't I take it? Because my parents refused to let me move to Washington, let alone move out of their apartment in Boro Park. I remember saying to my father, 'I can get home from Washington in six hours by train,' and he replied, 'You go to Washington and we'll never see you again.' "

Looking Forward by Looking Back

Backward-looking in character, the landsmanshaftn quickly fell out of step with the trends and directions of the immigrant Jewish experience in the United States. Despite some dispute over causes and results, there is no denying that first- and second-generation American-born Jews succeeded in assimilating into the mainstream of American society. By 1900 the Lower East Side was no longer the "last stop" for East European immigrant Jews, and by 1920 it was no longer even the first stop for many new arrivals. Sophie Drucker, who came from Poland after World War I, recalls that her parents went straight from the dock to an apartment in the Bronx, and she did not see the Lower East Side until she was taken to the Yiddish theater many months later. This experience was not atypical of immigrants who came over from the Pale after the turn of the century.

The social and economic mobility of immigrant Jews and their children in the decades after World War I, and to a much greater extent after World War II, is hardly a new story. Sophie Drucker was born in a shtetl in 1902. She was married in 1924, and her two children were born in 1926 and 1929. The children enrolled at City College and NYU in 1944 and 1946, respectively, and by the 1970s her grandchildren, reared in the suburbs of Long Island, were attending college at the University of Chicago, UCLA, and Cornell. Meanwhile, her two children, both professionals, faced such difficult decisions as choosing between a winter vacation in the Bahamas or a summer trip overseas (to which their mother always remarked, "I never felt the need to go back"). The story of these three generations may seem overly stereotypical, but it is not without foundation in the experience of many immigrant and American-born Jews.

While the shtetl mentality of the landsmanshaftn exerted a limiting influence on the assimilation and Americanization of their members, those limitations do not appear to have been passed on to succeeding generations. The same people who were most reluctant and resistant to accommodate themselves to the influences of American society proved willing and able to push their descendants into the mainstream of American life. They propelled them into education, into professional careers, onto a variety of paths that led both upward and outward from their own, marginal existences in the inner-city neighborhoods of New York. The result was the development of a dichotomy between the European-born immigrants and their American-born descendants, opening up great possibilities for the latter while posing profound difficulties, at times, for the former.

To gain a clearer perspective on this problem, let us return to the meeting of the Boyerker Society in March 1980. During the meeting an especially troublesome issue was debated at great length. The voices were often emotional, and to an outsider who did not understand Yiddish, some members of the society might have seemed quite angry. The debate went on for several hours, with members being interrupted and even shouted down. On several occasions the president of the society banged his gavel repeatedly in a vain attempt to restore order, then gave up any sense of decorum and simply screamed for quiet (to no avail). Like many of the smaller landsmanshaftn, the Boyerker Society had adhered over the years to its own version of *Robert's Rules of Order*, which consisted of yielding the floor to whoever could yell the loudest.

The debate finally subsided because of the exhaustion of the participants. The question was not resolved, nor would it be resolved in the near future. The issues were very complex and perhaps incapable of resolution or even comprehension by this small group of elderly people. This is because the problem, in all its implications, represented in microcosm the sum of sixty years of life in an alien culture.

It should be noted that, petty welfare schemes aside, the Boyerker Society, like most of the smaller landsmanshaftn, had existed primarily as a debating society. The members argued about jobs and housing in the 1920s and 1930s, about World War II and Israel in the 1940s and 1950s, about children and grandchildren in the 1960s and 1970s (especially the 1960s). But now they have reached the 1980s, and many of the earlier problems have either solved themselves or become irrelevant over the passage of time. The current argument was no longer about jobs, except to marvel at those few hardy old-timers who were still working part-time ("off the books") to supplement "the Social Security." The argument was not about housing, since the surviving members of the society had long ago laid claim to comfortable, rent-controlled apartments in the Bronx or had been ensconced in South Florida condominiums through the generous impulses of their children. The argument was not about Israel, because the society was recognized de facto as a chapter of the United Jewish Appeal and always made an annual contribution to the Jewish state. The argument was not even about children, because most of the children were by this time grandparents themselves, and nobody could talk sense into grandchildren. The argument for the 1980s was about space. This was not an argument about the space required to "do your own thing," or about the space necessary to help develop that "special relationship." It was an argument about cemetery space, and it had reached a critical point.

Sometime in the late 1920s, shortly after the Boyerker Society was organized, a burial plot was purchased in Beth David Cemetery in Elmont, Long Island, right on the border of Queens and Nassau counties (see map on page 165). The purchase and maintenance of cemeteries was the chief function of the landsmanshaftn from their beginnings, and even though the Boyerker was a smallish society, the members felt compelled to acquire their own private cemetery. Until 1947, individuals or groups could purchase plots in cemeteries in New York; each plot was regarded as the private property of the owner. The plot could hold as many graves as the owner(s) desired, and burial within the plot could be limited to any particular family or group. The plot purchased by the Boyerker in Beth David was just one of several thousand such plots sold to landsmanshaftn and other communal organizations. Within the boundaries of their own private cemetery, members of the Boyerker Society could stand on hallowed ground which was truly their own.

At the time the plot was purchased, Queens was the frontier of New York City, and Nassau County in the modern sense did not even exist. Not a single member of the Boyerker Society even lived in Queens, and in fact many sections of that borough were still off limits to Jewish residence. But many members of the Boyerker were moving into neighborhoods in Brooklyn, such as Bensonhurst and East New York, and these areas were not that far from the Queens border. Although nobody lived near the cemetery, it was accessible from the city, and the land was relatively cheap. Rather than paying higher prices for space at one of the older, more established cemeteries in Cypress Hills, the Boyerker Society, always a little more in step with the times than other landsmanshaftn, purchased land for 320 graves in Beth David.

Initially, the cemetery in Elmont was entirely adequate for the society's needs. Most of the original members of the Boyerker were in their twenties and thirties (now difficult to imagine), and the cemetery was utilized at first only to bury a few aged parents and grandparents who had not long survived the rigors of escape from Russia or the trauma of resettlement in America. In fact, the cemetery primarily served as a memorial to and a symbol of the original shtetl of Boyerke, for every year the members of the society took the occasion to gather at Beth David for a service to honor their fellow villagers who had perished in the pogroms of 1919–21. In 1930 the society erected a granite monument in the rear of the cemetery listing the names of all the martyrs of the pogrom years. The cemetery's use during the early decades was best summed up many years later by an original society member, now in his eighties, who said: "When I was young, my parents took me to the cemetery, but I didn't understand. Then, when I grew older, every time I went to the cemetery I became afraid. Now that I am really old, when I stand at the cemetery I say to myself, 'Better him than me.' "

The dilemma facing the Boyerker landsmanshaft arose simply and naturally from the passage of time and generations, which nobody had the power to alter or prevent. By the late 1950s, when the original members of the society had all passed through middle age, space in the cemetery had begun to run short. At about this time the Boyerker Society —although nobody alive today will take responsibility for the decision—realized that it was necessary to purchase more cemetery space. All the cemetery plots in Beth David had been bought up, however, and the entire cemetery had been transformed from farms and marshes into one of the most intensely suburbanized zones on the East Coast. Beth

David Cemetery was now ringed by split-level housing tracts, shopping malls, and multilane highways which formed the approach roads to Idlewild (later Kennedy) International Airport. During the postwar period, Elmont had been transformed from the frontier into the gateway to New York, and land for any use, especially for burial plots, was only to be had at a premium price.

The Boyerker Society still had a number of unused grave sites in its cemetery, but the members knew they would not have enough space for the long run, especially for second- and third-generation members. So the society went shopping around for a second cemetery and found it way out on Long Island, in the town of Bethpage, nearly 20 miles from Beth David and more than twice the distance of the original cemetery from midtown New York. But at the time it didn't seem to matter that the new cemetery was so far away. The land was cheap, everyone had a car, the Jews had "conquered" Queens and parts of Nassau County, the children were all moving out to the suburbs anyway, and most important, the new cemetery would not be needed until the original members were long gone and buried at Beth David.

The Boyerker landsleit had made a fateful miscalculation, although it was no fault of their own. Like everyone else in America who had lived through the Great Depression, including the architects of the Social Security Administration, the original members of the society assumed they would all be dead and buried before they reached their seventieth birthdays. On that assumption, the Bethpage cemetery—the "far out" cemetery, as it was called—was destined for use only by the descendants of the society's original members, many of whom had joined only because the $24 annual dues was an inexpensive means of pleasing and honoring their parents. Unfortunately, a few of the second- and even third-generation Boyerkers had predeceased their parents. Worse yet, some of the original members were vigorously alive and well (or not so well) into their eighties and even their nineties. When it was all figured out without the benefit of an actuarial table, as near as anyone could guess, the Beth David cemetery no longer contained enough graves to hold all the original members of the Boyerker Society. At every funeral during the last few years—and the number of funerals increased in inverse proportion to the number of surviving members—a few persons could be seen walking around the cemetery, heads down, counting the remaining unused plots. The issue for the 1980s, spelled out at every meeting in strongly worded terms, was as follows: Who will be buried "close in," and who will be buried "far out"? The rejoinder of one member during an argument at the March meeting to "die sooner" did not suffice to close the debate.

The passions that inspired this debate can be better appreciated if we pause for a moment to examine the actual layout of the Boyerker Society cemetery and the manner in which it has been utilized. The cemetery measures 140 feet deep by 100 feet wide. It is divided into twelve rows of eighteen graves, nine on either side of a path leading down the middle. The path extends from the front gate, inscribed with the names of the original members, to a granite pillar, memorializing the town's martyrs, at the rear. The path separates the men from the women—females on the left, males on the right. Except for eight double graves in the rear of the cemetery, which were purchased by the original officers of the organization and helped defray the expense of buying the entire plot, no spaces are reserved. Members are simply buried as they die, on a first-come, first-served basis. In the fifth row of male graves, for example, lie the remains of nine individuals, of whom only two were related to one another, as distant cousins.

The refusal to differentiate between family groups within

the Boyerker cemetery was not accidental and is, in fact, a feature common to many landsmanshaft cemeteries. The Brestowitzer Independent Society, which was organized in 1907 and buried its first member in its Mt. Carmel Cemetery in 1918, divided its plot into male and female sections until the 1930s. The Neshwiser Benevolent Society began burying members in Mt. Carmel in 1905; it placed men and women in adjacent graves but made no distinction between families and did not segregate family plots from the rest of the deceased membership. The landsleit of Boyerker and other landsmanshaftn considered themselves to be a community, in death as in life. Although the difficulties inherent in family affairs often intruded upon and complicated society relationships, the members of Boyerker regarded their organization as something that transcended particular family ties. This clearly evoked the traditions of the shtetl, and the layout of the Beth David Cemetery followed practices that had long been carried on in the shtetl. The Boyerker cemetery in Beth David and the obsession of the original members to be buried within its boundaries reflected the desire of these immigrants to sustain to the end of their lives the memories, habits, and cultural instincts of their origins.

But there was an even more profound current running through the Boyerker cemetery debate, for which the attempt to remain together in the "close in" cemetery provided a convenient rationale. The real underlying fear of the old immigrants, as symbolized by the threat of burial in the "far out" cemetery, was that once deceased and removed from life, they would be forgotten by their children and grandchildren. Notwithstanding the fact that many of their children had already moved away, the members of the older generation intuitively knew that when they died, only the Beth David Cemetery would remain as a visible symbol of the society's existence. The society in an active sense would cease, and its memory would be resurrected only when mourners came to the cemetery. "Who will pray at my grave if I am buried far out?" anguished one elderly member of the society, whose family was not truly known for its religious devotion. The reality was that this person's children had never exhibited any great interest in the society, had never come to meetings or visited the cemetery anyway. But symbols in this respect were much more important than substance. People would come to the old cemetery even if they were visiting someone else's grave. But to have one's remains and one's monument placed far away from the old cemetery meant abandonment; it represented an objective break with a tradition to which these people had clung and with which they had identified themselves over the entire course of their lives. The consequences of this breakdown were not to be contemplated with ease. The original members of the society had buried their parents, husbands, wives, friends, and even (God forbid) children within the confines of a place that reflected the continuity of their lives and provided a symbol of stability in a society that continuously changed in ways they could barely comprehend.

The cemetery represented the end of a cycle that could never be repeated. When the last original member of the society was laid to rest, the society would die with him. Occasionally, the realization of that fact intruded into the deliberations of the society, provoking a special brand of black humor—a typical defense against thoughts about the unthinkable. Like most of the smaller landsmanshaftn, the Boyerker Society had been exceptionally frugal in its affairs, a frugality which characterized the personal lives of the members as well. Consequently, although the annual dues were only $24 and had not been increased within anyone's memory, the society's treasury in 1980 actually contained about $10,000 in ready cash. This sum represented more money than the entire life's savings of any original member, and the question of how to spend it lay beyond anyone's comprehension. Several of the younger-generation members had suggested that the society make a lump-sum donation to Israel or purchase equipment for an old-age home in the Bronx where a few of the landsleit had unfortunately been required to pass their final years. But the older members were resistant to such ideas, and vague rumors frequently surfaced that "so-and-so" was just hoping to hang on to become the final surviving member in order to come into possession of the entire stash!

Greatest Strength and Greatest Weakness

The Boyerker cemetery debate was different in form but not in substance from controversies that arose in most landsmanshaftn during their twilight years. The subject matter varied from society to society (although the question of money was an element common to most), but the essence of the problem was always the same: a way of life was coming to an end, and there was no possibility of prolonging it. The landsmanshaftn were organizations in a legal sense; some had incorporated, they tried to file tax returns, they owned property (cemeteries) and other meager assets. But most of these organizations had never become formally *institutionalized*. A few of the societies remain active today, having managed to involve their younger generations in a wide variety of social and benevolent activities. For that matter, several landsmanshaftn have experienced an actual revival with the recent appearance of the Russian Jews. But for the most part, these organizations could not be maintained apart from the tight web of social relationships that existed between the original members. Such relationships could only be defined by the limits placed on the lives and life-styles of the members themselves.

These limits were spelled out in a debate that took place at a meeting of another small landsmanshaft, a society that, like the Boyerker Society, had been reduced to a handful of elderly members meeting monthly at the UJA. A younger member, a man in his fifties, had come to the meeting intent on getting the older members to sponsor a social event that would attract more persons from his generation to involve themselves in the activities of the society. "After all," he said, "some of us want to continue the good work of the society," a comment that was met with grudging but somewhat uncomprehending assent. Speaking very slowly and clearly in English, so that the older generation would understand what he was trying to say, he proposed the following: the society would sponsor a one-day trip to Atlantic City. A casino would provide the bus, and for a small fee everyone would get a box lunch and free admission to the gambling areas. For those who had no interest in gambling, there was always the beach or the boardwalk. Before he finished outlining his scheme, the speaker noticed that most members of his elderly audience were beginning to murmur among themselves. Fearing that he was losing their attention, he reached for his trump card and shouted, "It's a terrific idea. My synagogue has done it twice, and we get more reservations than there are seats on the bus."

The room fell silent, an unusual occurrence for a meeting of this normally garrulous group. Several lifelong members rose to speak but only mumbled vague comments about the length of the trip and the cost of the excursion. Then two women stood up and, walking to the back of the room, told the others that it was time to pour coffee and have some cake. A wave of relief swept over the group. It was obvious that nobody wanted to take a bus to Atlantic City, but neither did anyone want to insult the younger member, who had come to this meeting and several previous meetings specifically to present his idea. One of the women took a coffeepot and began walking alongside each member to pour coffee into the little styrofoam cups on the table. She paused at the elbow of the oldest male member of the society, whose opinions, intelligent or not, were often the "last word" on important issues. "Well, Hymie," she asked, "what do *you* think of the idea?" The man to whom the question had been put was clearly on the spot. His answer, now eagerly awaited by all, would have to accommodate both the resistance of one generation and the insistence of another. Without looking up or changing expression, he leaned back in his chair, shrugged, and muttered, "America *goniff.*"

America *goniff,* a thief, a place where the children could spend their money on trips to Atlantic City in a private bus while their parents bitterly complained about a recent increase in the subway fare; a place where the streets were "paved with gold" but where the food was unclean (not kosher). America *goniff* was both the attraction and the contradiction of the landsmanshaftn. The societies came into existence because their members could only respond to the opportunities of America in the most limited terms. The societies would ultimately cease to exist because those limits did not outlive their members. The strength of the landsmanshaftn was also their greatest weakness.

I I

Out of the Shtetl

Snitkiv my shtetl,
The size of a yawn.
It's not on the map,
Not even a scrap.
—J. L. Malamut,
Snitkiv Mein Shtetl

THE ORIGINS of the landsmanshaftn in New York go
back to the shtetlach of the Russian Pale. Along with the
urban ghettos of Eastern Europe, these tiny villages were the
starting points for immigrants who came to America and
reconstituted their traditional social relations through the
medium of the landsmanshaftn. In order to understand the
attitudes and perceptions that shaped the landsmanshaft
experience, we must first examine the formation of those
attitudes in the shtetl and the more general development of
shtetl culture.

The culture of the shtetl was a product of the historical
circumstances of Jewish settlement in the Pale.[1] Since the
Middle Ages, the Jews of Western Europe had settled primarily in the cities, inasmuch as their talents and energies
had been traditionally devoted to such urban activities as
commerce and industry. The Jewish population in the Pale,
however, was not only concentrated in certain cities but also

43

scattered throughout the rural zone. In the villages, Jews also were the traders, merchants, and entrepreneurs, except on a much more limited scale than in the cities.

Jews had first been invited to settle in Poland during the thirteenth century by King Boleslaw the Pious for the purpose of reviving the national economy. Initially, Jews settled in the cities and port towns, playing a crucial role in the growth of the Polish economy throughout the fourteenth and fifteenth centuries. By the end of the fifteenth century, Polish Jews controlled large segments of the national economy, including many aspects of trade and commerce between Poland and other regions of Europe. They lived freely and openly in the cities and dominated the arts and intellectual life. This was a period when Jewish culture, education, and learning flourished.

The situation began to change after the middle of the sixteenth century. During the period from 1550 to 1650, Poland was torn by invasion and then engulfed in chronic civil war. As a result, the economy slipped into a long period of decline, largely reversing the economic and political achievements of the previous two centuries. As the fortunes of the Polish economy began to wane, so did the political power of the Polish monarchy. Poland was devastated during the Thirty Years War and slowly fell under the yoke of more powerful foreign interests.

With the decline in the power of the Polish crown, the fortunes of the Jewish community also reached a low ebb, and the special status accorded the Jews by the kings of Poland became a dead letter. Gradually, the Polish Jews were reduced to second-class status, losing their commercial monopolies as well as the protection of the Polish monarchy. The Jews had initially derived enormous benefits from their position as clients of a strong Polish state. When the state became weak, this client relationship left them all the more vulnerable to other pressures.

The final collapse of Poland occurred in the eighteenth century, when the country was invaded by the Russian army and partitioned between Austria, Prussia, and Russia. Eastern Poland, the region containing the largest proportion of Jews among its native population, was annexed to the Russian empire, and the last guarantees of political and economic freedom accorded by the Polish kings to their Jewish subjects finally disappeared. The Jews became just another captive population of the Russian tsars, without any claim to special status under their new rulers.

The period beginning with the rule of Alexander I in 1801 marks the beginnings of the "dark years" of Jewish life within the Pale. Anti-Semitism was an official doctrine of the nineteenth-century Romanovs, and they pursued this policy with a vengeance. A conscious campaign was undertaken at the tsarist court to reduce the social and economic status of the Jewish community within Russia as a means of bringing the new Polish colony more tightly under Russian control. Increasingly, Jews were shut out of business and enterprise in the larger cities and expelled from the smaller towns. Ultimately they would become a separate population, having social and economic relations only among themselves. Laws were passed restricting Jewish commercial activity, imposing quotas on the admission of Jews to educational institutions, denying Jews banking and credit facilities, dispossessing them of land, and limiting their right to practice their religion openly.

These early anti-Jewish laws were only a prelude to the more onerous restrictions imposed by the tsars on this captive population. A series of edicts passed at the end of the reign of Alexander I prohibited Jews from living anywhere

outside the Pale of Settlement, a region that embraced western Russia and eastern Poland, stretching from Odessa in the
south to the Baltic provinces in the north. Within the Pale,
Jews were forced out of their traditional roles as merchants,
craftsmen, and middlemen, with the result that the entire
population gradually collapsed into a general state of economic and social poverty. By the 1870s, the Jewish population in the Pale, variously estimated at between 5 and 6
million, was evenly split between urban ghettos and rural
towns. In the cities, the Jews were penned up in miserable,
poverty-stricken neighborhoods, while in the countryside,
they lived in backwardness and squalor.

This inexorable impoverishment of the Jewish population
in the Pale coincided, however, with the flourishing of Yiddish culture, learning, and political activity in the cities that
held large numbers of Jewish residents. Despite—or perhaps
because of—increased persecution, the urban Jewish population in the Pale developed a degree of cultural cohesiveness and political consciousness never before witnessed in
the history of East European Jewry. Partly this was the result
of political activity associated with the rise of Zionism and
socialism. Zionist beliefs found many adherents among the
Jewish population, while other Jews had already begun to
embrace the tenets of socialism. Both Zionism and socialism
struck a response among Jews already awakened through
the influence of Haskalah, an enlightened movement of
spiritual and philosophical reform that swept through the
Pale and contested the authority and control exerted by the
Hasidic hierarchy.

The Hasidic movement had arisen during the period of
turmoil following the decline of the Polish monarchy. The
founder of Hasidism was the first *tzaddik* ("righteous man"),
Israel ben Eliezer, known as the Baal Shem Tov. Born in

southeastern Poland in 1700, he developed by the 1750s a large number of disciples, to whom he imparted a philosophy that intertwined piety with the practical realities of everyday life. Revising the stance of the earlier Jewish mystics, he preached the redemption of the world through prayer, celebration, and energetic devotion, rather than messianic intervention. But above all, Hasidic belief turned on the notion of tradition and the maintenance of a society in which religious values remained supreme.[2]

While Haskalah and its two stepchildren, Zionism and socialism, made clear inroads in the urban Jewish culture of the Pale, the rural population remained shackled by the tradition, formalism, and religious piety defined by the Hasidic sect and its leadership. Thus the social and physical gulf separating urban from rural Jews was paralleled by a cultural and intellectual gap. Urban Jews became modern, secular, and political, while the rural population remained backward-looking. Whereas tsarist oppression produced dissidence and revolt in the cities, it accentuated the ignorance, resignation, and apathy in the countryside. Sholom Aleichem, the great Yiddish storyteller, captured the cultural backwardness of the shtetl in the following manner: "Stuck away in a corner of the world, isolated from the surrounding country, the town stands, orphaned, dreaming, bewitched, immersed in itself and remote from the noise and bustle, the confusion and tumult and greed, which men have created about them and have dignified with high-sounding names like Culture, Progress and Civilization."[3]

Not that shtetl Jews were incapable of being caught up in the social and cultural ferment that swept through the urban population of the Pale. Many young men and women from the shtetl found themselves drawn to the cities, to the universities, and to the cultural groups and the political parties that appeared and flourished during the nineteenth century. But getting involved in these sorts of activities usually required departure from the shtetl and a resolution never to return. A young villager who went to the city and became "infected" with the virus of modern ideas could no longer tolerate the slow pace and unchanging traditions of shtetl life, unless he came from a wealthy background and would one day return to take charge of the family's affairs.

One elderly immigrant now recalls that his first journey away from his shtetl occurred when he was drafted into the Russian army at the beginning of World War I. "I was wounded during my first campaign," he said, "and after convalescing in an army hospital was allowed to go home on leave. But after two weeks I was so bored that I returned to my regiment early." The shtetl did not on its own have the capacity to stimulate modernization and progress; it could only receive these impulses in vague and transmuted forms from the cities, which was not enough to alter the foundations of its existence.

Shtetl Culture, Shtetl Consciousness

What elements made the experiences of shtetl life so inappropriate as a model for dealing with the pressures and possibilities of immigrant existence in New York? The answer lies in an examination of the cultural and religious habits of the shtetl population, habits formed by the social and economic conditions of the Pale. Most important was the fact that although shtetl Jews lived in the countryside, they were generally denied access to land. They were involved in the usual artisan, craft, and commercial activities, but were able to replicate urban commerce and trade only on

48

a greatly reduced scale; and their landless existence promoted a psychology of fear and insecurity.

A brief anecdote from the early life of a shtetl resident illustrates the situation exactly. This individual was considered by the other members of his landsmanshaft to be a great business success, a *macher* (big shot) of no small proportions. During World War II he had made money by cornering the market on some type of illicit commodity, and his ability to bargain and *shmear* (bribe) the proper officials was supposedly a talent carried over from his days as an itinerant merchant in the Pale. The fact that he traveled from one decrepit shtetl to another in a horse and wagon, instead of carrying his goods on his back like an ordinary peddler, only added greater luster to his presumed business acumen in the early days.

Near the end of his life, however, this now elderly immigrant confided the actual state of affairs regarding his so-called enterprise in the Pale. He said he was actually so poor, and made so little money, that he never slept indoors during his travels except when he returned to his native village. "The wagon was really something for me to sleep underneath rather than to carry goods," he recalled, "while merchants from the cities who came out to the villages took rooms at an inn or boarded in homes." So much for this legendary financial empire.

The point is that the shtetl economy usually involved only the most limited trade and contact beyond the confines of the village and its immediate surroundings. There was a certain degree of contact between Jewish tradesmen and the non-Jewish peasant population, because in exchange for farm goods, the Jews supplied or fashioned the implements, clothing, and commodities the peasants needed. But the recollections of shtetl dwellers are nearly unanimous concerning the extremely limited context of their economic activities. Partially out of fear, partially out of legal and social constraints, Jewish tradesmen and merchants focused their energies on business activities within their own communities and population, indulging in only limited and sporadic contact with the outside world.

The cultural and religious traditions of Jewish life also played an important part in reinforcing the self-enclosed nature of the shtetl economy. Communal activities were an essential aspect of Jewish life, because dietary and religious restrictions required the maintenance of kosher kitchens and religious and ritual institutions. Every shtetl had a communal bakery, which was used primarily on Fridays to produce bread for the Sabbath, when religious law forbade anyone to cook. There was also a communal "oven" to which housewives would bring food prepared before sundown on Friday and then return during Saturday to reclaim their food for the Sabbath-ending meal. Every shtetl also had a *cheder*, where young men studied the Torah and learned how to read and write. These communal institutions and others (such as the ritual bath, or *mikvah*) engaged the energies of the entire Jewish population and set it apart from the non-Jews in the community.

The composite picture that emerges from the memories of former shtetl residents confirms a general perception that life in the shtetl involved minimal possession of material goods and a basic lack of concern with socioeconomic mobility, no doubt reflecting the isolated nature of the local economy. Yet the shtetl did not exhibit the "culture of poverty" we associate with other backward rural zones. Shtetl poverty was not the poverty of a prerevolutionary Chinese village described by William Hinton, or the bleakness of a Mexican pueblo examined by Oscar Lewis.[4] These rural societies were characterized not only by an absolute lack of material possessions but also by a hopelessness that precluded any possibility of change or progress. In the case of the shtetl, on the other hand, circumstances combined to limit the degree of social and cultural development without altogether denying the possibility of change.

Perhaps a better approach to the problem of defining shtetl existence would be to examine the life and society of a "typical" shtetl within the Pale—in this instance, the shtetl of Aisheshuk, or (as it was known in Russian) Eiseskes.[5] The settlement was located 35 miles southeast of Vilna, the ancient capital of Lithuania; nearby were the cities of Lida and Grodno, both of which contained sizable Jewish populations. But the shtetl of Aisheshuk did not have a great deal of contact with these urban centers. Jews who lived in little villages like Aisheshuk rarely traveled to a large city more than once or twice in their lifetimes.

The population of Aisheshuk was somewhere between 3,000 and 6,000 at the end of the nineteenth century, of whom probably half were Jews. In other words, the shtetl held perhaps 250 to 300 Jewish families, which was the usual size of smaller rural settlements in the Pale. The Jewish and non-Jewish populations lived in the same village, but they did not live together. Theirs was a separate existence both physically and socially. The town was built around four streets which all led to a main square, the center of life in the settlement. The Jews lived on two streets, Vilna Street and Mill Street, and the gentiles lived on Radu Street and "Goyishke" [Gentile] Street (which no doubt had an official name but none of the Jewish residents knew what it was). The actual population of the shtetl was mostly Jewish, however, because many of the gentile residents worked on farms in the surrounding countryside.

The Jews who lived in Aisheshuk and other small shtetlach recall meeting gentiles for the most part in the main square on market day. In Aisheshuk, the settlement came alive on the Thursday market day. Peasants from surrounding farms and neighboring villages brought produce to sell and trade or to be milled in exchange for implements and other goods to be taken back to the farm. The local Jewish merchants served as middlemen in these transactions, bartering and trading with peasants and using goods either fashioned in local workshops or purchased from itinerant peddlers who had come to the village from the larger towns. One resident of a settlement not far from Aisheshuk, who later came to America and opened a dry-goods business, recalled that he would go from village to village in the region, because each village held its local trade fair on a different day. He often made a profit through buying surplus goods in one settlement and then disposing of them several days later at another settlement where that particular item was in short supply.

Except for market day, Jews and gentiles in Aisheshuk lived apart and rarely mingled. A former inhabitant of the shtetl recalled that she first learned about Christian holidays when German soldiers occupied the village during World War I. "I saw for the first time in my life a Christmas tree. It was so beautiful with all kinds of little toys."[6] This woman could not remember any other personal contact with the gentile residents of the shtetl.

Living conditions for the Jews of Aisheshuk could only be described as primitive. The homes of Jews were constructed of wood; many residences were destroyed by a great fire that swept through the town in 1879. One former resident remembers: "Life was so primitive. . . . Water had to be brought in by a pail from a well, there was no plumbing at all. Heating and cooking was done on fireplaces with wood. The houses were dilapidated, the streets unpaved and dirty." Of the thirty Jewish-owned shops in the town square, most were so old that "the wood was green with age," and many were boarded up for months at a time.[7]

The Jewish side of the settlement did contain two buildings constructed out of brick, the synagogue and the yeshiva. The latter institution was founded in the early nineteenth century. It was a center of religious teaching of the *misnagdim* whose leaders preached a traditional form of worship in contrast to the emotionalism and ecstacy of Hasidic practices. The Chief Rabbi of Vilna, who was the leading proponent of the Misnagdim in Poland, established the Aisheshuk yeshiva specifically to train adherents who would go out and propagate his doctrines.

The yeshiva provided a certain degree of cultural sophistication for Aisheshuk that other, more isolated shtetlach did not enjoy. Its presence made the population of Aisheshuk intellectually more heterogeneous than populations in shtetlach that were totally controlled by the Hasidic rabbinate. It also allowed a certain degree of outside influence to penetrate the settlement, insofar as scholars and students from the surrounding cities came to Aisheshuk to teach or enroll in the yeshiva's program.

But the importance of the yeshiva in influencing the social and cultural attitudes of the local Jewish population should not be overstated, for this link to the outside world was very tenuous. It did offer an awareness of Jewish issues and provide some understanding of how Jewish life in other communities was evolving. But it did not bring the entire outside world into focus. Jewish residents of Aisheshuk were still generally ignorant of goings-on in society at large, or even among their non-Jewish neighbors in the shtetl. The yeshiva was a decrepit institution that always tottered on the brink of insolvency. It never enrolled more than fifty students at a time (despite one local resident's claim that it was one of the "great yeshivot in the world"), and it would be entirely destroyed in the pogroms of 1919–21. Like everything else in the shtetl of Aisheshuk, the yeshiva operated on a small scale, and its operations did little to open the village up to the outside world.

Another village whose former residents have provided memories not unlike those of the residents of Aisheshuk was the shtetl of Skala. Located in Galicia on the Russian border, Skala was similar to Aisheshuk in many respects but also had its own particular history and development.[8] Skala is located on the Polish side of the Zbrucz River, about 20 miles north of the point where the Zbrucz flows into the Dnestr. In the eighteenth century, the Skala was described as a "Jewish town surrounded by suburbs, populated mostly by Ukrainian peasants," with a total of 362 inhabitants.

The village fell within the domain of the Polish noble family of Goluchowski, which had always held important positions at the royal court. The Goluchowskis were also the largest landowners in the region and depended upon the Jews of Skala for a wide variety of commercial transactions, a relationship that no doubt dated back to the early conditions of Jewish settlement in the zone. Count Goluchowski owned a village brewery, which was leased to Jews, and the flour mill, which was operated by a Jewish family. The products from these enterprises were mainly exported abroad, and several Jewish families had kin in Western Europe who acted as export agents for the goods produced in the settlement. Jews in Skala also owned a whiskey distillery and an oil press for the production of industrial lubricants.

The Jews of Skala included two families, the Drimmers and the Seidmans, who had acquired landowner status in the nineteenth century, but the others were petty tradesmen, artisans, merchants, and shopkeepers. It should be added that the elevated status of the Jewish gentry carried little weight outside the shtetl or among the enemies of the Jews. When the Nazis massacred nearly all the residents of the town in 1942, three members of the Seidman family and four members of the Drimmer clan were among the long list of victims.

By the twentieth century, the village of Skala was no longer an exclusively Jewish enclave. The town now contained a Greek Orthodox church and a Catholic church, the latter being the largest and most imposing structure in the settlement. The town also had six synagogues, a number that reflected a religious split within the Jewish community. Skala had always been a Hasidic village; in fact, this part of Galicia was the native region of the Baal Shem Tov. But during the nineteenth century there had erupted an acrimonious dispute between the followers of Reb Israel of Rosanoy and those of the Rabbi of Wizhnitz, and the population had remained divided until World War II.

Immigrants from Skala recall that the village had a limited but active social and intellectual life. Social activities included lectures and celebrations, as well as the occasional appearance of theater troupes from the large cities. The children were all educated in the local Talmud Torah, and young men from the more enlightened and affluent families were sent to study in the *gymnasium* (academy) at Czernowitz. But the shtetl also had its share of poverty and backwardness. Residents of Skala began leaving for America as early as 1890, and they left because the village held little hope or future for most of the townspeople. After the oldest *shul* in Skala burned down in 1911, not enough funds were collected to complete the construction of a new building on that site. The desolate, half-finished structure was used by a group of poor Skala Jews who established a small open-air synagogue in one of its corners.

Although Aisheshuk and Skala were typical of smaller

shtetlach, they hardly represented the entirety of shtetl existence. The Pale had many larger Jewish settlements, often the size of small cities, with substantial populations supporting all sorts of economic and cultural activities. The village of Bialystok, whose residents formed the first landsmanshaft in New York, supported seven synagogues and three yeshivot. It also had a hospital maintained by contributions from the various chevras in the town. The shtetl of Knyszyn, in Poland, had an orchestra and a string band; the latter performed nearly every weekend for private parties or community-wide festivals. An immigrant from Lithuania recalls that his shtetl had a modern, fully equipped volunteer fire department, and a former resident of a shtetl near Warsaw remembers a legitimate theater where troupes from the big cities "opened in New Haven" before moving onto the national circuit. The Galician shtetl of Rohatyn is described by a former resident as "no hodge-podge of streets and little huts, as in most of the towns of Poland and Russia, but wide, tree-lined streets around a big square in the very center of the town."

The living environment of the large shtetlach was indistinguishable, in the main, from the Jewish ghettos in the major cities of the Pale. Perhaps the villages did not contain extensive working-class neighborhoods like those found in Cracow and Warsaw, or large university and professional populations like those in Vilna and Kiev. But the larger shtetlach were often centers of regional trade and commerce, and their communities supported such cultural institutions as legitimate theaters and newspapers. The size and economic importance of these villages linked them to the major cities of the Pale and connected their inhabitants with the social, cultural, and intellectual influences of the outside world. The larger shtetlach did not therefore suffer from the cultural backwardness of smaller, more remote villages, although they were never cosmopolitan centers in any sense of the word.

Typical of the larger, more urbanized shtetlach was the village of Swislocz in the Grodno region of Poland.[9] Known in Yiddish as Sislevich, the town had a population of more than 2,000 Jews at the beginning of the twentieth century. Most of the streets were unpaved, but there were sidewalks around the central market square, and many of the larger homes were multistory brick residences. There were sixty wholesale and retail establishments in the village, and a railroad connected the town to the provincial capital of Bialystok, although some tradesmen were prosperous enough to bring their goods all the way from Warsaw.

The town was surrounded by little villages inhabited by White Russian peasants, and many of the Jewish townsfolk made their living by supplying the rural population with essential iron goods and other types of nonfarm commodities. But the major economic enterprises in the town were the eight leather factories, which together employed more than 400 workers; all the skilled workers were Jews. Beginning in 1901, a series of strikes called by the local Bund took place in these factories, culminating in a bitter four-month stoppage in 1908. This last action involved union organizers from all over the province and at one point resulted in the appearance of the army to keep order in the town. In the aftermath of the strike, which ended with a complete victory for the factory owners, many of the skilled workers emigrated to Canada and the United States. This episode illustrates the difference between Swislocz and Aisheshuk or Skala. Swislocz's size and economic development produced the kind of political ferment that was characteristic of the large industrial cities in the Pale.

Aisheshuk and Skala were not representative of larger towns such as Swislocz, nor were they by any means typical of the really small shtetlach, such tiny dots of settlement as Cholmetch, Heinsk, Krivka, Lutzk, Rayoz, Sobolivka, and Vishmeritz. These and countless other minuscule shtetlach together contained perhaps one-quarter of the total Jewish population of the Pale. A visitor at a landsmanshaft meeting was surprised to discover that most of the society's members had actually come from shtetlach all over a wide region. "You see," he was told, "we named our society after the largest village in the area. The other shtetls were too small."

The little shtetl of Kasrilevka, the fanciful setting for Sholom Aleichem's stories about rural life in the Pale, typifies these tiny villages. Instead of the four streets that ran through Aisheshuk, the fictional shtetl of Kasrilevka had only two. In fact, there was only one real street; the other was a large alley that bisected the street at the midway point of the village. The layout of the shtetl was simple: Jews lived on one side of the street, gentiles on the other. The center of the settlement contained just two establishments, an open-air market and a horse market. On the outskirts of the village was a communal bathhouse, and at the opposite end stood the mill. (Nobody who resided in the shtetl could recall any other things of note beyond what has been listed above.) Sholom Aleichem described the shtetl as "houses built on the slope of a hill, and the rest . . . huddled together at the base, one on top of the other, like the gravestones in an ancient cemetery."[10]

So Aisheshuk and Skala become prototypes for an examination of shtetl life, falling somewhere between the two extremes of the large town and the tiny isolated hamlet, combining social and cultural elements characteristic of both. When all is said and done, we know a good deal about the shtetlach of Aisheshuk, Skala, Swislocz, and other villages of that size because these settlements were large enough to produce a record of their existence. These villages exist to this day, and immigrant survivors in the United States can still be found whose memories allow a reconstruction of life in those settlements.

Even in the smallest and most poverty-stricken shtetlach, in villages too small to have left substantial record, life was distinguishably different from that of non-Jewish rural communities. For in the tiniest shtetlach, the Jews retained an active sense of their written tradition. In part, this difference was the result of a system of religious belief that emphasized the historical and cultural continuity of Jewish existence. A more important difference was the fact that Jews in the most remote and isolated villages of the Pale were literate, whereas illiteracy was a fundamental component of rural life in the rest of Russia and elsewhere.

In accounts of nineteenth-century Russian peasant life, illiteracy and superstition always emerge as dominant leitmotifs. Virtually every European who traveled through rural Russia remarked on the cultural backwardness of the peasant masses.[11] The same phenomenon is captured in the semifictional reminiscences of Maxim Gorki and the sharp historical analyses of Trotsky.[12] But perhaps the most potent example of cultural backwardness and illiteracy is provided by the American historian Geroid Robinson, who journeyed through the Ukraine in the aftermath of the Russian Revolution. At one point his convoy stopped in front of a village, and a group of local village "notables" came out to greet the travelers. During the exchange, Robinson noticed a newspaper lying beside the door of a hut, picked it up, and began perusing its contents for news about the revolution. The peasants became somewhat agitated at his behavior, and he was told they were afraid he might take the newspaper with him when he left the village. The newspaper was regarded as a precious item in the settlement not because it contained news of the outside world but because it was used to wrap homemade cigarettes![13]

Illiteracy did not, for the most part, exist within the Jewish population. Nearly every young man could read Hebrew from the sacred texts, and most men could read and write Yiddish and the local vernacular language. Literacy in the shtetl cut across class and gender lines, with most females also acquiring rudimentary reading and writing skills. The poorest of the poor shtetlach contained a synagogue and a *cheder*, and usually managed to support the full-time activities of a rabbi and a *melamed*, a person of generally low esteem who gave simple lessons to young children for little pay.

In larger villages and towns, particularly those with a yeshiva and rabbinical bureaucracy, teaching and learning were often the most important local "industries." Even Jewish men who were not full-time rabbinical students were involved, to varying degrees, in the constant ritual of study that surrounded the activities of religious life. Although there was a growth of secularism in reaction to Hasidism during the nineteenth century, religion and religious learning were still integral components of shtetl society, and former shtetl residents, men and women alike, carry with them the memories of countless hours of study in dimly lit classrooms or in makeshift quarters elsewhere in town. Even if this learning was solely rudimentary or religiously oriented, it was enough to distinguish the Jewish population from the gentile peasants, most of whom spent their whole lives without comprehending the written word.

Although it is usually offered as a sufficient explanation, the tradition of shtetl literacy did not flow only from the nature and practice of religious belief. Literacy in the shtetl also reflected the economic roles played by Jews in the local community. Even in the smallest and most backward shtet-lach, Jews were the tradesmen, peddlers, merchants, arti-sans, and shopkeepers. Jews in the shtetl were the economic link between city markets and gentile peasants. Conse-quently, their occupational survival depended upon literacy, which would not have been the case had most Jews been farmers or landowners.

We can better appreciate the unique economic position of the Jews if we compare Aisheshuk and similar shtetlach to non-Jewish rural communities at an analogous state of eco-nomic and social development. For example, the village of "San Lucás" in southern Spain had the same number of residents in the 1930s as lived in the shtetl of Aisheshuk in 1890.[14] "San Lucás" was located forty miles from the pro-vincial capital and, like Aisheshuk, had four large streets that bisected the village at a central plaza. Aisheshuk held its market day on Thursday; the weekly market in "San Lucás" was held on Saturday. The peasants in Aisheshuk planted beets; the peasants of "San Lucás" planted olives and cultivated wine. The shtetl had its yeshiva; the pueblo of "San Lucás" had a small monastery of the Franciscan order. Neither village had lighting or plumbing, and both maintained only minimal contact with the outside world. The crucial difference—if we compare Aisheshuk to rural settlements in Spain, Sicily, Yugoslavia, or France—is that of the 500 families who resided in the typical Spanish peasant village, perhaps 475 were directly involved in working on the land. They owned land, rented land, grazed their animals on land, or cut and hauled wood from land. The few households that did not derive their livelihood from some kind of farm or forest enterprise were headed by persons who performed certain other tasks indispensable to the farm community: miller, forger, shopkeeper, shoemaker, tailor, weaver, prostitute, and priest. The preponderance of local residents who worked the land was common to every rural society in the world except for the rural Jewish society of the Pale.

In most villages of the Pale that contained Jews, only a few Jewish residents worked on the land. The rest depended upon the labor of a gentile peasant population for their own economic well-being and security. But they lived apart from the peasants, and they did not control what the peasants produced. As a result, their perception of life was circumscribed by the immediacy of risk, causing decisions to be made carefully, deliberately, and fearfully.

Recounting their lives in the shtetl, former residents of the Pale do not focus on the poverty or isolation, although both elements were constant aspects of the local environment. Rather, recollections invariably center upon the genuine sense of limitation and the basic lack of security that came from landlessness. "My shtetl was a poor shtetl," recalls a former resident of Viliusk in Lithuania, "you can be sure of that. We never had more than just enough, and we were never sure if we would have even that much." A resident from a prosperous shtetl in Rumania, whose father was the local miller and notary, once said, "There was just one of everything in the village, so you took no chances because you might lose it all."

The Shtetl Awakes . . .

This sense of limitation and insecurity diverges from much of the current literature written about life in the shtetl world of Eastern Europe. The accepted version of shtetl life is based on an idealized recreation of a bucolic existence that minimizes the alienation of shtetl Jews and exaggerates the sense of cultural and religious identity. Such standard accounts as *The Shtetl Book* or *Life Is With People: The Culture of the Shtetl* portray the village as an impoverished and backward little society, but emphasize its idyllic and enduring qualities.[15] They show life in the shtetl as played out according to unquestioned rules defined by religious and cultural traditions that embraced the totality of existence and continuously reaffirmed all social and economic roles. According to this view, the shtetl, with its songs, piety, and veneration of tradition, was a place of refuge from the outside world, a place where survival demanded adherence to an immutable way of life that kept everything in its place and under control.

This approach to shtetl life transforms the realities of the shtetl into a quasi-romantic myth. The myth is based on a stereotypical, one-dimensional portrayal of shtetl Jews as different from other rural populations only insofar as their religious beliefs and customs bound them together in a community from which a positive view of life emerged. Notwithstanding the limitations imposed by poverty and isolation, life in the Pale (seen in this way) was ultimately transformed into a spiritual experience. This spirituality compensated for material privation, providing the moral strength for the maintenance of culture and tradition from one generation to the next.

Religion and spirituality *did* play an important role in the community, defining social relations among Jews as well as rationalizing the relationship of Jews to the gentile population. Religious belief and tradition allowed the Jews to create a hierarchy of values and ideals that infused some of the most menial and senseless aspects of rural life with a sense of importance, transforming the mundane and monotonous into a higher level of existence and thought. There is no doubt that religion provided a bulwark against the alienation and insecurity of daily life.

Yet if religion and tradition formed a protective web against the real world, they also rendered shtetl Jews unable to comprehend this world in its true dimensions. To the extent that religious and cultural cohesion ameliorated the isolation of the shtetl, it also accentuated the fear and suspicion of anything outside it. The result was that inhabitants of the smaller shtetlach were psychically unprepared for the waves of violence and terror that engulfed their villages during the latter part of the nineteenth century. These same people brought those same fears and insecurities with them when they left their villages and made the long journey to America to begin life anew.

The insecurities and fears of many rural Jews were not, however, characteristic of the outlook of the urban Jewish population. In the cities, Jewish workers and students had become imbued with Zionist and socialist ideals. Both credos were dynamic, proclaiming an alteration of the status quo through the building of mass political movements to effect economic and social change. For Zionists, the message was escape to the Promised Land. For socialists, the aim was to create a promised land within the Pale.[16] The Zionists embellished their credo with a certain amount of socialism, and the socialists based many of their beliefs on assumptions shared with the Zionists. Whichever course they chose, adherents effectively separated themselves from the conservative outlook of traditional religious and social beliefs.[17]

The militancy and agitation of socialists and Zionists culminated in a broad wave of dissidence, demonstrations, and strikes in the urban centers of the Pale. By the 1870s the strikes had turned violent, with increasing numbers of Jewish workmen resorting to outright defiance of the authorities and conscious acts of industrial sabotage. By the late 1880s the Social Democrats had organized strike funds and union cells among Jewish workers in every industrial area. Strikes led by Jewish workmen in 1893 and again in 1895 resulted in the formation of the first national Jewish trade union, the Universal Union of Bristle Workers. The situation worsened during the first decade of the twentieth century, when agitation by Jewish radicals fed into a general upsurge of political militancy, culminating in the Russian Revolution of 1905. During and after the revolt, Jews were imprisoned en masse in the dungeons of the tsar or sent into exile in Siberia and abroad. The Pale was dubbed by one government official as "a hotbed of revolutionary activity."[18]

The rural population of the Pale did not sleep through these developments, but neither was it truly awake. For the most part, socialism and Zionism made only limited inroads into the shtetl prior to 1914. These alien doctrines only penetrated the consciousness of the shtetl population when a local resident returned from the city carrying some of these strange ideas in his head. The people of most shtetlach were too isolated, too backward, and too unsophisticated to accept a world view based upon dynamic notions of social change.

On the other hand, modern currents of thought and political action did enter the shtetl in a diluted form, through the medium of Haskalah. The shtetl proponents of Haskalah considered themselves "modern" in every sense of the word. They were mostly the wealthier members of the community, whose social and economic status led to some degree of contact with the outside world. They eschewed the traditional religious piety of the Hasidim, sent their children to secular schools in the larger towns or big cities, and generally attempted to copy the mannerisms and cultural attitudes of the urbanized Jewish bourgeoisie. But Haskalah was not a political doctrine or a strategy for political action. It was an intellectual link between the shtetl and the world around it for those Jews whose lives allowed them to become involved with the world beyond the shtetl. But if the intellectual stirrings within the shtetl produced a handful of residents who saw the advantages of leaving the village and setting their sights on the possibilities of progress on the outside, this was not typical of the bulk of the rural population. Most of these rural Jews remained within the villages, unable to develop a modern consciousness to carry with them when their shtetl was finally destroyed.

But Too Late

The great wave of violence that would ultimately destroy shtetl culture in the Pale erupted in the Crimea in 1871.[19] A much more serious outbreak of violence occurred in 1881, following the assassination of Alexander II by a group of terrorist revolutionaries that included several Jews. The 1881 pogroms resulted in the slaughter of more than 50,000 persons before the government belatedly reestablished order in the Pale. The anti-Jewish violence was spearheaded by the Union of the Russian Nation (the notorious "Black Hundreds"), who recruited local goon squads in every region and town. Behind these "spontaneous" massacres could be discerned the acquiescence—if not the active connivance—of tsarist officials, whose anti-Semitic rhetoric and laws grew increasingly virulent. Government policy gave further rein to local henchmen and hooligans, who knew that violence and slaughter directed against Jews would be rationalized and condoned.

Anti-Semitic violence in the Pale erupted again in 1903 and 1905. These years marked the most serious incidents, but there was constant abuse and intimidation throughout the entire decade. The anti-Jewish laws that had been promulgated by the earlier tsars were enforced at the local level in whatever manner seemed most expedient at the time. Statutes requiring Jews to leave a particular locale or give up their interests in a particular business became incitements to further violence and slaughter.

The pogroms that occurred prior to World War I were but a prelude, however, to the mass slaughter and destruction which broke out in 1919. With the onset of the Bolshevik Revolution and the collapse of political authority throughout Eastern Europe, the Pale became a no-man's-land. As civil war engulfed the region, the Jews were caught between contesting factions, and a new wave of massacres took place from which hardly any city, town, or village containing Jews was exempt. Between December 1918 and April 1919 more than 60 separate pogroms took place in the Ukraine, resulting in the deaths of more than 250,000 Jews. Unlike earlier pogroms, which occurred in haphazard fashion, this new wave of violence left entire villages destroyed and whole regions pillaged in an organized and systematic manner. The shtetl of Ladyzhenko, near Kiev, held 1,600 Jews on the eve of the pogrom. The day after the village was invaded by Cossacks, there remained only two survivors. The shtetl of Tetien had a Jewish population of more than 6,000; over 4,000 were murdered during the pogrom, including scores of women and children who were hiding in the main synagogue when the Cossacks burned it to the ground. The list of atrocities committed during 1919–21 is endless and includes almost every type of torture and violence that humans could suffer at the hands of other "humans." Sometimes survivors escaped the mass slaughter only because there was not enough time to finish the killing, or because rifle cartridges were too expensive, and the grisly job had to be done by hand. In all, there were more than 1,500 publicized incidents of mass violence in the Pale during 1919–21, along with countless episodes of slaughter and pillage in shtetlach too small to command attention from the outside world.

The reasons behind this great wave of pogroms have never been adequately explained, just as the history of the rural Pale has never been analyzed in detail. The horror of the pogroms was recognized at the time, and worldwide campaigns were mounted, with scant success, to avert the ultimate disaster.[20] But once the pogroms ended, and the survivors were relocated or returned to their native villages, the entire episode began to recede from the consciousness of a public that wanted to forget the political and social turbulence associated with World War I.

The pogroms can be partially explained by the fact that they were not isolated events but the culmination of nearly a century of official and unofficial persecution and terror. Another important factor was the general economic and social dislocation that accompanied World War I and was aggravated and prolonged by the effects of the Bolshevik Revolution. But the intensity of the pogroms underscores the unique position of the Jews within the rural Pale—particularly the Jews who lived in the smaller and more isolated shtetlach, who were set apart, both culturally and physically, from the larger society around them. The local peasants perceived the Jews as an alien population. Nor were the Jews capable of overcoming this basic social antipathy. In addition to being viewed as outsiders, Jews were also seen as petty exploiters, the result of their role as middlemen and merchants. Indeed, Jews were often utilized by local officials to perform the odious tasks of public administration, such as tax collecting, precisely because they stood apart from the peasant population.

Mired in a life of poverty and isolation, cast in the role of exploiter, real or imagined, the Jews in the small shtetlach came to regard themselves as an alien population surrounded by enemies. In some shtetlach, the situation was not so extreme. The Jews of Skala, for example, participated on equal terms with gentiles in the political life of the town and maintained harmonious social relations with the non-Jewish population. But the memories of the townsfolk of Skala, in this respect, are more than outweighed by the innumerable stories of persecution, intimidation, and isolation recounted by so many former shtetl dwellers. Threatened by the world around them and trapped by the poverty of daily life, Jews in the small shtetlach developed a strategy of survival that reduced risks to the minimum and required that every decision be weighed not in terms of the opportunity for success but against the possibility of failure.

Fear of change, avoidance of chance, and minimizing of risk were the linchpins of a basic social philosophy and psychology that Jews carried from the small shtetlach to the New World. For the shtetl Jews who eschewed such attitudes, the banality of shtetl life was resolved by going to the cities or emigrating to America of their own free will. But the majority of shtetl dwellers never viewed such options in positive terms. They remained in their villages until events beyond their control forced them to leave, and when they left, they literally ran for their lives. They arrived in New York having left shattered families and villages behind, but with their limited and fearful perceptions of life still intact. These perceptions and the experiences that formed them would become the motivating force behind the emergence of the landsmanshaftn in New York.

III

Years of Settlement,
Years of Strain

The New World turned things upside down.
—A. Cahan,
The Rise of David Levinsky

IN 1908 a penniless young immigrant named Harry Fish-man arrived in New York, having departed three months previously from his native village in the Ukraine. Many years later, in recounting the events of his first day in New York, he said: "I got off the ferry from Ellis Island at the Battery. Everything was so big. I didn't know which way to turn. The city, the buildings, the noise was too much to take in. Then I saw a group of men standing in a circle around another man who was handing them each a slip of paper and a dollar bill. The man was recruiting a work gang to go to New Jersey and unload a ship at the pier. So I got in line and signed up for a day's work. We were put on a ferry and went across the harbor to New Jersey. I worked all day and night but never got paid, so the next morning I took the ferry back to New York and started all over again. I like to say that I got off the boat in New York not once, but twice."

This story graphically portrays the immediate dilemma

that confronted immigrants arriving on the shores of the New World. They were faced with a wholly new situation and could either learn to adapt quickly or face the possibility that they might not survive. For many shtetl immigrants, moreover, life in the Old Country simply had not prepared them for the upside-down world they would find, nor could they even comprehend the types of decisions they would be forced to make. An immigrant who had made the wrong decision summed up the whole situation as follows: "If I had known it would be so bitter for me here, I wouldn't have come. I didn't come here for a fortune, but where is bread? What can I do now?"[1]

Added to the limitations imposed on immigrants by their experiences in the shtetl was the fact that they arrived in New York at a time when the city was experiencing its most dynamic period of growth and change, a far cry from the unchanging nature of life in the Old World. From 1880 to 1920, New York grew to become not only the largest city in the United States but also the most important port city in the Western hemisphere and the financial capital of the globe. By the early 1920s, when the East European migration came to an end, New York had developed into the world's first megalopolis, containing an uncountable number of competing social groups within its massive population. What did New York offer the new immigrants from Eastern Europe? What types of problems and possibilities lay in store for them as they attempted to adjust to this new way of life? The answers can best be appreciated through a brief survey of the city's economic and social development during the period of the Great Migration.

The New World Challenge

In 1900, New York was not only a magnet for the world's humanity; it was also a magnet for the world's supply of goods and commodities.[2] Each year the port handled nearly half the tea and three-quarters of all the coffee, sugar, cotton, silk, and wool entering the United States. It also expedited the shipment of nearly half the volume of all goods entering and leaving America. This unprecedented concentration of commerce quickly made the city the world's leading banking and insurance center. In addition to its commercial activity, New York was also a major hub of manufacturing, with 70 of the 185 largest industrial concerns in America located within its environs.

The growth of international finance and trade was more than matched by the expansion of the city's internal economy. By 1915, New York's population had increased to more than 5 million people, with several million more residing in adjacent cities and towns within the metropolitan area.[3] This population explosion led to an unparalleled growth in retail trade, as well as to the expansion of the service and wholesale sectors. On the eve of World War I, New York accounted for 10 percent of the entire manufacturing output of the United States and an even higher proportion of wholesaling activity. The city's industrial output was not concentrated in a few major industrial enterprises but was spread out among thousands of small workshops and loft factories.

The development of industry and commerce and the increase in the numbers of city residents resulted in the expansion of the city's physical boundaries. As late as 1880, the City of New York consisted only of Manhattan Island, while much of the outlying regions of the Bronx, Brooklyn, and

Queens remained undeveloped, open land and farms. By 1900 the city's political boundaries embraced all five present-day boroughs, and with the exception of Staten Island and the eastern part of Queens, near the Nassau County border, all these outlying areas were beginning to be filled up. Between 1880 and 1920 the Bronx increased its population ninefold, Brooklyn's population grew to five times its earlier size, and Queens showed a fourfold increase. Each day, more than 3 million persons rode subways, buses, and trolleys into the central city, and the "rush hour" in and out of Manhattan had already stretched well beyond sixty minutes each morning and afternoon.

All of this unplanned and unprecedented growth coincided with the steady influx of European immigrants into New York. By 1915 the number of New Yorkers of German and Irish descent, who had formed a majority of the city's population just after the Civil War, was exceeded by the combined total of immigrants from other regions in Europe. The city's population grew from 1.5 million to over 5 million in less than 50 years, and nearly all of this increase reflected the outpouring of humanity from Eastern and Southern Europe, particularly Italy and the Pale.[4]

The dramatic growth of the city, together with the disproportionate increase in the number of poor and unskilled inhabitants, produced widespread misery and deprivation. Immigrants jammed into tenements on the Lower East Side and other ghetto neighborhoods, and the congestion produced crime, vice, and disease. In 1890, Jacob Riis estimated that 330,000 persons lived in a square mile of slum housing, with the density of some areas exceeding 700 persons per acre. This made certain immigrant neighborhoods more crowded than Dickens's London or even Bombay.[5]

Municipal authorities responded to these conditions in a

sporadic manner. The city built roads and erected street-lights, but orphanages, hospitals, and welfare institutions remained largely the responsibility of private endeavors. The city with the highest population density in America had less than 5 percent of its total land area set aside for parks, and most of them were undeveloped. The city's population included 1.5 million children under the age of 12, but there was only one playground for every 12,000 of them.[6] To the extent that the conditions of life and work improved over time in New York, this was largely the result of a general increase in economic activity and a consequent rise in the overall standard of living. It was only in the decades after World War I that government stepped in with major public-service programs to ameliorate the plight of the poor.

For the new immigrants, the overwhelming insecurity of the situation was compounded by the unfamiliarity of the surroundings. People moved from job to job, if they could find work, and they often labored for days on end without knowing if they would get paid. One elderly woman recalls that her husband found work in a greengrocery, but when payday arrived the proprietor told him that he was short of cash and could only give him the equivalent of his wages in groceries. "From then on," she chuckled, "we had plenty of potatoes to eat, but no money to spend."

Unending insecurity and uncertainty were the harshest realities of New York life for new immigrant Jews. Economic privation and material scarcity were factors common to poverty everywhere, including the shtetl, but life in the Old Country at least had a certain unchanging character. There, people lived and worked together throughout their entire lives. In every respect, life in New York was at the other extreme. Brothers and sisters who had been together since birth were now thrown into a variety of makeshift living arrangements, often boarding with different families and changing residences every week. People who had labored in the same workshop or neighborhood in the Old World now faced the prospect of changing employers and work locations several times each year. The frenzy of immigrant life in New York, its rapid and unforeseen change, was the antithesis of the shtetl experience, and all the traditional definitions and habits were suddenly without meaning.

The continuing influx of Jews from the Pale resulted in a rapid expansion of the scope of Jewish settlement within the city. By the end of the Great Migration, there was hardly a neighborhood in New York that did not contain Jewish residents. In 1890, most immigrant Jews were living on the Lower East Side. In 1920, on the other hand, only 40 percent of New York's Jewish population still lived in Manhattan, while 37 percent lived in Brooklyn, and 17 percent resided in the Bronx. Queens now held 5 percent of the city's Jews, or nearly 100,000 persons.[7]

The movement of Jews away from the Lower East Side, however, did not alter the style and pace of life for those who went to live in other neighborhoods. Immigrants who moved to Brooklyn or the Bronx brought with them the same attitudes and habits that defined the style of life on the Lower East Side. By 1900 many immigrant Jews were stepping off the boat and going directly to Brooklyn, where Brownsville was fast becoming the largest and most intensely settled Jewish community in the entire city. Brownsville was considered by some to be even a worse ghetto than the Lower East Side, with an even larger number of sweatshops, tenement hovels, itinerant peddlers, beggars, and gangs of wayward youths. The violence and bitterness of the cloakmakers' strike in 1910 exposed the poverty and misery of immigrant existence throughout the city, but the worst instances of labor strife occurred in the streets and factories of Brownsville.[8]

Even as the expansion of the immigrant population into outlying boroughs extended the wretched conditions prevailing in the Lower East Side ghetto, it also presented opportunities for economic and social progress. As the Jewish population swelled in the decades prior to World War I, the city's internal economy experienced a corresponding growth. No matter how poor, the masses of new immigrants from Eastern Europe needed clothing, shelter, and food. The result was an upsurge in retailing and wholesaling throughout the city, but particularly in newer neighborhoods. Nearly all of the tradesmen, wholesalers, and retailers who catered to this expanding immigrant market were recent immigrants themselves and were often people who had engaged in the same types of activities back in the shtetl.[9]

Jewish tradesmen who were able to take advantage of the expansion of the internal market and respond to the needs of the immigrant population experienced a degree of economic and social mobility that was virtually impossible and incomprehensible in the Old World. In 1880, 56 percent of all Russian-Jewish households were headed by manual laborers, while 39 percent were headed by petty tradesmen or white-collar employees. By 1905, 54 percent of all Russian-Jewish households were still headed by persons involved in manual labor, reflecting the masses of new immigrants who had arrived in New York after 1890. But among those Russian Jews who had been in America for twenty years or more, only 33 percent were still classified as laborers.[10] In other words, within a generation after their arrival, nearly half the Russian Jews who had started life in America as laborers had managed to move up the socioeconomic ladder.

Not only did immigrant Jews achieve a much higher standard of living after their move to the New World, but American society also offered them a variety of paths upward. The new immigrants could not yet enter banks, security brokerage houses, or major corporations, which were just then being penetrated by the established German Jews. But immigrants could enter the myriad mechanical, petty industrial, and manufacturing trades that dominated the city's productive sector. They also took over entire sectors of wholesale trade and totally controlled retailing in their own neighborhoods. The movement of Jews into the Bronx and Brooklyn resulted in the growth of an immigrant real estate market, and Jewish entrepreneurs became the primary speculators in the rapid buying and selling of building lots for new home construction. In Brownsville the price of residential lots jumped from $50 to $3,000 in just a few years, and real estate deals between Jewish brokers were literally made on street corners.[11] As soon as the houses were completed and occupied, Jewish tradesmen moved in and established wholesale and retail networks to provide goods for local consumption.

Economic mobility went hand in hand with cultural assimilation, which, in turn, bred the possibility of further economic success. This was particularly true among the laborers, who quickly grafted onto American culture as a means of enhancing their strength relative to the factory owners. The Workmen's Circle and the Bund actively recruited members to join the effort to "become part of American society and correct its evils," according to an early Workmen's Circle manifesto. Even the political system offered possibilities for mobility through the use of patronage and the power of the immigrant vote. Before World War I, only "uptown" Jews of German descent could entertain political ambitions, but the uptowners were mindful of the importance of immigrant votes, and they courted immigrant political support with great fervor.

Yet the expansion of the city's economy and the possibilities of increased social mobility did not wholly ameliorate the basic insecurities and fears of immigrants, particularly those who had just arrived from the smaller villages in the Pale. The pace of New York life was too chaotic, too quick, and too overwhelming to allow any immediate adjustment to take place. In the shtetl, for example, nearly all social and economic activities had centered around the home. The house was a workshop, a small store, or a place to keep goods. Because the home also served as a workplace, economic affairs were family affairs. Wives, children, and any others who inhabited the shtetl home were included in the work process as an inseparable and integral aspect of daily life.[12]

When the shtetl was replaced by the stoop, this traditional relationship gave way. It is true that many of the early immigrants worked at home, supplementing a meager factory wage with piecework labor carried on late at night on a sewing machine or a lathe set up on the kitchen table. Oftentimes groups of women from the tenement would gather in an apartment to sew, knit, or sort textile goods. But as the economy expanded and production became automated, the house and workplace were increasingly divorced from one another. Immigrants began moving into neighborhoods that had a clear residential character. These Jews traveled to the workplace by day and returned to their homes at night; each day's trip, which could last an hour or more, might represent a greater distance than many immigrants had traveled in a lifetime of work back in the shtetl. Work also lost its familial character, and the phenomenon of husband, wife, children, and relatives laboring together gradually became a dim memory of the past. "I always worked with my father in the village," recounts one elderly immigrant, "but I never worked with him again after we came to New York. I got a job in the jewelry district [where he eventually owned a large showroom] and my father remained in a grocery store near our apartment in Harlem."

This story typifies the initial experience of many shtetl immigrants. To the extent that it was possible, they began by attempting to arrange their new lives according to familiar customs and traditions, but they soon realized that Old World practices would have to be replaced. Barter disappeared in favor of cash, family labor gave way to individual effort, English replaced Yiddish, and all the other old habits began to change. But how did one make the decisions that were required in order to survive such changes? Which decisions were right, and which decisions were wrong? The shtetl population lacked the experience, awareness, know-how, and understanding of this new society, which could only come with the passage of time. Until that happened, they had to survive on a thin edge, where the smallest mistake might be fatal. The wrong choice could mean the end of everything.

It was this dilemma, multiplied by the tens of thousands of immigrants who confronted it, that explains the origins of the landsmanshaftn in New York. For the landsmanshaftn held out the possibility of making such choices within an environment of security and hope. Surrounded by like-minded people who shared the same problems and viewed the world in a similar fashion, the immigrant could have each decision reviewed by others who had made or would make similar decisions about the same types of issues. If the key to survival lay in minimizing risk, then it became an objective necessity to spread the risk among as many people as possible.

The Immigrant Response

In 1938 the Yiddish literary scholar Isaac Rontch published a survey of landsmanshaft organizations under the auspices of the WPA Federal Writers Project. This book, written in Yiddish, represents the only specific study of the landsmanshaft phenomenon up to the present time.[13] Rontch and his associates made contact with 2,468 separate organizations, of which perhaps half were independent landsmanshaftn whose membership consisted of individuals from the same village or region in the Pale. The remaining organizations included chapters of fraternal societies such as the Order Brith Abraham, Workmen's Circle branches, family circles, and neighborhood benevolent associations.

By the time Rontch's work was published, many smaller societies had already ceased to exist. Since many landsmanshaftn were originally outgrowths of neighborhood chevras, the quick pace of change in living patterns had led to the disappearance of many smaller societies, along with the storefront synagogues to which they had been attached. In addition to the many societies that had disbanded by the 1930s, there were many landsmanshaftn that were still active but not large enough to draw the attention of Rontch and his fellow writers.[14] If many East European immigrants came from shtetlach too small to be remembered, they also formed landsmanshaftn that were too small to survive for any period of time. For these reasons, Rontch's work cannot possibly convey the breadth of the landsmanshaft experience among immigrant Jews in New York.

A vague sense of the richness of landsmanshaft existence can be gleaned from the names of the societies themselves. Often a society would split into several branches or separate organizations, each retaining the name of the shtetl of origin but adding a descriptive title to denote a specific type of membership. For example, the Piaterer Progressive Benevolent Society was a secularized and probably left-wing off-shoot of a more politically conservative or religious landsmanshaft. The First Independent Staroznitzer Bukowiner Sick and Benevolent Association had separated from an earlier organization which itself had become "independent" by breaking away from a parent body. Nearly all the early landsmanshaftn excluded females from active membership, allowing a woman to appear on the membership rolls of a society only if she was the wife, daughter, or widow of a male member. But women soon founded their own organizations, and many of these female auxiliaries similarly split as the aims and philosophies of their members changed and diverged.

Despite these developments, which reflected a certain recognition of modernity, the landsmanshaftn as a whole remained mired in the Old World view of things. Yiddish remained nearly the universal language at meetings, even if records were occasionally kept in English. Many societies broke away from initial affiliations with orthodox synagogues but retained a basic sense of religious orthodoxy, particularly when a society activity, such as a funeral, involved actual participation in religious rituals. Most of the societies only ate kosher food at their meetings and avoided overt manifestations of Americanization. Nearly all retained a basic identification with the shtetl or region of origin.

The Old World antipathy toward New World society was reflected in nearly every aspect of landsmanshaft activity but was most evident in the groups' conservative attitude toward trade unions and other labor issues. An exception was the Breziner Sick and Benevolent Society, which inserted a bylaw in its constitution stipulating that "if any member shall be found working in a shop at the time of a local strike therein, such working shall be considered immoral conduct for which such member may be expelled." Generally speaking, the landsmanshaftn were notorious for their lack of working-class consciousness, enabling employers to manipulate the workers' landsleit sentiment as a means of keeping labor peace in their shops and shutting the union out. In *The Rise of David Levinsky*, Abraham Cahan relates how his fictional hero formed a landsmanshaft in his factory, aware that such an organization would undercut efforts to unionize the work force:

> All this, I confess, was not without advantage to my business interests, for it afforded me a low average of wages and safeguarded my shop against labor troubles. The cloakmaker's union had come into existence, and, although it had no real power over the men, the trade was not free from sporadic conflicts in individual shops. My place, however, was absolutely immune from difficulties of this sort—all because of the Levinsky Antomir Benefit Society.[15]

Cahan created a fictional character in David Levinsky, but his comments about the role of the landsmanshaftn as a defense against the radicalism of the unions were drawn from his own experiences. As editor of the *Daily Forward*, he published in the "Bintel Brief" column many letters from immigrants decrying the backwardness and conservatism of the landsmanshaftn. One such letter, published in 1910, states that during the cloakmakers' strike, a committee from the union appeared at a landsmanshaft meeting to make an appeal for funds. The society's treasury had been inoperative for six months (a not unusual occurrence among the smaller landsmanshaftn, which were chronically short of funds), and only a special tax on the membership would produce the necessary donation to aid the union's cause. The letter writer concludes: "A motion was raised to tax the brothers at the next meeting, but it was defeated by the members with the argument that each one could, of his own free will, make his own contribution to the strike."[16]

Other Jewish organizations, particularly labor unions, were clearly aware of the negative and anti–working class tendencies of the landsmanshaftn and went out of their way to reject the landsmanshaft mentality among their own members. "Whenever anyone stood up at a meeting and addressed his fellow workers as 'landsleit' or 'brother,' we would boo and hiss and remind him that we were comrades first and foremost," recounts a retired Bund activist. "You couldn't trust the members of the societies, because when all was said and done, their loyalties were really to themselves. They were just small-town Jews." The unions made a fetish about learning to speak English, for how else could a workingman bargain with his employer or argue with a judge for his rights? The landsmanshaftn, on the other hand, never spoke English and usually avoided any mass organization or activity that was built around economic or social issues.

The attempt by the landsmanshaftn to maintain traditional attitudes and beliefs not only provoked animosity and conflict between the societies and other organizations, but also resulted in generational disputes within the landsmanshaftn themselves. Younger immigrants strove to acclimate themselves to the new social order, while the older generation remained fundamentally tied to a pre-migration mentality. Many younger immigrants were not active in their parents' societies during the early years because they perceived the landsmanshaft as being too religious or too conservative to suit their needs. If the landsmanshaftn were not actively anti-socialist, they simply ignored labor issues, leaving little room for participation in the landsmanshaft by members who were politically active or committed to larger causes.

One result of this conflict between the conservatism of the older members and the activism of their children was that many first-generation immigrants actually joined their societies quite late in life. "My father wanted me to become a member when I got married," recalls an immigrant in his eighties who came to America as a teenager, "but I was too busy working, and the society was too conservative for me. I once went to the landsmanshaft and asked them to join me at our union parade, but nobody would go with me."

This individual ultimately returned to the landsmanshaft fold, becoming an active member of his society in his fifties, when nearly all the original members had passed away. He had never truly assimilated into American society, spoke English only haltingly, and had achieved only minimal success as a petty entrepreneur. Very quickly he was elevated to the presidency of his society and then ran its affairs for the next twenty years, carrying on in the best Old World tradition and loudly excoriating the more assimilated members for their obsession with becoming "Americans."

The obsession to become an American had characterized this man's own life when he first came to New York and had resulted in his refusal to join the society until he was well into middle age. There were a number of reasons for his abrupt turnabout, chief among them the birth of the State of Israel and the terrifying awareness of the Holocaust, events that provoked the deepest and most visceral feelings of fear and hope. But there was another, more subtle reason why this man's generational conflict was ultimately resolved in favor of the landsmanshaft. Like many immigrants, he had attempted to achieve a modicum of financial success, only to discover that he would never rise above the bottom rung of the business ladder. Once he realized his own limitations, he chose to survive by minimizing all risks and resorting to his most basic instincts. While he did not join his society in a formal manner until his later years, he never truly lost the landsmanshaft mentality.

This is not to say that basic problems of life in America lay outside the concern of the landsmanshaftn, or that issues of social welfare and economic justice were never raised. To the contrary, the meetings of most societies were taken up by endless discussions about housing, work, and other dilemmas that everyone faced. But when immigrants characterized the landsmanshaftn as being too conservative, they were not speaking about the content of landsmanshaft discussions; rather, they meant the context in which these discussions were held. With rare exceptions, every issue debated at a landsmanshaft meeting was analyzed in personal terms, with scant reference to the non-landsmanshaft world and with only passing interest in how other groups or organizations were dealing with the problem. Most landsmanshaft members were not overly concerned about the fate of the unions, or the masses, or the society around them. They were concerned with their own individual struggles, but most of all they were concerned with the survival of the landsmanshaft itself. A member who felt drawn to a movement or issue that transcended the society's narrow concerns quickly fell out of step and broke away from the landsmanshaft.

A Society Is Born

The world of the landsmanshaftn has disappeared, but a reader can gain some appreciation of that world by vicariously "attending" a few meetings of the Progress Mutual

Aid Society (PMAS), which was formed in 1905.[17] The membership was drawn from several smaller Polish landsmanshaftn that had gone out of existence at the end of the nineteenth century, hence the absence of a place-name in the title. The PMAS was a secular society, but the membership spoke Yiddish, and many of the group's functions were carried out within the context of Old World, orthodox traditions. The society met every month (and sometimes more than once a month) until it was disbanded in 1961. For a brief moment it will be revived again.*

The first session of the PMAS was held in a small meeting room in a building on 107th Street and Third Avenue on July 13, 1905. We do not know how many persons attended the meeting, but we do know they were all men. The society would not allow a female to attend any of its meetings until it had met over sixty times and had been in existence for more than five years.

At the initial meeting, the society's first officers were elected. They were Abraham Schiller as president, Behrend Cohen as vice-president, George Jonas as financial secretary (the reader should bear this name in mind for future reference), Hyman B. Cohen as treasurer, and, as trustees, Nathan Marks, Leo Reiman, and Isaac Simon. In all, the society first had seven officers who were elected by acclamation. Within three years, the society would have fourteen officers, although the number of members would not substantially increase. Murphy's Law operated even within the smallest landsmanshaftn.

The manner of electing these original officers also requires

---

*The PMAS was chosen as a "model" landsmanshaft because it was the one society whose archive at YIVO was virtually complete, including minutes of every meeting held between 1905, when it was started, and 1961, when it was disbanded. Consequently we can reconstruct an entire "history" of its existence.

a brief comment. Not a single position was contested, although each individual was formally nominated and had to accept nomination before a single vote was cast by anyone on his behalf. The number of contested elections in landsmanshaft political history is very slight. In many societies it was often difficult to find people who were willing to serve the brethren, and as the membership grew older, it was not unusual for a particular landsmanshaft officer to find himself taking on, de facto, a lifetime position. But on the rare occasion when an election was contested, all elements of civility and fraternity were likely to collapse. The experiences of the PMAS, as we shall see, were no exception to this rule.

To return to our first meeting in the summer of 1905, it was agreed that the society would meet monthly except in August. It was also decided, after the election for officers, that yearly dues would be $2 per family. Since the society had a list of 166 prospective members which had been drawn up prior to the meeting, this meant that the treasury began to operate with the sum of $332. From this amount had to be deducted $20 for the certificate of incorporation, $7.75 for framing said certificate, $3.25 for printing stationery, $1.50 for stamps, and $3.75 for rental of the meeting room. The PMAS now faced the world with a war chest of $295.75. Not surprisingly, the meeting ended with an exhortation from the newly elected president, Mr. Schiller, to go out and find new members. Just before adjournment, the president also appointed two committees, one to secure a permanent meeting room and the other to draft a set of bylaws. It should be pointed out to those readers unfamiliar with landsmanshaft procedures that everything was done on a committee basis. No problem was too minute or insignificant to warrant anything less than committee attention.

The second meeting of the society took place on October

2, 1905, at 1664 Madison Avenue. It was a brief meeting, taken up primarily with a long discussion on the report of the meeting room committee, which had found a suitable room on East 104th Street in a building known as the Harlem Terrace. The landlord, Mr. Rand, would allow the society to rent meeting space for $25 per year, broken up into four quarterly payments of $6.25 each. A motion to sign the lease was actually carried, and the financial secretary, Mr. Jonas, was instructed to disburse the first quarterly payment from the society's bank account. This event set a significant precedent which, as we shall see, was soon forgotten. As time went on, it would become increasingly rare for a committee report to meet with instant approbation by the society's membership. Only the most skilled parliamentary maneuvering would lead the society to take positive action on any issue unless it was absolutely necessary. After all, with the dues collected from all the members, the society now had a bank balance of more than $400 and would soon be moving into very serious and weighty discussions about extremely significant issues. Quick decisions were not the stuff of which landsmanshaft debates were made.

At the third meeting, held at the Harlem Terrace on November 20, the bylaws were brought up for discussion. A portion of the bylaws, dealing with the official name of the society, the requirement for monthly meetings, and other procedural matters, was adopted. But the bylaws committee was instructed to continue its work, because the society's growth would necessitate many revisions and amendments as time went on. The membership also agreed at this meeting to give the financial secretary, George Jonas, an annual salary of $25, beginning with the first session in 1906. Mr. Jonas thus became the highest-salaried member of the society hierarchy, an issue that would come back to haunt the membership in the years ahead. Before closing the meeting, the president made another appeal to increase the membership, and this was underscored by the appointment of an official membership committee consisting of "Brothers B. Cohen and Nathan Marks." The society, after four months of existence, now had seven officers and three committees. Since attendance at most meetings was usually less than thirty persons, this meant that perhaps two-thirds of the active brethren were actually engaged in some form or another of society affairs.

At the fourth meeting, on December 18, 1905, the membership committee gave its first formal report. "Bros. B. Cohen and Nathan Marks reported that they visited several members still out from the society and they succieded and having three of them to pay in, and the rest will pay up and be with us very soon."* The society also took a major step forward at this meeting by appointing an entertainment committee, whose first chairman was George Kinsburg. This meant that the society was on its way toward becoming a true landsmanshaft, inasmuch as it was beginning to develop the types of activities that would bind its members together over the course of their lives. It also meant that each meeting would have another item on the agenda, in this case the monthly report of the entertainment committee, thus increasing the scope for debate. Since a major function of the society was to provide a monthly opportunity for lengthy discussions about whatever had to be discussed, the emergence of yet a fourth committee after just four meetings was a healthy sign.

The entertainment committee, which had seven members

*The errors in spelling, grammar, and usage found in quoted landsmanshaft source material reflect the style and flavor of the immigrant idiom, and are directly transcribed from actual society minutes, letters, and conversations.

(making it the largest of all committees), weighed in with its first report at the fifth meeting, in January. The chairman, "Bro. Geo. Kinsburg, stated that the Committee has decided to run a Dance and pacage [sic] party for the benefit of the society and that they can procure the Hall in Harlem Terrace for the sum of $10. After a *long* discussion [author's italics] it was moved and seconded to give the Committee the full power to run the same and charge 11¢ for tickets and 15¢ for hat check for each gents, ladies to furnishe the packages."

It should be added that giving the women responsibility for providing the refreshments marked the first time that females were mentioned in any capacity in the society's minutes. Having come up with the society's first entertainment activity, the entertainment committee, obviously embarked on a major enterprise, was enlarged from seven to eleven members. At the next monthly meeting, in February, the committee would be enlarged to fifteen members.

In March, during the society's seventh meeting, it was agreed to pay the cost of sending postcards each month to advise the membership of the following month's meeting. Clearly, the society had now grown beyond an association of individuals who could notify other members of its activities by word of mouth. At the eighth meeting the president asked for a minute of silence to note the death of "Bro. M. Frankenstein," the first member of PMAS to pass away since the society's founding. The practice of calling for a minute of silence whenever a member's death was announced would continue almost to the end of this society's existence.

Sometime before the ninth meeting, on May 21, 1906, the PMAS held its first function, and it evidently was a success. We know this because at the May meeting the entertainment committee reported that expenses for the dance had been $57.70 and income had been $106.48. The meeting was spent primarily on a long discussion about the bylaws, which were still being developed by the bylaws committee. The society had been in existence for less than one year, and it could hardly be expected to decide such a profound question as its own legal structure in such a short period of time. Accordingly, the president instructed the bylaws committee to revise completely its earlier draft and report back to the members at a later date.

We now move to the first meeting of the society in 1907. By this time the Progress Mutual Aid Society was beginning to come into its own. A motion on death benefits was debated, and it was agreed that the society would pay $100 to the heirs upon the death of a male member and $50 to the heirs upon the death of the wife or widow of a member. The membership in 1907 comprised 108 members in "good standing," meaning dues had been paid on time, and 60 members not in "good standing"; in addition, there had been 32 suspensions and 7 deaths. The yearly dues had been increased to $9, payable at $2.25 per quarter. If a member did not pay his quarterly dues for more than two meetings after the remittance date, he was suspended. At the January 1907 meeting, 21 members were suspended for nonpayment. This alerts us to the fact, mentioned earlier, that many immigrants joined landsmanshaftn but quickly moved on to other types of organizations that better suited their needs.

The minutes of the seventeenth meeting, held February 18, 1907, contain a significant notation. For the first time since the society was organized, a weekly sick payment was made to a member. The PMAS paid $5 weekly for no more than ten consecutive weeks to any member in good standing who could prove that illness prevented him from working. There was also a lump-sum payment allowed for cases of "terminal illness." The society's willingness to expend $50 for the illness of a member was quite generous. The First Bratslaver Society paid only $8 for six weeks in any one year, and a member had to be sick for two weeks before receiving benefits. The Breziner Society would pay $8 for up to twenty weeks, but only if the treasury held an excess of $2,000. "Bro. H. Marks" became the first recipient of a payment from the PMAS provident fund, and thus the society added benevolence to entertainment as essential activities for the remainder of its existence.

The third essential activity, the maintenance of a cemetery, would also be initiated at this meeting. Responding to the fact that the ranks of the society had already been depleted by seven deaths, including that of the first president, Abraham Schiller, the members decided "that a committee of three be appointed to look for a suitable Burial Ground for this Society, and to bring in estimates at our next meeting." The president also stated his intention to look for an undertaker who would be in charge of all society funerals, a decision no doubt motivated by the payment of $12 to an undertaker for the rental of a hearse and carriage for a member's funeral the previous month.

At the eighteenth meeting, in March, the records show sick payments of $15, including a two-week payment to one member. Thereafter, sick payments would become a regular feature of the society's business, as well as a drain on the society's finances. In the long run, this matter would become a problem of major proportions. The following month's meeting was highlighted by the announcement that thirteen more members had been suspended for nonpayment of dues.

By May, the burial ground committee still had not settled on a suitable plan for buying burial space for the society. The committee "reported progress," however, and was told to make a further report at the next month's meeting. The May gathering did result in the formation of yet another committee, but its life span would be relatively brief. "The president announced that he recieved a invitation from Bro. Samuel Prince to represent the Society at the celebration of his Golden Weding." After a surprisingly brief discussion, a three-man committee was appointed to purchase a "suitable present" for Brother Prince. The Prince present committee dutifully reported at the June meeting that it had "purchest a Gold Headed Cane for the Brother. It was regular moved and seconded that the committee shall go to the Bros. house and present the same to him in behalf of the Society."

At the July meeting, the one issue of note was the official rendering of financial accounts. The society had actually managed to accumulate cash assets of $2,741.93, along with the intangible value of the framed charter of incorporation, which was hung on the wall at the beginning of each meeting. When a society member died, the charter was draped in black cloth for thirty days. The assets of the society were now so large that every decision became doubly serious and could only be taken with the greatest of care. Such a huge surplus also inspired certain members of the organization to hatch more grandiose plans.

The first such plan came to light at the August meeting. After the burial ground committee again "reported progress," an idea was put forth "that the Progress Mutual Aid Society shall run a theater party for the benefit of said society. After a long discussion pro and con between the members present, it was regular moved and seconded the recomodation be send back to the committee." Here we detect the beginnings of a generation gap. Success at the landsmanshaft game had gone to the heads of some members, and they were quite prepared to mount a major campaign to enlarge the activities of the society as well as its spending. But cooler heads prevailed. The theater party was an idea whose time had not yet come.

The resistance to an extensive entertainment program was underscored by a motion made at the meeting in September. Five members, including the financial secretary, George Jonas, and the group's elder statesman, Samuel Prince, had formed a rump committee for the purpose of accelerating the search for new members. In a petition to the society, they said: "We recommend that members sons from the ages of 18 to 25 years and being single, be admitted to this Society without any initiation fee." This petition tells us that at least a certain segment of the membership was beginning to acknowledge the fact that the society was not drawing in the younger generation. But this concern cannot have been shared by the majority, since the petition never made it to the floor for actual debate.

In November, nine months after it had first begun deliberations, the burial ground committee submitted its report. "Bro. Isaac Simon reported that this society can purches ground at Mt. Carmell Cemetery at $100 per plot. The committee was then authorized to meet at the cemetery and select a plot of 25 [graves] and take an option on same." The entertainment committee, which also reported on its ongoing deliberations at the meeting, did not achieve a similar degree of success. It recommended that the society hold a "Public Instolation" of new officers and a dance, but after a "Long discution" the report was rejected and the committee was told to come up with a new plan. The entertainment committee was still thinking in terms too grandiose for the society's rank-and-file.

One would have expected the December meeting to witness a triumphant announcement by the burial ground committee that a cemetery plot had been purchased at Mt. Carmel. After all, its recommendation to "take an option on same" had sailed right through the previous month's meeting with hardly a disclaimer. But such expectations were far removed from landsmanshaft modus operandi. Indeed, an issue as important as the cemetery, perhaps the single most important activity of the society, could not be settled easily. After all, the bylaws were still being discussed after more than a year, and the entertainment committee's last two schemes had met with nothing but rejection. So why should the burial ground committee get away with anything less in the way of argument and dispute? In fact, it didn't.

The December meeting began with a startling announcement. Acting on his own, the society's vice-president, Bernard Phillips, had visited the cemetery to look at the $100 plots. Phillips stated that "it was not satisfactory for this Society but this Society can purchers on the same Cemetery in Section D plots for $180 a plot." The announcement created an uproar. Motions and countermotions flew thick and fast. It was proposed to buy twenty-four plots at no more than $190 a plot; the motion was amended to buy only twelve plots. Then the amendment was withdrawn, and the original motion was put to a vote; it lost, 12–8. The burial ground committee, its own proposal now in shreds, asked to be discharged. This motion carried by 10–7, several members apparently having left the meeting, which had dragged on for nearly four hours. The final result of ten months' work was that the society still did not have a cemetery and didn't even have a cemetery committee.

But the cemetery problem would not go away. In fact, it was becoming a critical issue, for at least three more members had died in the past several months. The first session in 1908, which was the twenty-eighth meeting of the society, began as January meetings always began, with the installation of new officers. It was then announced that the cash assets of the society were $3,105.72. The new president's first official act was to appoint a new burial ground committee of five members to "procure suitable burial ground." The meeting room committee, the society's first committee, was revived for the purpose of looking for a more suitable (that is, cheaper) monthly space.

By February there was action on all fronts. The entertainment committee reported "further progress." The meeting room committee reported that a larger room had been found at the Star Casino, but the rent was $38 per year. The members immediately voted to sign another year's lease at the Harlem Terrace. Now came the much-awaited report of the new burial ground committee. Evidently the influence of Brother Phillips was still strong. The committee proposed "that this Society purches 12 plots of ground at Mt. Carmel Cemetery not to exceed $175 per plot and to give the committee the power to make contract for same and make a payment of 1,000 dollars on the purches." The report created another uproar. After all, an entire meeting had been spent debating a motion to buy plots at $180, and the idea had finally been defeated. Now it was back on the table again. The issue was simply too hot to handle. Not only was the proposal defeated, but its defeat was followed by the passage of a motion to postpone the entire question for a period of eighteen months.

In March the society once again debated the bylaws and decided after lengthy discussion that the issue could not yet be resolved. For more than two years various bylaws had been discussed and rejected. But nobody was in a rush to bring the matter to a conclusion. The membership did act decisively on one issue at the March meeting, however, by voting to increase the salary of the financial secretary, George Jonas, to $40 per year. Mr. Jonas was the only officer who had held his position from the society's inception, and clearly he was regarded by his peers as an indispensable cog in the bureaucratic machinery of this landsmanshaft.

In June 1908 the society once again launched a drive for new members. This time it was agreed that all new members between the ages of eighteen and thirty would be admitted free of charge until the following January. The motive behind the search for new members was not simply to compensate for the gradual diminution in membership strength. Rather, it was clearly recognized that the society's activities were resulting in higher costs. One such activity was the sick fund. Every month the financial secretary reported that sums of ten, fifteen, or even twenty dollars were being disbursed to members who were too sick to go to work. This steady drain on the treasury forced the society to modernize its procedures for running the sick fund. At the July meeting the society agreed to engage the services of Dr. Joseph Mark, who, in exchange for a yearly salary of $25, would visit all sick members once a week and report their medical condition to the monthly meeting. It was obviously assumed (erroneously, as it turned out) that the doctor's salary would be more than justified by avoidance of false claims of illness.

Despite the society's decision in February to table the cemetery question for eighteen months, the issue refused to die. At the same July meeting, Brother Isaac Simon "then stated that this Society has a good chance of purchecing a buerial ground at half price and select your own plots at $100 per plot. It was then regular moved and seconded that a committee of 3 be appointed to see the grounds and report at our next meeting." Mt. Carmel was evidently running a sale on cemetery space, and this overrode parliamentary niceties.

In October the new burial ground committee presented the results of its work. Lo and behold, the committee proposed that the society buy twenty-four burial plots in Section D of Mt. Carmel at $190 per plot, putting $1,500 down and carrying the balance at a mortgage of 6 percent. In other words, the new committee had resurrected the proposal made by Vice-President Phillips the previous December, the selfsame proposal that had led to the decision to table the question in the first place.

The argument raged again. A minority of the membership put forth a motion to table the entire issue, but this was defeated 16–7. A motion to implement the plan of the new burial ground committee was then carried by precisely the same margin, 16 yea and 7 nay. The cemetery issue was settled, but only in the minds of the majority. Hy Cohen, a member of the original burial ground committee formed nearly two years previously, "then got up and protested the legality and action against purchising the Buerial ground claiming that this Question came up some time ago, and it was tabled for 18 months." But the majority held fast. Brother Cohen's objection was overruled by the president. But Mr. Cohen was adamant. The minutes of the following month's meeting, on November 16, 1908, contain the following entry: "Communication received from Bro. Hy Cohen our Treasurer resigning as a member of this Society. After some discussion it was regular moved and seconded that the Secretary notifys Bro. Hy Cohen that we could not except his resignation untill his accounts is audited and the balance of moneys held in his possetion turned over to the Society." In December the president would announce that Brother Cohen had turned over $26.05 to the society and that his resignation had been accepted. Hy Cohen's concern for legalities had obviously fallen on deaf ears.

In 1909 the society moved its regular meeting place to

Grossman's Hall at 109 East 116th Street, at an annual rent of $40 per year. Clearly the society was shifting into high gear. It had rented a fancy new hall. It had purchased cemetery space at a premium price. It was even paying for the services of a full-time medical practitioner. At this point, things were getting too big for the mere mortals of the Progress Mutual Aid Society. Its vast wealth was sure to create serious problems. The first such crisis occurred at the March meeting, an event that might be called the "Jonas affair."

George Jonas had been the society's first and only financial secretary. He was, in 1909, the only officer who had served continuously since the first meeting in 1905. He had guided the society through its difficult early years and had managed a financial operation that had grown from initial assets of $332 to more than ten times that amount. He was neither a bookkeeper nor an accountant, but he did have a special method for balancing the books and keeping the accounts—so special that no other member of the society could understand it. This alone made him indispensable and accounted, in part, for his annual reelection.

If only the society had remained a small organization and had not taken on such important financial burdens as a cemetery and a sick fund, perhaps the Jonas affair might never have occurred. But as costs mounted and money began to run short, the issue of finances reached critical proportions. Sometime between the February and March meetings it was learned that George Jonas was the financial secretary for more than one landsmanshaft. Added to this potential conflict of interest was the fact that he evidently had fallen into the habit of commingling society funds, with the Progress Mutual Aid Society winding up on the short end.

On March 28, 1909, the society faced up to the crisis by

calling an emergency meeting. Jonas failed to appear at the meeting but sent a letter to the members which was read in his absence. "To the officers and members of the Progress Mutual Aid Society. Brothers! I was instructed by your President to call this special meeting and I am sorry I cannot be with you. I have some other business to attend to this evening [he had never missed any of the previous forty-two meetings of the Society]. I do not see any sense in calling this meeting. If some of our members are in doubt in regards to the financial matters in this society for the reason of the conflict I have in another society I would therefore demand that my books and the account be given to a special accountant for the past three years for the time this Society is in existence so that the members of this society will be able to sleep sound. This can be done before our next meeting." Despite his immigrant background, Jonas was a skilled political tactician: when everyone knows you are guilty, claim total innocence.

The strategy did not work. A motion was made and passed to remove Jonas as financial secretary and to appoint an acting secretary in his place. Of course, such a serious matter required a committee inquiry. Accordingly, a special committee was appointed to investigate the books and report at the next regular meeting. But a month later, at the April meeting, the special committee reported that it was unable to decipher Jonas's bookkeeping methods. Consequently, a motion was made and carried to have the president engage an "expert accountant" to go over the records and make a full report to the members at the May meeting. It was noted that the fee for the "expert" should not exceed $25.

At the May meeting the accountant appeared before the assembled members to render his report. After a thorough presentation, his advice was simple and straightforward: the society needed to start a new set of books. At the same meeting the society agreed to enlarge its medical staff from one to three doctors. Dr. Mark would remain on the staff, but his practice would be limited to "uptown members." A second physician, Dr. Streep, would check the sick claims of "Brooklyn members," and a Dr. Zucker would be responsible for reporting on sick claims by "downtown members." The society had not grown in membership to any great extent. But the appointment of the two additional doctors does tell us that its membership was becoming more geographically dispersed, a phenomenon common to all the New York landsmanshaftn.

The ghosts of past activities continued to plague the brethren of the Progress Mutual Aid Society. At the July 1909 meeting, a brief letter from George Jonas was read. He submitted $25 to the society as "part of what he owes" but stated that he was unable to pay the balance. This was followed by a report of the burial ground committee. Evidently Brother Hy Cohen had been correct in protesting the wisdom of the decision to buy space in the D Section of Mt. Carmel Cemetery, because the society found itself unable to meet its payment for the space. It was decided to advertise in several Jewish newspapers the desire of the society to sell twelve of its plots, and a campaign was started to sell as many plots as possible to members of the society as well.

The next meeting began with a report from the burial ground committee to the effect that the newspaper advertisements had not turned up a single offer to purchase land from the society. In desperation, the members voted to sell plots to members at $225 apiece, which was barely more than the original price the society had paid Mt. Carmel. Burial plots to nonmembers were priced at $275, but there was scant hope of outside sales. In its search for funds, the society also endeavored to force George Jonas to clear up his past debts. The president read a letter from Jonas stating that he was still unable to pay what he owed, and the members responded by immediately voting to notify their past financial secretary that "if the money is not paid by the 16th of August the society would take action against him at once."

Now the group was ready to hear the report of the entertainment committee. Having been previously rebuffed on their ideas for a theater party and an installation ball, the members of the entertainment committee once again sought to commit the society to entertainment on a grand scale. This time the committee recommended that the society sponsor a dance which would include a drawing for prizes to be donated by fellow members. The plan had been in the works since the previous November. But ten months of deliberations by the entertainment committee were not enough to sway the majority, and the plan was rejected.

Undaunted, the entertainment committee produced, at the next meeting of the society in October 1909, a backup plan that was more in line with the limited vision of the majority. A motion was made to sponsor a pinochle game at Lexington Hall. Tickets would be 50 cents for each participant, and all members were asked to donate prizes. The motion carried, and for the first time since April 1906, the society was prepared to renew its commitment to social activities on a large scale. But even a pinochle game at 50 cents a head almost proved too much to bear. The November meeting was entirely taken up with a debate on how to sell tickets, a special meeting was called on November 30 to push ticket sales even further, and at the regular December meeting the pinochle game was postponed because a large number of tickets remained unsold.

Sometime early in March the vaunted pinochle game was finally held. At the March meeting the entertainment committee, flush with success, reported that the game had resulted in net profits to the society of $70.50. The membership was so gratified by the work of the committee that at the April meeting a motion was carried that actually committed the society to hold at least one formal function each year. Furthermore, every member of the society was to be assessed an extra dollar a year in dues, which would entitle him to receive tickets to the event. The perseverance of the entertainment committee had finally paid off. From now on, its work was recognized as integral to the society.

The Progress Mutual Aid Society now had a sick fund, a cemetery, and an organized entertainment program, but it still lacked one element that was characteristic of nearly all landsmanshaftn in New York. That element appeared for the first time at the June 1910 meeting, in the form of a motion (which was carried) to appoint a committee "to try and organize an auxiliary composed of wives of members." After five years, the society was about to open itself up to the participation of women. Typically, however, their participation would be strictly limited to an auxiliary organization whose basic structure, bylaws, and finances would be determined by the men.

At each subsequent meeting, from July until November, the committee on the ladies' auxiliary reported progress, but no definitive decisions were made. After all, what was the rush? But at the November meeting, for the first time, thirty-five women actually came to the meeting and were allowed to sit in the back of the room while the deliberations over old and new business were carried on. At the December meeting, a delegation of women appeared and announced that a slate of officers for their auxiliary had been elected, with Mrs. Annie Cohen to serve as president. So the women now had their own officers. But they still did not have an organization, since the committee on the ladies' auxiliary reported further progress but was not quite ready to present a formal report. In fact, it would take nearly two more years for the auxiliary actually to begin functioning. Not until November 1912 could the president announce that the ladies' auxiliary was in the process of organizing. To that end, the treasurer was instructed to release $18.75 from the society's account, to be given to the women as a basis for beginning their own finances. Shortly before the meeting ended, a committee representing the ladies came into the hall, "with the object of ascertaining the status of the $18.75 held by the Society, and they were informed that same would be turned over to their Treasurer." The women were now on their own.

Having finally granted the women separate (but not equal) status, the society turned in December to the business of electing officers for the year 1913. This meeting, which would represent a watershed for the society, was prompted by a continuous undercurrent of dissatisfaction over the services of Dr. Joseph Mark. For the first time, a position of leadership within the society—in this case, the position of "uptown doctor"—was actually contested. Dr. Mark stood as usual for reelection, but he was confronted by a second candidate, Dr. Julius Goldsmith.

When the meeting began, it was noticed that many more members than usual were in attendance. In fact, there were over fifty persons in the room, whereas most meetings failed to draw more than two dozen. Moreover, many of the members were quite new to the society—indeed, had never previously been to a meeting. In anticipation of a bitter electoral contest, the friends of Dr. Mark, who included the president of the society, had "packed" the premises. Realizing that they were outnumbered, Dr. Mark's opponents resorted to a time-honored parliamentary trick; they stalled for time by raising questions about the legality of the proceedings. Joseph Radin led off by making a motion that members who had been initiated at that meeting not be allowed to vote. But the president and his allies were in firm command. The motion was ruled out of order, and when Brother Radin attempted to appeal the ruling, he was "refused recognition." Maurice Feiger, whose two brothers were, respectively, recording secretary-elect and trustee, then made a motion to disallow the vote of any member who had not attended two or more meetings of the society. But the president held firm and also ruled Feiger out of order. At this point the vice-president, Leo Rosenberg, demanded that Feiger's motion be reconsidered, but he too was declared to be speaking out of turn.

The election for "uptown doctor" commenced under general pandemonium. When the ballots were finally tabulated, Dr. Goldsmith received 25 votes, but Dr. Mark, having managed to hold together his coalition, returned 30. The ballots of Brothers Juster, Rosenberg, Feiger, and Alexander were counted as "protested." Following the vote, Leo Rosenberg made a motion "that the election of Uptown Doctor be set aside and be declared illegal, and a new election called for, on the ground that the new Brothers had no right to vote." The president refused to recognize the motion, but Rosenberg, undaunted, promised to raise it again at the next session. The election meeting had lasted for nearly five hours, and it had been the most difficult and argumentative meeting in the entire history of the society.

The society convened a special election meeting on January 9, 1913. But before the electoral proceedings could actually begin, the president produced a slip of paper that created a veritable sensation among those assembled. The paper was a court order, an injunction restraining the society from holding the special election. Dr. Mark had retained an attorney who had gone into court and asked that the society "show cause" why the election should be held. The president had managed to get the court date postponed until January 13, but the whole issue had taken an unprecedented turn. This was not just a member threatening to sue over nonpayment of dues, or a member admitting he was unable to pay back money he had stolen from the treasury. Those were simple, informal matters that could be handled through traditional methods of discussion and compromise. This was a court order, an intrusion into the affairs of the society by The Law. Dr. Mark was, in fact, a member of the society, but he was also a businessman, a man of the world, a man who knew how to use modern ideas and modern devices for his own purposes.

But what were the doctor's true purposes? There was a principle here, and the principle involved $25 that Dr. Mark believed he was owed for his services over the coming year. On the other hand, a majority was now clearly of the opinion that the problem had gotten out of hand. So a deal was struck between the two warring factions. Dr. Mark agreed to stand for election but to relinquish all financial claims against the society if the election did not go in his favor. At the same time, his opponent, Dr. Goldsmith, withdrew his name from the ballot and was replaced by a compromise candidate, Dr. Kramer. In the voting, Dr. Mark received seventeen votes (including one ballot that had his name written twice and was therefore disallowed), while Dr. Kramer mustered twenty-four votes and was named "uptown doctor" for the year 1913. The crisis was resolved, the breach was healed, and the society went back to business as usual.

A Society Dies

The 845th regular meeting of the Progress Mutual Aid Society was held on September 13, 1961, at the home of the president, Milton Benjamin, on Davidson Avenue in the Bronx. The brief agenda held only two issues. First, the handful of members voted to reimburse the president the sum of $10 for the cost of refreshments served at the meeting. Then the society debated a motion to strike the following statute from its bylaws: "This Society shall not be dissolved as long as seven (7) members are willing to continue the same under the present name and charter." When the society was first organized, it had taken more than three years to write the bylaws, but now its most important clause was stricken after a five-minute debate. Now the society was ready to terminate its affairs.

The Progress Mutual Aid Society was officially dissolved in 1964. Each member in good standing was entitled to receive two grave sites in the society's cemetery. The society had existed for fifty-one years, and counting regular meetings, emergency meetings, ladies' auxiliary meetings, and formal social functions, its members had assembled together on more than a thousand separate occasions. Indeed, over the entire history of the society, not a single month had gone by during which some of the active members had not gotten together for some occasion or other.

The reasons for the birth of the Progress Mutual Aid Society and other landsmanshaft organizations lay in the social homogeneity and insularity of their membership. The members brought with them to America the same language, customs, traditions, outlook, and expectations. When they arrived they all encountered a society that held out the possibility of survival but on terms which were totally different from—indeed, largely antithetical to—the demands and requirements that had shaped their lives in the Old World. The PMAS and other landsmanshaftn thus became mechanisms for "filtering" these new experiences and challenges for a collective psyche that could only absorb such stimuli gradually and in a limited fashion. Moreover, social interactions within the PMAS had the effect of reducing these alien experiences to petty and minute issues which, in the process, became understandable and controllable by all.

The history of the PMAS encompassed World War I, the Great Depression, World War II, the Holocaust, fifteen American presidential elections, the civil rights movement, the age of television, and countless other local, regional, national, and international events and crises. But one reads the minutes of society meetings in vain hoping to find mention of *any* of these events. References to things American or, for that matter, to anything not directly germane to society affairs were vague, muted, and offhand. During a meeting in 1947, for example, a motion was made to collect money for the State of Israel, but the matter was never raised again in formal fashion. The society could spend meeting after meeting debating the purchase of a cemetery plot but disposed of the Holocaust in less than half an hour.

There was only one issue that remained at the forefront of all society deliberations and activities over the entire course of its existence, and this was how to maintain the bonds between members that allowed them to cope with the moments of greatest personal trauma: illness and death. This issue and this issue alone was the lifeblood of the society's existence, as it was for all the landsmanshaftn. Nothing that occurred in the outside world could alter the fundamental reality that every member of the society would someday become old and would someday die. When such events occurred, the membership had to rely on its most basic cultural instincts, which life in the New World had eroded but never quite eradicated. Reliance on the society thus became a survival strategy adopted by people who intuitively knew that no other course was available to them.

The seemingly endless arguments that swirled around the most petty affairs attracted certain people to the landsmanshaftn, but they also made these same organizations anathema to others, who considered such concerns claustrophobic, old-fashioned, and somewhat absurd. Could one imagine a gathering of upwardly mobile, acculturated immigrants spending eight months arguing about the purchase of cemetery plots for $9 apiece? Would a young, aggressive second-generation physician go into court to force the payment of a $25 fee?

Such questions reflect an attitude toward life that cannot be comprehended today, but neither could it have been explained consciously when these questions were being debated. The members of the PMAS wrestled with such questions because they came from a world which other immigrants had quickly forgotten and which their children would never know. At the same time, the members of the PMAS and other landsmanshaftn could not cope with a world in which such questions were *not* asked. The members would never be capable of adjusting to new attitudes or new ideas, and as long as they could breathe life into their society through continuous debate, the claims of their new world never even had to be acknowledged.

The discussions and affairs of the PMAS thus become an artifact that offers potent assistance in analyzing the thorny problem of assimilation. Statistics on intermarriage, education, religious affiliation, and linguistic usage will be presented in the following chapters, but these data do not help us to comprehend the issue in fully human terms. The statistics are only signposts; they tell us *when* things happened and *how fast* they happened, but they do not tell us *why* they happened. The figures externalize the question, so to speak, and leave us on the outside looking in, assuming the existence of attitudes and perceptions without really knowing their content. If the members of the PMAS met more than a thousand times to discuss what they considered to be the most important issues of their lives, then we must take those discussions at face value.

The problem is that there *were* other issues of importance to other immigrants and to the children and grandchildren of the landsmanshaft population. Consequently, these people did not show up at the meetings; their discussions and debates encompassed other issues and were held in other contexts. Just as the minutes of the meetings of the PMAS tell us in tedious detail what was going on within these organizations, so they tell us nothing about what was going on outside. In the following chapters we shall examine some events that occurred in the world outside the landsmanshaftn. Having looked inside the societies to learn why they were formed, we will now begin to look outside to discover why they withered away.

IV

The Old World Shatters

The condition of the Jews in Poland is desperate,
in the Ukraine it is hopeless.
—Report of a Joint Distribution
Committee relief team sent to
Eastern Europe in 1920

THE MOST important world event affecting the landsmanshaftn was the decimation of the Jewish population of the Pale during and after World War I. Although 2 million Jews departed from the Pale during the Great Migration, nearly 4 million residents were left behind. But in the years 1880–1920, more than a million East European Jews died as the result of famine, pestilence, warfare, and the organized violence of the pogroms. This calamity effectively shattered the original homeland of America's Jewish population, completely, eradicating many smaller towns and villages. Henceforth, Jews from Eastern Europe constituted the one ethnic population in America without a home base on the other side.

The turbulence in the Pale was the only major occurrence in the world outside the landsmanshaftn that was able to penetrate the inner consciousness of the societies. Until 1920 the societies were, in many cases, appendages of villages and communities that still flourished in the Pale. Most societies retained active and continuous contact with the regions and shtetlach whose names they bore, and most immigrants who arrived in New York first made contact with a landsmanshaft whose members already knew of the newcomers' impending arrival. Consequently, the reaction of the landsmanshaftn to the pogroms was an instinctive response to a situation that happened in the outside world but could be defined within the landsmanshaft context. The intense connection between the landsmanshaft and the shtetl was the most potent factor in the efforts by American Jews to provide relief for the ravaged regions of Eastern Europe. Unfortunately, no amount of help could redress the situation. The extent of the destruction and misery was greater than anyone in America could imagine.

Into the Pogrom Land

In the early months of 1920, a relief team of the American Jewish Joint Distribution Committee [JDC] arrived in the Pale to organize the campaign to save the East European Jews from annihilation. The JDC had been established by Felix Warburg and other German-Jewish philanthropists in 1914 to spur relief efforts in Eastern Europe, and by the end of World War I the work had taken on a critical urgency.[1] The situation of the Jews had become precarious. As early as 1918, reports had surfaced in the Western press about the atrocities committed against Jewish communities throughout the region. By 1919, however, random violence had been replaced by organized campaigns of mass slaughter. The civil war of 1919–22 resulted in wholesale destruction, with more than 200,000 lives lost in pogroms during those years.

The leaders of the JDC relief team, Professor Israel Fried-laender and Dr. Meyer Isaac Leff, quickly realized that the Jews had become human pawns in the struggle between the Polish and Bolshevik governments to retain the loyalties of their local populations.[2] The Polish government was clearly abetting, if not actively directing, the anti-semitic reign of terror as part of its strategy of inciting the local population against the Bolshevik regime. An American aviator employed by the Polish air force told a JDC official that he had flown behind the Bolshevik lines and dropped propaganda leaflets telling the local population to rise up against its "natural enemies, the Communists and the Jews." Meanwhile, the Bolsheviks, never particularly sympathetic to the Jewish problem, were more than willing to sacrifice the welfare of the Jews in order to divert local hostility from their cause. This meant that the Jews of the Pale were caught in the middle, unable to appeal to any government in the region and too isolated and weakened to mount any sustained campaign of self-protection.

An assistant medical officer of the JDC team, Dr. Harry Plotz, sent his observations to Felix Warburg, the JDC chairman. Visiting a Jewish refugee camp in Kiev in October 1920, Dr. Plotz counted some 2,000 people "practically starving of hunger. They were lying on the ground crying for bread—men, women and children were all living in a small, partly-destroyed barrack, sleeping on the floor without bedding or covering. In some rooms there were no windows there were no toilet facilities and the stench was unbearable. Lice were crawling from person to person. Adults with tuberculosis and typhus were lying on the floor. There were many pogrom victims limping about with open, infected wounds."

Professor Friedlaender was killed by Bolshevik soldiers

at the Polish front in June 1920. His associate, Dr. Leff, continued to travel throughout the Pale for the remainder of the year, visiting scores of towns, villages, refugee camps, hospitals, and orphanages, in an effort to assess the full dimensions of the problem. In Lithuania he found more than 10,000 refugees, all "practically penniless," including more than 3,000 orphans. Over 30 percent of this refugee population suffered from typhus, a common symptom of malnourishment. After traveling all day to visit an orphanage in a small Lithuanian town, Dr. Leff discovered that, just prior to his arrival, the building had been sequestered for use as a barracks for Polish officers, who had simply heaved the institution's orphan population out into the street.

Meyer Isaac Leff was both physically and psychically suited for the immense burdens he took upon himself when he agreed to travel through the Pale on behalf of the JDC. Born in a village near the city of Bialystok in 1888, he was an intellectual prodigy who was ordained a rabbi in his early teens. By the time he embarked on an active religious career, however, his intellectual ferment had grown beyond the bounds of religion, and he was increasingly drawn into political affairs, particularly of a radical Zionist nature. The result was a series of incidents involving the tsarist police, culminating in a headlong flight to America to escape a warrant issued for his arrest.

Once settled in New York, Leff began to study and teach at the Jewish Theological Seminary, but again his intellectual drive took him into new fields. He eventually switched to medicine, but he retained his interest in Zionist affairs while studying for his medical degree at Long Island College Hospital. After a brief visit to Mexico, where he worked as a physician for several American mining companies, he returned to the Jewish Theological Seminary, where he fell under the influence of Professor Friedlaender, a noted scholar and political activist. When Friedlaender was asked to head the first JDC relief team in Eastern Europe after World War I, he naturally chose his young associate, Dr. Leff, to carry out a medical survey of the surviving Jewish population.

When Dr. Leff returned to the Eastern European zone from which he had escaped some thirty years previously, he was no longer a youthful rabbi and political novice. He was now married and a father (his wife and son accompanied him to Europe but remained behind in Paris), and was a highly educated and cultured man. Furthermore, he was thoroughly committed to the ideal of Jewish survival, evincing a near-total obsession with the future of Jewish life both in Eastern Europe and in Palestine. But he was at the same time sensitive to the situation in which he found himself, and he was acutely aware of the potential difficulties and awesome responsibilities of his mission on behalf of the JDC. Consequently, his reports to the JDC were more than just a summary of medical conditions in the Pale. They were an incisive evaluation of the entire situation—political, economic, social, and religious—in postwar Eastern Europe.

Commenting many years later on his experiences in Eastern Europe, Dr. Leff recalled that the overall feeling which enveloped him from the moment he arrived in the Pale until the moment he left was one of constant peril and fear. Despite the fact that he traveled throughout the zone in the uniform of a United States army officer (he had been granted a temporary commission for the duration of the trip) and carried a diplomatic passport, he knew that, at any moment, he might be accosted by bandits, robbed, and killed. Recounting his experiences to his son, he summed it all up by saying, "We were always surrounded by bandits on all sides." This fear was heightened by the murder of Professor Friedlaender, who had been stopped by a Bolshevik patrol in the no-man's-land on the Polish frontier and then summarily executed when he attempted to flee his captors. Leff and several other JDC officials spent three harrowing days traveling from one border post to another, attempting to verify the incident. After enduring constant threat and harassment, they were led to a shallow, unmarked grave by the side of a road, where they performed the grim task of exhuming and identifying Friedlaender's body.

If Leff, traveling through the Pale under official protection felt such fear and anguish at the brutalities he witnessed, one can only imagine the fear felt by local inhabitants who were the objects of that brutality. Yet despite the mass sufferings and privation, the Jewish population, particularly in the larger cities, retained a vitality and willingness to carry on a full range of social and economic activities that surprised all observers. Indeed, the JDC relief efforts were frequently hampered by the internecine feuds and rivalries between competing local organizations. In his native Bialystok, Dr. Leff found that "money is spent rather liberally on institutions and projects which are not at all connected with relief. These activities include Yiddish classes for adults and children and the Yiddish theater. When we had a conference with the executives of the Kehillah [local communal leaders] and they were asked why so little attention and money is being paid for relief they replied that they were in principle opposed to 'schnorrers' [freeloaders]. When I told them that the American point of view is that a 'schnorrer' must also live and that we are mainly interested in the alleviation of the needy they replied that owing to the fact that the Kehillah is a democratically elected institution that would take orders from nobody. One man said that rather than submit to American interference he would refuse American money though this might cost a few Jewish lives, it would be worth it, as long as no 'schnorrers' are created." Here we encounter echoes of the selfsame narrow and independent mentality of the American landsmanshaftn, and not without reason. After all, in his travels Dr. Leff encountered many persons whose relatives and friends had just recently left the Pale for America.

In the face of unprecedented brutality and terror, the local Jewish communities of the Pale often retained a sense of dignity and were able to apply themselves to the daily task of surviving in a world that was crumbling around them. But this was not usually the case for the more isolated Jewish populations in the smaller towns and shtetlach of the Pale, where resistance to the pogroms was minimal. Of course, there were examples of extreme heroism. A survivor of a shtetl pogrom in 1919 recalls that when the Cossacks first came to his village, "all the men came out in the streets with rifles, and the Cossack column turned immediately around and galloped down the street." But more typical was the experience of Norman Gilmovsky, whose family, along with all other Jewish residents, was ordered to leave the Polish village of Hancewicze in 1918. First the village was occupied by a regiment of Cossacks, who ordered the Jews to line up at the railroad station to board a freight train for a journey to points unknown. "In the meantime," recalls Gilmovsky, "peasants from the surrounding villages streamed into Hancewicze, waiting until they would be free to pilfer and loot. Within hours after we left, everything in that little township was carted away."[3]

Perhaps the most telling comment about the situation of the shtetl Jews was made by Dr. Leff, in a report to the JDC concerning relief efforts in Minsk. He noted that the Jewish community in Minsk, despite privation and persecution, was still able to organize relief efforts, maintain a rudimentary degree of political organization, and even continue to operate local schools. But in the countryside, he wrote, "cases of death from starvation are common. Many eat grass." Clearly, the age-old gap between city and village, between modernity and backwardness, was producing a tragedy of untold human dimensions for the surviving residents of the rural Pale.

The Landsmanshaftn Respond

Upon receiving reports of widespread distress from Eastern Europe, the JDC began to enlarge its campaign to secure relief funds, a campaign that had been started during World War I. In terms of both money and energy, the task would be immense. In April 1920, Dr. Leff estimated that medical supplies alone for that year would require expenditures of more than 2 million dollars. This figure did not include the costs of feeding, clothing, housing, and possibly evacuating the Jewish population. Nor did it include the much greater costs of rebuilding villages and towns that were obliterated or severely damaged during the onslaughts. (Relief workers estimated that more than 100,000 dwellings had been rendered uninhabitable during and directly after the war.) Moreover, it was obvious that the entire cost of relief would have to be borne by outside authorities and organizations, since no government in Eastern Europe was prepared to undertake relief efforts on behalf of its own Jewish population.

The task of saving East European Jewry fell primarily

upon the shoulders of American Jews. The United States government had established an American Relief Administration, under the direction of Herbert Hoover, but the moneys dispensed by this organization went to all European civilians affected by the war; of these, the Jews were only one of many deserving groups. Consequently, the JDC began a massive effort to raise money, which culminated in a September 1920 memorial service for Professor Friedlaender at Carnegie Hall. Over the previous eighteen months, nearly $25 million had been collected, and between 1919 and 1924 the JDC received total contributions of more than $45 million.[4]

Contributions to the JDC relief effort came from every segment of the Jewish community in America, including the landsmanshaftn. Indeed, over the entire postwar period, more than 1,200 landsman societies contributed a total of $7 million to the relief efforts in Eastern Europe, or an average of nearly $6,000 per society.[5] Some of the larger groups, such as the Brisker Society and the Bialystoker Society, contributed tens of thousands of dollars, often assessing their members special payments to cover the costs. But even the smaller societies dug deep into their members' pockets to help share the burden of this enterprise. Societies with treasuries containing less than $1,000, societies whose annual dues were $5 per year or less and which included not a single family of any substantial means, managed to make large contributions to the JDC cause.

In addition to donating what was for most of the smaller societies enormous sums of money, the landsmanshaftn also engaged in a massive effort to save their families, friends, and native villages from the terrors of the pogrom years. This effort took many forms and involved the use of official as well as unofficial channels of communication. The various landsmanshaftn utilized the services and facilities not only of the JDC but also of HIAS [Hebrew Emigrant Aid Society], the YMCA, the Red Cross, and other voluntary relief organizations, as well as official government agencies both in the United States and abroad. But as we shall see, the relief efforts of landsmanshaftn went far beyond the services provided by formal charitable organizations. The landsmanshaftn went to great lengths to secure the safety of their landsleit on the other side, including sending delegations and individual members back to the native village with clothing, food, and funds.

It is impossible to estimate accurately the amount of money or effort expended by the landsmanshaftn on behalf of their besieged brethren in the Pale. The figure of $7 million cited above represents moneys collected by official Jewish relief organizations, most notably the JDC. This type of fundraising accounted for the bulk of landsmanshaft expenditures during the postwar period, but it represented only a minor aspect of the total landsmanshaft effort.

First and foremost was the problem of identifying the actual location of villages and populations in need of assistance. Initially, the JDC and other relief organizations preferred to work directly through government and agency channels. But this strategy was thwarted by the indifference or outright hostility of East European authorities, as well as by the chaos and instability resulting from the civil war. Consequently, by 1919 the JDC was forced to abandon its early efforts to serve simply as a conduit for moneys raised in America for Eastern Europe, and the committee took on the arduous task of directly administering relief funds and supplies.

The activities of the JDC and its field staff were heroic. The agency and its affiliates fed, sheltered, and clothed hundreds of thousands of refugees; rebuilt countless factories, workshops, schools, homes, and synagogues; facilitated the adoption of thousands of orphans; and operated medical facilities throughout Eastern Europe. The activities of the JDC extended far beyond the borders of the Pale, embracing relief of Jews in Siberia as well as support for the settlement of Jews in Palestine.

Both within and beyond the structure of JDC activities, however, the landsmanshaftn played their own vital role. The societies were the most direct link to those Jews within the Pale who were at the same time the most imperiled and the most difficult to save. Precisely because many of the landsmanshaftn represented the tiniest villages and shtetlach of the Pale, so their members had contact with the most remote and isolated communities. Many of the smaller shtetlach were not listed on maps, and their existence was known to the outside world only if a link had been maintained between the shtetl dwellers and their landsmen who had managed to escape abroad. The fact is that most of the landsmanshaftn in New York had maintained contact with their village of origin, particularly because many of the landsmanshaft members had been in the United States for only a few years.

Although the JDC played the major role in providing aid for the ravaged areas of Eastern Europe, its activities often followed in the wake of landsmanshaft efforts. On March 8, 1920, the JDC newsletter contained an analysis of the postwar relief efforts that had already been carried out by the landsmanshaftn. The purpose of this article was to develop the idea of establishing a separate landsmanshaft division within the JDC to coordinate relief efforts to Eastern Europe. Publication of the article coincided with the initial mission of Professor Friedlaender and other JDC staff members whose reports had already established the extent of the problem throughout much of Eastern Europe. The article stated, in part,

> The landsmanschaft relief movement, which assumed considerable proportions about a year ago, is spreading all over the country. New landsmanschaft organizations are daily springing up, and the work is assuming a more systematic form. Display "ads" calling for meetings, conferences and campaigns, announcing contributions, telling of delegates sent abroad, or appealing for funds, fill many a page in the Yiddish press. A new feature of this movement is the summoning of conferences of the various organizations of a certain parent city in order to unite them in one central landsmanschaft. Thus on February 22nd a conference took place in New York of all the Bobruisk societies, at which delegates from 23 cities, some as far west as Chicago, took part. The sending of special delegates abroad has become very marked of late. Such delegates are mostly sent by the landsmanschaftn of a large city assisted by those of its neighboring towns. The delegates generally take along collective and individual sums intended for the various communities and for private persons in their respective districts.[6]

This brief analysis of landsmanshaft relief efforts deserves comment, for it highlights some of the most important aspects of the landsmanshaft phenomenon up to the early 1920s. Clearly, the societies were a major force within the Jewish community, and their numbers were constantly growing. In addition, as the article makes clear, Jewish immigration to America had gone far beyond settlement in New York; for example, the landsleit from just one city, Bobruisk, had already settled in at least twenty-three cities throughout the United States. Moreover, most of the landsmanshaftn were still in frequent contact with their relatives and friends in the Old Country, hence the societies' ability to send personal representatives abroad with money to be spent for general relief as well as for payments to specific individuals. The article also notes another important element in the growth of the landsmanshaftn—namely, the extent to which many societies had already split into separate organizations, often reflecting geographical dispersion but also, because of divergent religious and cultural views within the immigrant population.

From March until September 1920, the JDC worked to establish an official landsmanshaft department to coordinate relief efforts undertaken by landsleit in the United States for their families overseas. But the JDC's effort to organize the landsmanshaftn under its own aegis was constantly frustrated, in part because of the reluctance of the landsmanshaftn to become part of a formal effort that involved adhering to fixed rules and guidelines. In this respect, the secrecy and intimacy that characterized the internal structure of many landsmanshaftn, particularly the smaller societies, carried over into their dealings with official Jewish relief organizations. The JDC was viewed as simply another manifestation of the outside world with which the landsmanshaftn had no desire for concrete involvement.

The conflict between the prerogatives of the landsmanshaftn and the requirements of the JDC was fought out in the Yiddish press. An editorial in the *Morning Journal* stated:

> Growing chaos prevails in the relief work of the American Jews. This chaos is due to the fact that each tiny landsmanshaft is trying to set up its own relief shop. Now the sentiment which actuates the landsmanshaftn is a power for good and as such should be encouraged. But the landsmanshaftn cannot give systematic assistance for reconstruction.[7]

While the *Journal* acknowledged the fact that the landsman-shaftn were not in a position to provide long-term assistance to the Jews in Eastern Europe, another Yiddish-language newspaper, *The Jewish Way*, took the opposite point of view:

> The landsmanshaftn are in revolt against the JDC because the latter do not consider the demands of the American Jews, the givers, nor the desires of the European Jews, the receivers. All Jews should rise up and aid in this revolt![8]

Several days later, a more moderate editorial appeared in yet a third Yiddish paper, *The Day*, which criticized the landsmanshaftn for their unwillingness to work with the JDC but noted that "they do a good deal of good because they are well acquainted with the persons and places."[9]

The editorial in *The Day* really got to the heart of the matter. Notwithstanding the enormous financial and organizational advantages of the JDC over the landsmanshaftn, the fact is that the societies represented the most important link to the masses of destitute and suffering Jews in the Pale. Indeed, the JDC staff took particular care to read every Yiddish daily for news about the landsmanshaftn as well as about events in Eastern Europe. Hundreds of societies placed ads in the various Yiddish periodicals seeking assistance from American landsleit; most of these ads contained descriptions of the situation in the home villages supplied to the landsmanshaftn by Jews still on the other side. The ads placed by the societies in the Yiddish press thus became a primary source of information not only for the landsleit but also for the JDC and other official relief organizations.

One reason why the landsmanshaftn were able to promote their own relief efforts was that the sending of money and representatives abroad offered commercial benefits for banks, steamship companies, and tourist agencies in New York. The same Yiddish papers that carried ads and appeals by the landsmanshaftn also carried notices from commercial enterprises promising to expedite passage and money payments for the delegates sent overseas on private relief missions. In August 1920 the Guaranty Trust Company took out large ads in all the New York Yiddish papers:

> If you contemplate sending a delegate abroad for the purposes of distributing your relief funds, we shall be glad to supply you with the information we possess regarding conditions in Europe, the methods of traveling and the difficulties involved. We shall also be glad to help your delegate through our foreign offices, representatives and correspondent banks. Letters of credit are issued which enable your delegate to carry and deliver the money in safety. Travelers' cheques are furnished to defray the expenses of the journey to and from Europe. Drafts are issued to any city desired, and we have always a supply of foreign money on hand. Our representatives will be pleased to call on you by appointment, if you desire it.[10]

The same newspapers carried ads for steamship passage on the Red Star Lines and ads placed by the American Express Company for a variety of travelers' services.

Despite the problems of communicating with the landsleit societies, the JDC formally established its Department of Landsmanshaftn, headed by Samuel Schmidt, in September 1920. The JDC staff began immediately to make contact with landsmanshaftn in New York and elsewhere. By the end of October, 97 societies had been persuaded to send more than $700,000 to Europe under JDC auspices, but this still represented only a tiny fraction of the money the landsmanshaftn were sending through private channels overseas.[11] In November 1920 a JDC official in Warsaw sent a

report to the New York office indicating that private landsmanshaft relief efforts not only were continuing on a massive scale but also were creating serious problems for the
overall relief efforts of the JDC. "A government minister
called to my attention," wrote the JDC official in Warsaw,
"the many annoyances caused to him by the representatives
of the various landsmanshaftn. He stated that there were
quite a number of people who were coming to this country
presumably for the distribution of funds representing various relief organizations. He stated that a number of them
were found near the front lines without proper credentials
and with large sums of money and that the local government does not feel that they can permit such an irregular
procedure."[12]

The concern of the JDC over the ad hoc relief effort of the
landsmanshaftn was intensified by the serious problems encountered by private landsmanshaft delegates when trying
to distribute money in the chaotic war-torn zone of the Pale.
Many delegates who went overseas never arrived at their
destinations; others were robbed, jailed, or harassed. Julius
Sklar, who attempted to return to the village of Lubeszow,
near Minsk, was arrested in Warsaw and robbed of $14,000;
he spent thirteen days in jail and was released only when he
became so sick that it was feared he might die in detention.
Isidor Burris, a resident of Brooklyn, attempted to bring
more than $40,000 to relatives and landsleit in a shtetl near
Vilna, but he was robbed of the entire sum after getting off
the boat in Danzig; another passenger who was carrying
money for his village near Minsk was arrested in Danzig.
Isador Cantor, who had set out for his native shtetl of
Chomsky, was robbed of over 5 million Polish marks.
Samuel Ring, bound for the village of Kartuz Bereza in
Grodno, was perhaps more fortunate. He did not lose the

100,000 German marks he was carrying to his landsleit, but he was stranded in Poland for more than six months and was never able to complete his mission.[13]

Some personal relief efforts undertaken by landsman-shaftn failed because of the motives or activities of the delegates. When a landsmanshaft representative arrived in a region or town carrying large sums of money, he attracted the attentions of many people interested not in helping to alleviate misery but in profiting from it. In regions where political conditions were chaotic and social unrest was extreme, there was ample scope for graft, corruption, profiteering, and monetary speculation. Many of the landsmanshaft delegates carried tens of thousands of dollars in American or local currency, and however positive their motives may have been at the outset, the end results sometimes proved disheartening. The JDC received frequent reports of abuses concerning the payment of funds to localities, some of which clearly could have been prevented. One landsmanshaft delegate who went back to his native village of Macjow, in Poland, distributed large sums of money to his landsleit but committed suicide, while still in the village, after discovering that his own relatives had defrauded their fellow villagers by using the money to reap huge profits through illegal currency transactions on the black market. The tragedy was compounded by the fact that this man had gone back to his shtetl not only for the purpose of distributing funds to villagers, but also to bring his wife and young daughter (whom he had left behind when he initially emigrated) back with him to the United States.

The JDC attempted to prevent such abuses by setting up guidelines regarding the personal and financial character of the landsmanshaft delegates whom the committee would sponsor overseas. If a candidate met the criteria, he would travel under official JDC auspices, carry "safe conduct" papers, and have recourse to help from local officials in the zone in which he was traveling. The JDC required a delegate to be an American citizen and to submit information regarding his background, family, and employment, personal references, a detailed itinerary of his travel plans in Eastern Europe, and a statement regarding the specific purposes for which he was returning to the village. In addition, the candidate had to sign a legal form requiring that he conduct himself according to official regulations, that he not undertake any financial or commercial dealings in Europe other than those approved by the JDC for the purposes of relief, and that he submit a detailed list of the persons to whom he was giving money as well as a report regarding the outcome of his trip. In many cases the delegate also had to submit a list of the shtetl dwellers who were members of the local relief committee, as well as their plans for distributing relief funds.

These guidelines at least helped to minimize chaos and abuses, but no set of regulations promulgated in a New York office could cover every situation that might arise in a particular shtetl. For example, in November 1920 the JDC was contacted by members of the Kovler Relief Committee, which represented landsleit from the shtetl of Kovel, in Poland. The landsmanshaft had a membership of nearly 400, and there were an additional 7,000 landsleit from Kovel and surrounding villages living in New York. They had received an appeal for help from the village, which they brought with them to the meeting at the JDC. The appeal read: "We, the representatives of the Jewish communities of the Kovel district have met to consider the question of immediate relief which our devastated communities are so badly in need of. The representatives of the JDC assisted us as far as possible, for which we are very grateful; but, friends and landsleit, too great is our need, . . . the calamity that has befallen us is without a parallel. You have probably read about the terrible pogroms and atrocities which have occurred in our district. The cruel pogromists spared neither babes nor women, neither the old nor the sick. Hundreds of men were killed; hundreds of women and girls were dishonored, and after undergoing fiendish tortures were put to death; many Jewish homes were burnt, and all the Jews possessed, all they had toiled to save up, was plundered or destroyed. Shoes and clothing, the very shirts people had on, were taken away, and many of the barefoot and naked are now in the hospital, their bodies swollen from hunger and cold.

"Brothers, if you still cherish some pity for us, if you do not wish those who have escaped from the hands of the murderers to perish from hunger, if you do not wish them to lose every human trait, we implore you to come to our aid. Spare no effort. Help us, think of us every day, every hour, every minute. Save your landsleit from ruin, shame and misery. Help us!"[14]

In response to this appeal, the American landsleit had raised more than $45,000 to be distributed in Kovel and the surrounding shtetlach. They had chosen a member of the society, Morris Gewirtz, to take the money back to Poland on their behalf. Most of the money was earmarked for specific individuals—brothers, sisters, parents, and friends of Kovel immigrants in America—but more than $5,000 had been set aside for general relief activities. Morris Gewirtz was a thirty-year-old printer who had migrated to New York in 1913. He still had family in the shtetl, as well as friends and former neighbors. On January 10, 1921, Gewirtz was issued a Polish visa in response to a request by the JDC, and on January 13 he sailed for Europe, arriving in Warsaw on January 30.

Matters took a startling turn shortly after Gewirtz arrived in Kovel. Within a week, he informed the local JDC official that he would not work through the village relief committee because its members were all "crooks." Instead, he had organized an ad hoc relief committee to help him distribute the funds. The JDC office in New York pressed its staff member in Kovel to try and ascertain whether Gewirtz was distributing the funds correctly, but the response was far from reassuring. Gewirtz had indeed organized his own relief committee, but it consisted of himself, his brother-in-law, his cousin, two former neighbors, and a former employer. Although most of the funds earmarked for distribution to particular individuals were received, the money allocated for general relief purposes was never accounted for. In addition, although Gewirtz had been carrying funds for some of the smaller shtetlach outside of Kovel, he apparently never went to those villages or made any effort to disburse that part of the money.[15]

Gewirtz never returned to the United States under official JDC auspices, although he may have come back at a later date by his own means. For several years after his arrival in Poland, the JDC received memos and reports that mentioned his involvement in all sorts of shady commercial activities related to relief work. In fact, the landsmanshaft delegate to the village of Macjow, who later committed suicide, evidently had discovered that some relatives who were profiteering in relief moneys had formed a short-lived business relationship with Gewirtz.

Other JDC guidelines actually made it difficult for the committee to work with a majority of the New York landsmanshaftn. For one thing, the JDC would not sponsor a delegate's trip unless he was carrying a minimum of $40,000 in cash or the equivalent in purchase orders for commodities. This was not an overwhelming sum of money for the larger, more prosperous societies. The Bialystok and Brisker societies easily raised many times that amount, and even some of the smaller societies were able to attain the minimal sum required by the JDC. The Musher-Baranowitcher Society, for example, had only a few hundred members and was in contact with perhaps another 1,000 landsleit in New York, but it had raised more than $41,000 cash before it came to the JDC. In addition, some of the smaller societies grouped themselves together in regional federations, such as the Ukrainian Federation, the Federation of Baltic Jews, and the Federation of Lithuanian Jews; this allowed them to muster the necessary funds for successfully meeting the JDC requirements. But most societies fell far short of the minimum cash required for JDC sponsorship and thus had to undertake relief efforts on their own.

By June 1922 the JDC had sponsored more than 800 relief missions by landsmanshaft delegates, who had distributed over $1.2 million in villages and towns in the Pale. By the spring of 1923 this number had grown to 1,084 sponsored missions, and it would rise to more than 1,200 by the end of the year.[16] Impressive as these figures were, the JDC was conscious of its inability to reach and work with a majority of landsmanshaftn in New York and elsewhere. Not only were many societies too small and too primitive to satisfy the guidelines imposed on their relief efforts by the JDC, but there were also many societies that remained wary of any official involvement with formal and quasi-official Jewish charitable organizations. The desire of many landsmanshaftn to avoid direct contact with the JDC reflected the instinctive fear of many immigrants regarding involvement with officialdom in any form, but it was also a vestige of the traditional antipathy between Jewish immigrants from Eastern Europe and the more established German Jews who formed the leadership and backbone of such established relief agencies as the JDC. The JDC clearly recognized the problem, but there was little it could do. At one point in 1923 the JDC staff attempted to initiate a public relations campaign in the Yiddish press, for the purpose of persuading East European immigrants that the committee's motives and activities were above suspicion. As a JDC staff member noted during the meeting called to organize the campaign: "The landsmanschaft societies are very often biased by information which they read in the Yiddish press, and the result is that at the least suggestion they come to conclusions regarding our work which are not altogether favorable."[17]

Partly in response to the changing economic and political situation in Eastern Europe, and partly in response to internal developments within the fundraising effort in the United States, the JDC liquidated its landsmanshaft section on June 1, 1924. (The entire JDC operation was reorganized the following year.) Nevertheless, over the previous several years, the JDC and its landsmanshaft section had managed to develop and sustain a relief effort of heroic proportions. Notwithstanding the chaos, uncertainty, and mismanagement that plagued many landsmanshaft delegate missions, the records clearly indicate that persons who arrived in a shtetl carrying money and commodities from landsleit in America often made the difference between life and death, or at least provided essential relief and support when they were most needed.

In February 1921, for example, the JDC sponsored the trip of a landsmanshaft delegate to the Polish shtetl of Horoszki. The New York landsleit had received a letter from the relief committee in the village, claiming that "the most part of the town is destroyed. People are in great distress. The murderous hands of Budeni's cavalry have destroyed an entire region and our town in particular." The funds donated for the relief of Horoszki came from three separate organizations: the Horadisher Bros. Benevolent Society, the Horadisher Branch 346 Workmen's Circle, and the organization that had no doubt been the original landsmanshaft from which the other two sprang, the Chevra Anshe Horadishutz. When the delegate returned to America, he told the JDC that he had found the village "burned, devastated, the population starving. There were almost 200 orphans."[18] No doubt the money he brought was sorely needed.

The JDC sent a landsmanshaft delegate to the village of Boryslav, in Poland, where a report had indicated there were more than 300 orphans along with some 3,000 other Jews in desperate straits. Upon arriving at the village, the delegate was taken on a tour of the various communal facilities in need of funds. The hospital had been entirely destroyed, and the school was in such bad condition and so short of funds to pay its staff that one teacher had actually collapsed and died from the effects of malnutrition while standing in front of a class. But the worst moment occurred when the man arrived at the orphanage. Children were waiting in a long line to be registered by the staff, and the rumor quickly spread that the landsmanshaft delegate was going to take them back to America. When the rumor proved groundless, many of the children began to cry and wail. The delegate later recalled that "little children cried loud and complained, 'Take us to America too.' They did not cease sobbing for quite a time."[19]

In some villages, relief funds from American landsleit were used to rebuild nearly every facility that played a role in the community's social welfare. In the Polish town of Janow, the landsmanshaft delegate gave money to the old-age program, which housed thirty elderly persons in private homes and paid for their board. He also distributed money to board 75 orphans in private residences and to purchase food for a kitchen that fed more than 350 poor children every day. Money was also spent to repair the mikvah and the cemetery, to establish a loan fund (kassa), and for direct payments to impoverished families and individuals. Most important, he was able to provide enough money to help the community organize a food cooperative. Food prices are very high in this locality, he noted. "Not only is the price high but food is often very scarce. Very often, indeed, has the town been faced with almost starvation conditions because of food scarcity."[20] The co-op, on the other hand, was able to purchase staples in large quantities at lower prices and store it for times of dearth.

The Kosower landsmanshaft in New York sent one of its members under JDC auspices with money for the home village of Kosowa. In addition to distributing individual remittances to family and friends, the delegate spent more than $5,000 on various communal facilities. As small a sum as $5,000 might appear today, the money actually enabled the town to reopen its children's kitchen, its orphanage, the Hebrew public school, and the mikvah. The money also subsidized the activities of the free loan society and the Red Mogen David, which dispensed free medical supplies to the indigent sick.[21]

Nearly every delegate who traveled to Eastern Europe on behalf of his society was entrusted with sums of money to be given directly to individuals still living in the shtetl. These payments were often quite small, sometimes no more than $20, but they represented an essential means of support for people who often had no way to earn a living and lacked the barest necessities. The JDC kept lists of these individual donations, which reflect the remarkable extent to which immigrants in America maintained contact with large numbers of relatives in their native villages and were able to know these relatives' needs. Morris Yapoliter, who lived on Fulton Street in Brooklyn, sent $115 to relatives in the shtetl: $30 for his brother, $25 for his sister, $25 for his sister-in-law, $25 to a nephew, and $10 for "two friends, Basse Fiesh and Zalman Alpinbam." Abe Maiden, in the Bronx, sent $100 on the same mission, to be divided between his mother, two brothers, a brother-in-law and the children of his sister.[22] In addition to giving cash directly to relatives in the village, landsmanshaft delegates, working with the JDC, arranged for tickets, visas, and other documentation to allow people to leave the shtetl and migrate to New York. Many delegates spent most of their time not in the shtetl but in various port cities, helping relatives apply for visas, booking passage on ships, and paying for room and board of prospective emigrants as they waited to make the trip to America.

Ties to the Homeland

From 1920 until 1924 the JDC sponsored and supervised the continuous outflow of people and money from America to Eastern Europe for the purpose of alleviating the plight of the Jews in the Pale. But this was only the tip of the iceberg, so to speak. What the records of the JDC and other major relief organizations fail to reveal is the extent to which the primary relief effort was carried out on a personal basis between the ravaged communities in Eastern Europe and their landsleit in New York. Both the reluctance of the landsmanshaftn to become involved with the JDC and the nature of the landsmanshaft relief effort are important signposts regarding the state of landsmanshaft development at the end of the Great Migration. The antipathy of the landsmanshaftn toward all formal organizations reflected the insularity of the membership, traits also common to the local relief organizations operating in nearly every shtetl. Without exception, every JDC official who journeyed through the war-torn zones of Eastern Europe found himself the target of mistrust, fear, and suspicion from the survivors, who were unwilling to submit to the dictates of any outside authority. JDC officials in New York encountered similar sentiments when they tried to organize American landsmanshaftn into a single coordinated campaign.

Although the Jewish population of Eastern Europe was devastated by the effects of war and pogroms, it was still in a position to carry out its own relief efforts by relying on traditional organizations and cohesive internal bonds, most of which were communal in nature and historically resistant to control from the outside. The same could be said about the independent stance of the landsmanshaftn in New York. Part of their aloofness from the JDC no doubt grew out of negative motives, but it had a positive side as well. The landsmanshaftn were able to mount a major relief effort on their own primarily because they did not need the help of others. In the aggregate, they represented the single most potent force within the Jewish immigrant community, both in terms of total membership and, more important, in terms of their intense links to the Pale. Many of the societies may have been financially weak, but most were of recent vintage; their numbers were still increasing, and many of their newest members were fresh from the other side, having just left kin behind them. To the extent that this contact with the native shtetl was maintained through the continued passage of immigrants, it served to augment the landsmanshaft relief effort to rescue relatives and rebuild Jewish communal life in Eastern Europe.

Another factor that aided the landsmanshaftn was their innate understanding of the social and cultural milieu to which relief effort was directed. Although the landsmanshaftn might have been culturally backward when measured by New World standards, they were perfectly in step with the cultural attitudes and habits of the Old World community. Unlike the JDC, whose bureaucratic and professional approach alienated many of the potential recipients of aid, the landsmanshaft representatives who journeyed to Eastern Europe could anticipate and respond to the peculiarities of thought and outlook they encountered. The instances of abuse (black marketeering, profiteering) might have appeared scandalous and unethical to the JDC, but these events also reflected the ability of the landsmanshaft representatives to reinsert themselves immediately and directly into the local culture. New immigrants who returned to the Pale intuitively understood the nuances, the customs, and the social dynamics of the villages they visited and the people with whom they dealt.

The years surrounding World War I were the high-water mark of landsmanshaft development and influence in New York; there were probably more societies with more enrolled members than during any other period in the entire century. Moreover, until 1923, the Jewish immigrant community, like every other ethnic group in America, still possessed an Old World base. To the extent that the existence of a homeland gave every ethnic group a greater sense of identity and an extra measure of security, the landsmanshaft population reaped such benefits more than any other segment of the immigrant Jewish community. But the effects of the pogroms and the ending of immigration opportunities to America after 1923 changed everything. Henceforth, security and cohesion for Jewish immigrants had to be achieved at the expense of—and in direct contradiction to—Old World culture and ideas. Those Jews who chose to remain tied to an Old World mentality found it increasingly difficult to rationalize their decision in functional terms. The landsmanshaftn were able to respond to events in the Pale because their members were still part of the Old World community. As that community increasingly passed into memory, the landsmanshaftn found themselves more and more unable to respond to events at home.

V

The New World Divides

For there is no denying that the very physical fact
of grouping large masses of Jews along sectional
lines of cleavage, is bound to produce a psychological effect, not entirely favorable to a complete
fusion of all Jewish elements in the Melting Pot
of the larger Jewish community of Greater New
York.

—*The Jewish Communal Register*
of New York City, 1917–1918

SOON AFTER World War I ended, a young man named
Sy Berkowitz was taken to a landsmanshaft meeting by his
brother-in-law, Murray Steinberg. The meeting was held in
a room on the Lower East Side, at an address Berkowitz no
longer remembers; this was the first such meeting he had
attended since arriving in New York several years earlier.
Climbing the stairs to the meeting room, the brother-in-law
turned to Berkowitz suddenly, and said, "Remember, Sy, the
secret password for tonight is ———." Berkowitz did not
hear the password that had been furtively whispered to him,
but he was not concerned. He didn't really want to get
involved in his brother-in-law's society, and he had agreed
to come in from Brooklyn only because his mother had
written to him from the shtetl telling him to go to a meeting
to locate some of her relatives.

Having reached the top of the stairs, he walked into a small, dimly lit room, where he found about a dozen men sitting around in a circle whispering to one another. They all turned upon his entrance and regarded him with a mixture of suspicion and reserve. He recognized and nodded to several familiar faces, taking the last empty seat in the room. "My God," he thought, "my brother-in-law wasn't kidding when he told me that his society kept their business to themselves."

All of a sudden he noticed that one man was slowly walking around the room, stopping in front of each chair, and whispering something into the ear of the occupant, who, in turn, quickly whispered something back. Now the man was standing in front of Berkowitz and whispering a brief, clipped question in Yiddish, to which Berkowitz was obviously supposed to respond. "What did you say?" asked Berkowitz, and the man, now somewhat angered, repeated, "What is the password for tonight?" Berkowitz, now flustered, rocked back in his chair, shrugged helplessly as all the eyes in the room bored in on his face: "Eh, eh, the password is . . . eh, eh, Berkowitz?"

This incident, minus the finale, was not uncommon at landsmanshaft meetings. The societies considered themselves separate from the world around them, and they often instituted strict and secret codes and rituals to instill a sense of exclusiveness among their members. This was communalism at its most primitive level, and it was reinforced by other forms of communal activity. In this context, it is ironic that the point at which the landsmanshaftn first began to fall out of step with the prevailing direction of immigrant life occurred at the same time that other Jewish groups in New York tried to re-create a basic form of Old World communalism known as the kehillah.

Originating in seventeenth-century Poland, the kehillah "combined, in its quintessence, a strong executive body and a wide-ranging network of voluntary associations."[1] The kehillah consisted of a group of local elected officials who appointed others to assist in governing the community. Generally speaking, the town rabbi, magistrate, teacher, clerk, and scribe were all paid officials of the local kehillah. Most community organizations—including the unions and guilds, the welfare and charity societies, and the merchants' associations—also were represented in the kehillah.

The kehillah actually had a dual role. On the one hand, it was responsible for controlling the affairs of the community, establishing and enforcing codes of economic and social conduct, regulating financial affairs, mediating both between and within various groups and associations, and overseeing the provision of municipal services. But during the eighteenth and nineteenth centuries, particularly in those areas of settlement where the yoke of tsarist rule was felt most harshly, the kehillah also came to represent the local community in its relations with the outside world. In effect, the kehillah became the overseer of outside interests within the local community, functioning, for example, as a tax-collecting agency for the Russian state. In this respect, the kehillah resembled similarly constituted local councils in peasant villages throughout the civilized world.[2]

By the middle of the nineteenth century the kehillah, as a formal institution recognized both internally and externally as the representative of local interests, began to fall into disuse. On the one hand, internal resistance to tradition, expressed politically through the growth of Zionism and socialism, robbed the kehillah of much of its local support; both the Zionist and the socialist movements drew adher-

ents away from the kehillah and often established independent organs of self-government that refused to acknowledge
the kehillah's authority. From the outside, the increasing
coerciveness of the tsarist government, expressed through
decrees aimed at raising taxes and enforcing political alle-
giance, undermined the efforts of the kehillah to maintain a
precarious balance between local and national interests. In
1844 the government abruptly abolished the kehillah and
instituted in its place an administrative entity known as the
Bureau of Jewish Affairs.

Yet despite these changes and pressures, the kehillah was
maintained, at least as a basic ideal. Even if it was modified
or abolished de jure, it retained de facto importance. The
kehillah, as such, might not meet formally and it might no
longer issue decrees, but everyone in the community still
acknowledged the importance of consulting with village el-
ders on the crucial issues of local life. In this respect, the
kehillah survived the economic and political changes of the
nineteenth century because the basic communalism of the
shtetl had not really been eradicated. Indeed, the dislocation
and destruction of the World War I years probably strengthened the kehillah, if only because in the wake of the pogroms, many communities reverted to their most primitive,
instinctive relations and attitudes. The dispatches of Meyer
Leff and other JDC functionaries who journeyed through
the Pale after 1919 are replete with references to the ad hoc,
informal village committees that sprang up in nearly every
settlement to undertake the task of reconstruction and
renewal of Jewish life. Some of these committees operated
as adjuncts to more formal organizations, such as labor
unions or Zionist groups, but many clearly were a product
of the energies of the surviving "notables" of the community (the rabbi, the teacher, and others), who naturally as-

sumed positions of authority and responsibility during the chaotic postwar period.

Communalism remained a fundamental force in Jewish life in Eastern Europe throughout the entire modern period. Not surprisingly, most East European Jewish immigrants brought many of these communal attitudes and ideas with them when they came to America. But in America—a land without pogroms, without physical violence or terror—the communal ethos began to die out. This is because the communal mentality could not withstand the subtle yet overbearing pressures toward assimilation and individualism imposed upon the immigrant population by the new culture. Communalism, as expressed through the kehillah, held a prominent place in the psyche and behavior of shtetl dwellers precisely because it enabled the Jews of Eastern Europe to survive as an alien, marginal population within the larger society. The formal abolition of the kehillah structure by the tsar in 1844 was intended to a break down this protective barrier. In America, on the other hand, Jewish immigrants faced a clear choice. They could remain marginal and unassimilated, retaining their fundamental Old World culture (including their communal outlook), or they could enter the mainstream of the New World society and gradually discard the traditional ways of the past.

This is not to say that communalism was immediately abandoned as soon as the immigrants walked down the gangplank and landed in New York. To the contrary, the growth and development of the landsmanshaft network was a potent example of the intensity of communal attitudes among the newly arrived immigrants. And the Jewish community of New York went even further: In 1909 a New York kehillah, ostensibly representing all the Jews in the city, was founded at a large meeting attended by 300 delegates.[3] The impetus behind this event was a scurrilous, anti-Semitic attack by the police commissioner, who had asserted the previous year that Jews were responsible for half of the crime that occurred in the city. Commissioner Theodore Bingham's attack, echoing both in form and substance the pogrom mentality of East European commissars, produced a shock wave within the Jewish community, galvanized the leadership of all segments into action, and even produced a brief rapport between uptown (German) and downtown (East European) elements of the Jewish population.

The New York kehillah attempted, on a broad scale, to emulate the activities of the communal organizations of the Old World. It set itself up as a self-supporting clearinghouse for Jewish welfare, as well as a representative of Jewish interests in the society at large. In other words, it was expected to function both as the arbiter of problems internal to the structure of New York's Jewish community and as the watchdog over Jewish concerns vis-à-vis the city. To these ends, the kehillah, at various times, established and operated bureaus of education, social morals, and industry. All three bureaus assumed the responsibility of collecting funds from the Jewish community and utilizing them to deal with the fundamental problems of immigrant life: poverty, criminality, inhumane working conditions, labor strife, and lack of education. In all these areas the kehillah was able to make positive advances in ameliorating social conditions, and it also succeeded in maintaining a certain degree of cohesion and cooperation among the various Jewish groups.

While the New York kehillah operated within a certain Old World sensibility, it was not an institution designed ultimately to maintain these traditions in the face of pressures for assimilation and change. To the contrary, the kehillah's founders and most of its leaders found themselves caught in the fundamental contradiction posed by the maintenance of a particular ethnic heritage within the context of an assimilationist society. Judah Magnes, the kehillah's guiding force, summed up the issue when he spoke of the need to retain the traditional heritage of the country of origin while becoming immersed in the "dominant culture of the land."[4] This ambivalence regarding the mission of the kehillah surfaced in virtually every program that it attempted to carry out, notably in the fields of education and labor arbitration, and it would be an underlying but nonetheless crucial factor in the decline and virtual disappearance of the kehillah during World War I. The kehillah was never able to surmount the gap between the fundamental social needs of its mass constituency (the immigrants) and the political objectives of its leadership (the German-Jewish establishment). For the most part, the leadership of the kehillah was drawn from the ranks of the city's Jewish elite (Magnes himself was associate rabbi at Temple Emanuel), which had the political and financial resources to organize and direct a body theoretically embracing the millions of Jewish inhabitants of the city. But the kehillah ostensibly represented the immigrant community, and while it attempted to formulate programs that would meet the needs of the immigrant population, it was never able to enlist or absorb that population's energies in its cause.

The reason for the gap between the leadership and the rank and file of the kehillah lay in the attitudes and history of the immigrant population. The downtown Jews never completely abandoned their traditional antipathy and suspicion toward the uptown German elite within the Jewish community of New York. Even in the shtetl, there had often existed a certain unease and hostility among the poorer residents toward their betters, a gap that was magnified in

America where class differences were reinforced by ethnic differences. The kehillah failed to take root within New York's Jewish community because the kind of intimate and insular forms of communal organization the immigrants sought to reestablish in the New World could never be grafted onto the large, impersonal, bureaucratic institution the New York kehillah came to represent. Given its ambivalent view of the immigrants' relationship to New World society, the kehillah could never satisfy the demands of its two basic constituencies. For those Jews who were truly bent on assimilation and social mobility, the kehillah was too timid and conservative. For those Jews who eschewed Americanization and assimilation, the kehillah represented an unnecessary and irrelevant attempt to superimpose a communal structure on a population that had already created its own personal forms of communalism.

Thus, even as the kehillah was experiencing a revival in towns, villages, and shtetlach across Eastern Europe, the New York kehillah was falling apart. Many of its activities, particularly in the areas of social welfare and education, would be brought under the umbrella of the Federation of Jewish Philanthropies, whose governing board included a large number of important German-Jewish figures, some of whom had previously lent their energies to the kehillah. The federation would eventually become the major social welfare agency for New York's Jewish community, and it would organize most of the important charity and relief work that is carried out to this day among New York Jews.

The disappearance of the New York kehillah in 1922, however, did not mean the end of communalism within the city's Jewish population, particularly among recent arrivals from the Pale, whose communal instincts were still fresh. Rather, the decline of the kehillah signified the fracturing of the Jewish community between two distinct populations: on the one hand, those individuals and groups who no longer had a need for communal organizations in their traditional form; on the other, those individuals and groups whose communal activities were too narrowly focused for inclusion in a community-wide organization.

As regards the former, the kehillah, in one of its last tasks, published in 1918 a comprehensive guide to Jewish organizations, the *Jewish Communal Register*.[5] This massive 1,536-page compendium contained the name, history, and function of nearly every Jewish organization in the city—or so its authors claimed. The document was prepared in response to demands during the war years for reform of the kehillah, and its analysis of the state of Jewish communal activities was to be the basis for a thoroughgoing restructuring of the body. The *Register* is no doubt the most comprehensive analysis created during this century of any large ethnic population in the United States, and a careful examination of its contents gives us a profound insight into the forms and structures of New York's immigrant Jewish community at a crucial watershed in its history.

At this time, religion still played the overwhelmingly dominant role in Jewish affairs. Of the nearly 3,700 organizations and groups surveyed in the *Register*, more than 1,100 were identified as congregations. Of these, 503—nearly half of all the congregations in the city—were located on the Lower East Side. Yet of these 503 Lower East Side congregations, only 77 actually occupied synagogue structures. The remainder conducted their devotional affairs in a variety of makeshift quarters, including storefronts, apartments, and meeting halls. In no other part of the city did so many Jews belong to congregations that did not occupy synagogue buildings. In Boro Park, for example, nearly three-quarters of the congregations were located in synagogue buildings. This difference clearly reflected the primitive conditions of life on the Lower East Side, where the activity of religious groups was still based on the intense interpersonal relations between members rather than on a more formalized and less homogeneous social structure that was emerging in the outer neighborhoods.

A second important difference in patterns of worship similarly reflected the social and economic distinctions between older and newer Jewish neighborhoods. Of the 1,127 congregations operating in the city, 343 (nearly one-third of the total), were not permanent, year-round institutions but instead temporary, "floating" groups of worshipers who came together on special occasions, such as the High Holy Days each Fall. Resistant to a year-round congregational commitment, many Jews would simply rent space in a hall or theater, pray together on the Day of Atonement (Yom Kippur), and then disband until the following year. Of the 503 congregations on the Lower East Side, only 71 were transitory. But on the West Side of Manhattan (an area that was filling up with an upwardly mobile Jewish population) nearly half the congregations were temporary in nature, and in Brooklyn temporary congregations accounted for nearly 40 percent of all synagogue groups. This difference clearly demonstrated the extent to which socioeconomic mobility and the movement away from the older, more traditional immigrant neighborhoods exercised a potent negative effect on Old World mores, drawing people away from their roots.

After religion, the second most important aspect of community affairs was education. In 1918 it was estimated that approximately 275,000 children were attending the first eight grades of the city's public school system. Of this total, only 65,000 (23.6 percent) were receiving religious instruction, in the form of weekday or weekend synagogue schools and Talmud Torahs, private establishments, institutional schools (such as those run by the Educational Alliance), and *cheders,* the last constituting a form of group tutorial rather than a formal educational environment. The statistics on Jewish education, like those on congregation membership, clearly demonstrated how the experience of life in America was gradually tearing away at the fabric of beliefs and practices the immigrants had brought with them. Not only were three-quarters of all Jewish children receiving no religious instruction (unthinkable in Old World communities, where religious instruction was usually the only form of education), but as one moved away from the inner-city neighborhoods to the more affluent outlying districts, religious education disappeared almost entirely. In Manhattan, for example, where most Jews still lived on the Lower East Side, 17 percent of the school-age Jewish youth were enrolled in some form of religious instruction, but in Brooklyn and Queens the proportion dropped to less than 12 percent.

While Jewish community institutions that attempted to maintain traditional patterns of belief and behavior were clearly in a state of decline, the same cannot be said for those organizations that attempted to promote a greater degree of social and cultural awareness about the new society. At the end of World War I, New York had 121 separate labor organizations, with an active membership of nearly 200,000 persons. These unions and locals were concentrated in the garment trades, which accounted for more than three-fourths of all Jewish union membership in the city. The garment trade unions ranged from such major groups as Local No. 9 of the Cloak and Suit Tailors Union, with 10,000 members, and Local No. 25 of the Ladies' Waist and Dressmakers' Union, with a membership roll of nearly 20,000, all the way down to the tiny Leather Suspenders Trimming Makers Union, with fewer than 300 members. Notwithstanding the preponderance of unions in the garment trades, Jewish labor organizations—including the Barbers' Union, the Waiters' Union (with over 2,000 members), and the Hebrew Actors Protective Union, whose Local No. 1 had just 125 members—embraced nearly every type of industrial and commercial activity in which Jews were employed.

New York's Jewish community also supported a wide variety of fraternal, benevolent, and social welfare organizations. Perhaps the best known of these organizations was the Workmen's Circle, or *Arbeiter Ring*, whose 240 branches in New York City enrolled more than 25,000 members. The Workmen's Circle, which was affiliated with the Socialist party, engaged in a broad spectrum of social welfare activities, with the aim of fostering a greater degree of self-reliance among immigrant workers and thereby easing their transition into the new society. Along with the Workmen's Circle, Jews also supported a number of fraternal organizations, chief among them the Independent Order B'nai B'rith, the Independent Order B'rith Abraham, and the Independent Order B'rith Sholom. Together, these three organizations enrolled nearly 120,000 members. Like the Workmen's Circle, they functioned primarily as welfare agencies, operating old-age homes, hospitals, and cemeteries and selling low-cost insurance policies to members for protection against the worst calamities.

The fraternal organizations, like the unions, consisted primarily of immigrants who were well on their way toward becoming Americans. Indeed, all of these organizations set themselves up as means through which the process of assimilation could be made easier for individual members. As the *Register* put it, "The Lodges of the various [fraternal] orders have been and still are the most valuable schools through which our immigrated Jews pass. Many have learned their English at their Lodge meetings."[6] Not only did the fraternal lodge and the Workmen's Circle set as their mission the more rapid assimilation of the immigrants, but in this respect they consciously chose to associate and identify with other public and private institutions of the society at large. In effect, they considered themselves representatives of the entire Jewish community in its dealings with the outside world, and they responded to any issue they considered important to Jews in their relations with the rest of American society. In some instances, these groups intervened actively in political affairs, and they all affiliated with other large fraternal, benevolent, and labor organizations that operated in the national and international arenas.

The "Hidden" Landsmanshaftn

Being a Jewish immigrant in New York, according to the findings of the *Communal Register*, meant coming into contact with a vast kaleidoscope of community organizations and institutions. According to the New York kehillah's own estimates, there was at least one religious, educational, benevolent, social, or recreational organization for every 400 Jewish residents in the city. Moreover, the majority of Jewish residents belonged to several such groups and made frequent use of the services provided by others. If a Jew bought a Yiddish paper for 2 cents in the morning (the going rate for all Yiddish dailies in 1918), he was one of at least 300,000 persons who read the Yiddish press each day. If he received a loan or an insurance payment from a mutual aid society or a lodge, this was part of more than $3 million in funds disbursed by those organizations each year. If he was sick, orphaned, or infirm, he would probably be cared for in one of the more than 30 hospitals, clinics, rest homes, and other medical facilities that annually spent nearly $6 million to care for the ill and indigent among the city's Jewish population. The statistics on Jewish community organizations published in the *Register* prove beyond doubt that hardly a single member of New York's Jewish population could go through daily life without frequently encountering Jewish agencies, organizations, and institutions designed to promote a better way of life.

But in one crucial respect, the portrait of New York's immigrant population and its resources provided by the kehillah was seriously flawed. For while the authors of the *Register* found numerous reasons to be concerned about the long-term trends in Jewish communal activity, which pointed toward the ultimate dissolution of the traditional social fabric of immigrant life, they neglected almost entirely the single most potent force for maintaining that traditional fabric, the landsmanshaftn. It was not so much that the leadership of the kehillah was unable to formulate a program for or policy toward the landsmanshaftn; rather, from the kehillah's perspective, the landsmanshaftn hardly existed at all.

Of the 1,536 pages of the *Register*, only 11 were devoted specifically to the landsmanshaftn. Moreover, while the *Register* contained in its exhaustive listings even the tiniest fraternal, welfare, educational, cultural, charitable, and recreational organizations (including the Literary Dramatic Club of Brooklyn, with only fifty members), it did not mention a single landsmanshaft by name. Many of the landsmanshaftn were lumped together with other types of mutual aid organizations. The *Register* noted that a large number of these organizations consisted primarily of landsleit and, while underestimating the number of landsmanshaftn by as much as two-thirds, did not pursue the matter further. Discussion of the landsmanshaftn as a distinctive phenomenon was confined to a brief description of the six national landsmanshaft federations, the Federation of Bessarabian Organizations, the Federation of Galician and Bucovinean Jews, the Federation of Oriental Jews of America, the Federation of Russian-Polish Hebrews of America, the Federation of Roumanian Jews of America, and the American Union of Roumanian Jews, the last-named involved only in overseas relief.

The large federations were hardly representative of the independent landsmanshaftn. They had come into existence primarily in response to the situation in Eastern Europe, and as national organizations they were able to muster the resources, both political and financial, to sustain a long-term relief campaign back in the homeland. But many local landsmanshaftn refused to affiliate with the national federations, or supplemented their connection to the larger organizations with their own personal relief efforts. Several federations supported major charitable institutions within the city, such as the Galician Federation's Har Moriah Hospital and the Russian-Polish Federation's Beth David Hospital, but such enterprises fell far beyond the scope of nearly all of the individual societies.

In truth, the *Register* neglected any mention of the real landsmanshaft phenomenon in New York precisely because most of the landsmanshaftn maintained a sense and practice of communalism that was antithetical to the objectives of New York's Jewish community leaders. The members of the individual landsmanshaftn were not interested in creating organizations that would allow them, in Magnes's words, to "saturate themselves in the dominant culture."[7] It is true that many landsmanshaft adherents were involved in other sorts of communal organizations and accepted help, as necessary, from many different welfare agencies at times when they were unable to maintain the dignity or security of their own lives. And even if the rank and file of the landsmanshaftn largely avoided contact with other organizations, most members made sure that their children were exposed to a healthy dose of Americanization through the efforts of the Workmen's Circle, the training schools, and the cultural agencies. Nevertheless, there were certain types of activities and traditions that could be maintained or expressed only within the context of the landsmanshaftn, and these activities found no place within an organizational structure that interposed itself as a halfway house between the Old World and the New. That the landsmanshaftn could have been almost totally ignored in the *Register,* which claimed to represent the sum and substance of all immigrant activity, serves as a potent reminder of the widening gulf within the Jewish immigrant community.

The most important communal functions carried out by the landsmanshaftn involved work and other economic activities. Like the societies to which most of them belonged, landsmanshaft members tended to be individualistic and independent in economic terms. This does not mean they were wealthy entrepreneurs. To the contrary, the limited financial resources of most of the societies reflected the impoverishment of the membership. But particularly during the latter part of the immigration period and the years following World War I, the immigrants who came to America, joined landsmanshaftn, and remained committed to their societies, tended to be petty merchants and proprietors (even if the proprietorship extended only to the front end of the cart wheeled through the street). If they were workers in the traditional sense, they were usually employed in small "ma and pa" shops, or in other establishments where the paternal or familial connection between owner and employee was strong enough to resist inroads from labor organizers or other outsiders.

The landsmanshaftn were heavily involved in many industrial shops during the early years, in part because of a calculated effort by factory owners to "import" new workers (who would accept lower wages) from a particular region or town in the Pale. In the 1890s nearly all the pants makers were landsleit from Rumania, while the children's cloak industry was dominated by members of several landsmanshaftn from villages around the city of Minsk.[8] But the early Jewish trade union movement set as one of its chief goals the elimination of the landsleit mentality from the rank and file, and by the 1920s the purge had been successfully completed in most areas of the garment trade and related industries. Industrial workers who came to America after 1910 often as not joined landsmanshaftn initially, but the strength and benefits of union membership usually impelled them to loosen their landsleit ties within a short period after their arrival.

As the landsmanshaft influence declined in the shops and the unions, it was strengthened in economic sectors that were emerging in response to the evolution of the city's economy and the changing character of the immigrant population. Particularly after World War I, the majority of new Jewish immigrants from the Pale no longer had made a conscious decision to emigrate away from their place of origin, but instead had been forced to leave Eastern Europe and would not have left if things had been otherwise. New immigrants who came from the small shtetlach that had been particularly vulnerable to the predations and chaos of the pogroms lacked any real working-class consciousness. And they came to a city which, by 1915, had already undergone its most dramatic phase of industrialization and commercial development, and now offered job opportunities not only in primary manufacturing but also in the secondary, service, and retailing sectors. Thus, many of the immigrants who arrived in New York during and after World War I found jobs as clerks or functionaries in the multitude of wholesale and retail establishments that sprang up in the newly expanding Jewish neighborhoods or were adjuncts to the growth of manufacturing and industry. The wholesale and retail trades, however, presented a set of economic requirements much different from those of the shop. If the landsmanshaft connection retarded the development of class consciousness and labor advancement in factories, it was definitely an advantage for the petty entrepreneur or the man who had dreams of becoming one. The landsmanshaft connection enabled a small shopkeeper to set up shop, because he could borrow space, fixtures, and even inventory from his landsleit; it enabled him to learn the distribution and market patterns of his particular commodity; and it enabled him, if his business failed, to go back to work for one of his landsleit shopkeepers. For example, the members of the Krakinever landsmanshaft in Brooklyn, who operated small dry-goods stores, got together and bought their goods in bulk from factory owners, thus receiving a better price and ensuring a higher profit when they retailed their wares. The Progressive Monasterzyska Society, consisting of diamond cutters and diamond setters, many of whom over time became proprietors of small wholesaling outlets in the jewelry district, similarly exemplifies the use of landsmanshaft connections to expand a commercial base.

The individualistic, parochial, and politically conservative tendencies of most of the smaller landsmanshaftn were not just a function of Old World customs and traditions. They also reflected the selfsame qualities of the landsmanshaft membership, which was gradually turning away from the blue-collar occupations of the early immigrant era to more "gray-collar" forms of work. This trend toward petty entrepreneurship, shopkeeping, and merchandising was evident after 1920 not only among landsmanshaft members but also throughout the city's entire Jewish population.

Many immigrants who came to America and went into the shops would remain workers until the end of their lives, but they were no longer immigrant workers; rather, they were American workers from an immigrant background. On the other hand, the small entrepreneurs and petty shopkeepers who formed a sizable segment of the immigrant population did not necessarily move in the same direction. Some of them, certainly only a tiny minority, managed to rise to commercial prominence through a combination of hard work, diligence, exploitation of their employees (and landsleit), and a good dose of luck. If they remained immigrants in their homes and habits, they also learned how to operate in the larger world around them. Others tried to go the route of individual entrepreneurship, failed, and then fell back into the ranks of the working or service classes, some nourishing to the end of their lives the dream of regaining their entrepreneurial status.

A sizable part of the non–working class population, however, quickly achieved a minimal level of economic success, and once having done so, never moved upward or downward again. They remained tied to their little shops, and their fortunes, in turn, were tied to the fortunes of the neighborhood in which they operated. They served a small, definable clientele who depended upon these shopkeepers and merchants for the right goods at the right price, just as the shopkeepers depended upon their customers for their daily sales. In essence, they created the ethos of a shtetl economy (or many shtetl economies) within the city; and not only were they content to operate within this economic milieu for the rest of their lives, but they also certainly feared to expand beyond it. This population formed the natural base of long-term landsmanshaft affiliation, and it would only disappear when the small, self-evolved neighborhood economies began to disappear as well. Moreover, the members of this economic class were daily made conscious of the extent to which they controlled nothing beyond the narrowest perimeters of their own economic existence, and their landsmanshaftn thus became a crucial mechanism, socially and psychically, to counterbalance the insecurity of their daily lives.

Alongside the communal economic rationale for landsmanshaft membership were the social and familial aspects. The social aspect of the landsmanshaftn provided their members with a continuous dose of Old World customs and culture, primarily through the device of maintaining the meetings of most societies on the Lower East Side. Even when a majority of the city's Jewish population lived far away from Delancey and Essex streets, this original neighborhood of immigrant settlement retained its fundamentally Old World character. Consequently, a visit to the Lower East Side for the monthly or bimonthly landsmanshaft meeting was a means of reasserting the bonds to the traditional culture. The Lower East Side still had a plethora of shops, restaurants, theaters, and other public facilities that catered to a Yiddish-speaking and basically non-Americanized population. One could eat a meal in the hundred or so kosher East European restaurants, purchase ritual foods (matzoh and wine) for the holidays, watch the Old World artisans in their skullcaps making prayer scrolls and shawls, rummage through the stalls of Yiddish booksellers, or take in any one of a dozen or more Yiddish theatrical productions. The Grand Street Theater, at the corner of Grand and Chrystie streets, was an imposing five-story building whose plays often starred the Adlers. Several blocks away, on East Houston Street, stood the Thomashefsky Theater, which staged a wide variety of Yiddish repertory, usually starring the great Thomashefsky himself.

The fundamental vehicle for Old World culture, however, was the Yiddish press. In 1917, five Yiddish daily papers in New York sold a combined total of more than 300,000 copies each day, of which Abraham Cahan's *Daily Forward* alone had a circulation of nearly 150,000. Along with the five main Yiddish dailies, there were a dozen weekly and monthly periodicals; trade journals for butchers, grocers, and farmers; a long list of union papers; local neighborhood papers in Brownsville and East New York; and even several magazines for juveniles. The Yiddish press spanned the entire gamut of the immigrant community, and the landsmanshaftn utilized it extensively to promote their own organizations. Every issue of the *Forward* and the other major dailies contained notices from individual societies about meetings and other social events. Owners of meeting halls advertised space for rent to attract the landsmanshaftn, as did cemetery owners trying to sell plots to the societies.

The Yiddish press, which deserves its own study, was as vigorous and lively as the community that supported it. The newspapers reported extensively on events of interest to immigrants, both in America and elsewhere. The papers were the main source of information about developments in the Old World, both through news dispatches and through letters from individual readers. Editorials concentrated particularly on local economic and political matters. An editorial endorsement on election eve was a decisive factor in the next day's outcome at the polls—or so every politician whose name appeared on the ballot in an immigrant neighborhood believed. Yiddish periodicals were also the main forum for news and opinion about labor disputes and union activities, at a time such issues affected virtually every immigrant household.

Most of the city's landsmanshaftn continued to meet on the Lower East Side even when their membership had dispersed to neighborhoods throughout the city. As we shall see, the long-term trends represented by this geographical dispersion would eventually undermine the cohesion of many landsmanshaftn, but during the early decades of the century the connection between the societies, the Lower East Side, and the Old World held firm. The Jaslowitzer Progressive Young Men's Society met twice a month at 257 East Houston Street, even though most of its members lived in the Bronx. The Independent Kassower Society came together at 30 East 1st Street, although its members were primarily living in Brooklyn. Similarly, the Independent Stavisker Benevolent Society held its meetings on Forsyth Street, despite the fact that only a handful of its members after World War I still lived in the area around the meeting hall.

The attraction of the Lower East Side as a place of social contact for the landsmanshaftn did not extend to the more formal Jewish communal organizations, which quickly began to move away from any reliance on the resources of the inner city to support their social and cultural affairs. By 1920 most of the larger Jewish labor unions had bought or purchased vacation enclaves in upstate Rockland or Sullivan counties, and weekend excursions to these country retreats during the spring and summer months became the usual form of communal social activity for these organizations and their members. The Workmen's Circle operated several summer camps in the Catskills for members' children, and many offspring of landsmanshaft adherents recall being sent to these camps during the summer while their parents stayed behind and tended their shops and small stores in the city. The social activities of many unions, particularly the left-wing organizations, were outgrowths of union activity itself. Picnics and gatherings were often adjuncts to the parades and demonstrations that took place on labor holidays, such as May Day, or in the aftermath of an organizing or political campaign.

The communal web of landsmanshaft activity underscored its role in the maintenance of family relations. Although many younger Jews migrated to America with their wives, children, and older relatives in tow, many others came alone. More often than not, immigrants came to America after World War I as individuals, their family units in the Old Country shattered by pogroms. Many immigrants joined a landsmanshaft in the hope of finding the warmth and conviviality of the family life they had left behind in the Pale. Just as many shtetl dwellers had lived their early years within an extended family circle in their native village, so their landsmanshaft became an extended family in the New World. The landsmanshaft not only helped families to remain together, but it also helped families to come together. The societies performed the vital task of finding eligible mates for unmarried or widowed members. So did the traditional marriage brokers who advertised their services in the Yiddish press, but the landsmanshaftn added at the same time a touch of familiarity and personal concern.

It was difficult for a landsmanshaft member whose

spouse had passed away to escape remarriage, since the societies had a vested interest in keeping the basic social fabric intact. The story has it that in a particular society, a member's wife who lay on her deathbed instructed her husband to marry the widow of another former member, saying, "She is a good woman, she made a good home for Morris and she'll make a good home for you." The man protested in vain to his dying wife, who was quick to overrule his objections, admonishing him to "think of the children and don't feel guilty when I'm gone. You can even give her all my clothes to wear." But as the poor woman drew her last breath, her husband stood up and frantically shouted, "How can I marry Sadie? She takes a size six and you wear a size ten!"

The question of death—and of the social and religious requirements that surrounded the funeral of a Jew—was the single most important factor in explaining the survival of the landsmanshaftn in the face of so many competing institutions and organizations. The problems of life, as we have seen, could be handled through a multiplicity of agencies, institutions, and strategies, but the problem of death and the care of the deceased offered fewer possible solutions. For one thing, orthodox religious ritual required that the body be interred within twenty-four hours after death (except for the Sabbath, when no funerals could be held and all cemeteries were closed). Religious rules also mandated that the body be wrapped in a special shawl woven for the occasion, and placed in an unadorned pine coffin constructed entirely of wood. In addition, orthodox custom required that the body of the deceased be kept at home, because some form of prayer or silent devotion and attention was to be maintained by relatives and friends until the actual burial occurred. In the aftermath of the funeral, the relatives of the deceased were required to spend seven days in mourning (shivah), during which time a nightly prayer service would be held.

These religious and cultural requirements could only be fulfilled within an intensely personal context. The need to place the body in the ground within twenty-four hours meant that a great number of financial and social tasks had to be accomplished at a time when the immediate family of the deceased was least able to undertake these responsibilities. The requirements of the shivah period meant that at least ten men, the minimum number for a minyan, had to assemble each night to pray for the dead. Another burden was the cost of the funeral, which the family, in many cases, lacked sufficient resources to cover. This problem had been handled in the Old World, through the institution of the *chevra kadisha*, or community burial society. When immigrants first came to New York they reconstituted their chevras as adjuncts to synagogues, albeit on a much more limited scale than had previously existed in the shtetl. By the 1920s, however, most of the smaller chevras had gone out of existence, much as the smaller synagogues and congregations were also beginning to collapse. For the most part, the responsibilities of the chevras were taken over by the landsmanshaftn, and they remained the primary vehicle for dealing with death among immigrant Jews until at least the late 1930s.

The landsmanshaftn were also the primary purchasers of cemetery space in the city for the immigrant population; in fact, many societies were organized primarily for the purpose of buying burial plots, which was always cheaper when bought on a group basis. But even more important than financial considerations was the personal element associated with a landsmanshaft funeral. Each society appointed a *shames*, who was responsible for making sure that the grave

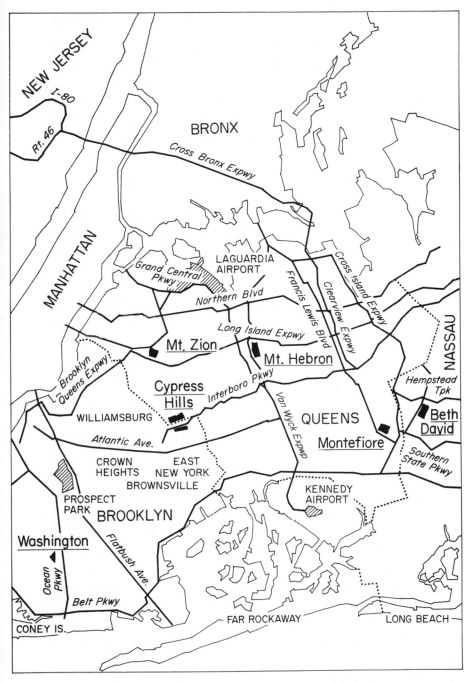

Landsmanshaft Cemeteries in New York

was dug on the day when a funeral was scheduled to take place. He would arrive at the cemetery ahead of the procession and hearse, arrange for a crew to dig the grave at a specific location which he chose within the boundaries of the society's plot, and then supervise the actual burial procedure, including jumping into the open grave after the casket was lowered, in order to crack open the pine planks (in accordance with orthodox ritual) before the dirt was shoveled back on top.

The first cemetery that sold space to the landsmanshaftn was the Washington Cemetery in Brooklyn, located on Ocean Parkway between Boro Park and Bensonhurst. Opened in the 1850s, it sold its first society spaces in 1869. Initially, most of the society plots were sold to fraternal lodges and synagogues, but many of these eventually became benevolent societies or landsmanshaftn. One of the earliest organizations to purchase space was the Nichwitzer Chevra, but in 1889 the society changed its name to the Progressive Brethren of Meshivis. Similarly, the Chevra Rofei Cholim Krakauer Society within a decade became the Krakower Benevolent Society.

In the late 1880s and the 1890s, East European landsmanshaftn began to buy large amounts of cemetery space in the Washington Cemetery, a testimony to the first large wave of immigrants who had begun to arrive from the Pale. In 1891, for example, cemetery space was purchased by the Independent Wilner Association, the Independent Kletzer Brotherly Aid, the Independent First Odessa Benevolent Association, the Independent United Brethren of Pomevisch, the Independent Kurlander Benevolent Society, the Independent Grodno Sick Support Society, and the Independent Minsker Association. Many of these organizations had evolved from smaller, more religiously affiliated chevras or burial societies, the latter having begun to disappear from the roster of purchasers of space in the Washington Cemetery.

Not only was the city's Jewish population becoming dominated by immigrants from Eastern Europe; it was also becoming much larger. The result was that the Washington Cemetery soon began to run out of space. In 1893 a second Jewish cemetery was opened. This one, known as Mt. Zion, was located in Maspeth, Queens, less than 2 miles from the heart of the Williamsburg ghetto. In fact, Mt. Zion and Mt. Washington cemeteries were located at opposite sides of what would become the Jewish immigrant "belt" in Brooklyn, an area stretching from Williamsburg along the East River to Brownsville and East New York on the border of Queens. By 1920 this area would contain more Jews than could be found in any other urban spot in the world (see map, p. 165). Mt. Zion sold off nearly all its available land within fifteen years after it first opened, and the space was sold primarily to landsmanshaftn. It also sold a large parcel to the Workmen's Circle, which bought space in nearly every Jewish cemetery in the city, as did many of the other Jewish benevolent organizations and labor unions. Mt. Zion was overwhelmingly a landsmanshaft cemetery, and its character, layout, and design clearly reflect the mores and culture of the landsmanshaftn at what was the high point of their existence.

A visit to Mt. Zion Cemetery today brings us face to face with a cultural tradition which, like the members buried within its walls, has long since passed away. The society cemeteries exhibit a minimum of concern for aesthetics, comfort, or grace. In the older plots, particularly those that were completely filled in by the 1930s, literally every inch of space is taken up by graves. There are no walkways, no space between monuments or headstones, no landscaping, no benches or other ornamental features. The headstones are in Hebrew (and some in Yiddish), many without dates, and it is often difficult to tell where the burial plot of one society ends and another's begins. One is struck by the fact that these cemeteries make no attempt to hide or obscure their essential function: to provide a minimal space in the ground for the departed.

Few if any landsmanshaft burial plots allowed for family groups or had spaces reserved for the next of kin. People were simply buried as they died, with little or no attempt to distinguish between them on the basis of wealth (of which few had any), social status, or prestige. The crowding together of graves in this pell-mell fashion was itself a reflection of the poverty of immigrant life. Since each society purchased its plot for a lump sum, it followed that the more graves that could be dug within its boundaries, the less would be the overall cost for each society member. Consequently, a cemetery plot in Mt. Zion that was designed to hold 120 graves might actually wind up with 130 or 140 burial sites, including perhaps a foot or two of space on the edge of the plot that had not yet been purchased or used by another society.

Nearly all the available space in Mt. Zion was purchased by 1907. Two years earlier, space in Mt. Carmel Cemetery in Cypress Hills had been opened for purchase by societies. Cypress Hills had been a nonsectarian cemetery from the 1850s, but it became a specifically Jewish cemetery once large numbers of Jews wanted to be buried in separate plots. Mt. Carmel was located adjacent to Crown Heights and East New York, neighborhoods into which Jews moved when they first began spilling out of the Williamsburg and Brownsville ghettos. Unlike Mt. Zion and the older section of Washington Cemetery, however, Mt. Carmel was not completely "Old World" in layout. As early as the 1920s, many of the plots had already abandoned the narrow, crowded appearance of the older cemeteries. Now there were larger headstones, wider spaces between graves, and decorative shrubbery and landscaping.

The real change came when Mt. Hebron Cemetery was opened on the grounds of the older, nonsectarian Cedar Grove Cemetery in 1909. This cemetery was located in Flushing, Queens, more than 4 miles to the west of Cypress Hills, and farther away from the "inner city" neighborhoods of Brownsville and Williamsburg. At this date there were very few Jews living in Queens, but the growth of the city's population had foreclosed the possibility of opening new cemetery space in Brooklyn. The first cemetery space in Mt. Hebron was sold to the Lubliner Society in February 1909, and the first burial in the entire cemetery was of a member of the Lubliners, Morris Kosakevitch, who was interred on April 13, 1909. In the same year, two smaller cemeteries were opened, the Montefiore Cemetery in Queens and the United Hebrew Cemetery in Staten Island.

Most of the early cemetery space in Mt. Hebron, as in other cemeteries, was sold at the front of the cemetery, within easy walking distance of the main gates. But as one moves farther away from the main gates into the sections opened in the 1920s, a change becomes apparent. The cemetery plots that were purchased and organized by societies after 1920 are no longer "Old World" in appearance. Instead, they begin to look more modern and secular. Headstones are much larger; there is space between graves; paved walkways allow mourners and visitors to pass unimpeded through different sections; shrubbery and landscaping begin to take on a "suburban" look. Moreover, the inscriptions on cemetery gates and headstones are no longer in Hebrew but also in English.

The last cemetery the Jews opened in New York was Beth

David Cemetery in Elmont, on the Queens–Nassau border. Beth David, which opened in 1918, was more than 6 miles east of Mt. Hebron and nearly 10 miles away from the edge of the Jewish ghetto in Brooklyn. Although it opened before Jews began moving in large numbers to Queens and the suburbs, its location clearly foreshadowed the future geographical dispersion of the Jewish population in New York. In addition, the cemeteries that arose within it clearly reflected the processes of assimilation and acculturation. There are almost no traditional plots within Beth David, and those few which began as "Old World" burial places were very quickly transformed into more modern cemetery plots, often after fewer than ten or fifteen persons had been buried within their boundaries.[9]

As with the older cemeteries, most of the space in Beth David was sold off to societies, but here again one sees a clear divergence from earlier patterns. While Mt. Zion is occupied almost entirely by chevras and landsmanshaftn, Beth David has almost no chevras; many of the society cemeteries are, in fact, the burial plots of family circles and other non-landsleit groups, such as private benevolent agencies and civic organizations. In addition, many of the individual cemetery plots in Beth David are unused. Societies in the 1920s would purchase a plot, bury a handful of members, and then either go out of existence or bury only a few members at a later date (the rest of the membership and their descendants would be buried elsewhere). For example, the cemetery of the Kolozsvar and Vicinity Sick and Benevolent Society was purchased in 1925, and nine persons were interred in orthodox fashion in the first row between 1926 and 1933. However, the rest of the cemetery contains only a few family plots scattered over the grounds, with a few burials in the 1950s and 1960s and then several graves from the 1980s. Obviously, this society, like many others, was not able to sustain either its traditional customs or the support of its membership for more than a decade after the plot was bought.

The Most Sacred Task

Cemeteries can evoke powerful feelings of mourning and death, but the Jewish cemeteries of New York transmit to us an equally powerful message about life. Other physical artifacts have been obliterated or uprooted, but these cemeteries still represent a true "sociology" of immigrant culture and development in the century since Jewish immigrants first began to arrive in large numbers, established communities, and established cemeteries to serve those communities. For example, most of the early synagogues were abandoned long ago, and only a handful remain to be seen in their original locations.[10] Indeed, if one travels through the old immigrant ghettos such as the Lower East Side, Williamsburg, and Brownsville, one sees that the physical, cultural, and ethnic transformation of these neighborhoods in less than three generations has wiped out nearly all but the faintest traces of Jewish immigrant life. But this is not the case with the cemeteries, since the physical evidence—the types and layout of graves, the style of inscriptions—remains immutably preserved.

Walking through Washington, Mt. Zion, and the oldest sections of Mt. Carmel and Mt. Hebron cemeteries, one moves instantly backward in time to an era when the Jewish community in New York still exhibited nearly all the cultural attributes of the Old World. These older cemeteries, like the surrounding ghetto neighborhoods, are densely populated and lack any latter-day concerns for appearance, comfort, and convenience. The styles of the headstones and the layout of the plots conform to a basic framework of religious orthodoxy and Old World culture, just as the original immigrant neighborhoods were dominated by Old World and orthodox styles and designs.

The Jews who buried their relatives and friends in these older cemeteries had a consciousness still directly linked to their origins. Even though many immigrants quickly adopted certain American ideas and attitudes, the core of their existence, their most fundamental cultural instincts, remained largely unchanged. For the cemetery had been a center of life and social interaction within the shtetl. Only the cohesiveness of the shtetl could absorb the trauma and pain of death. If the cemetery could no longer serve as the central focus of life in the New World, it still harbored within its grounds the most basic sentiments and instincts of a population that had been severed from its true roots.

The early cemeteries also offer the most potent reminder of the extent to which the landsmanshaftn dominated the social network of immigrant life. The landsmanshaftn owned nearly all the space in the older cemeteries, and they controlled the layout and organization of these properties. Indeed, there is not a single individual buried in Mt. Zion or the older sections of Mt. Hebron who was not a member of some type of immigrant benevolent society, usually of an independent landsmanshaft. Between 1890 and 1905 it was extremely difficult for Jewish nonmembers to find a burial place in New York, unless the mourners were willing to follow the casket to the outer reaches of Staten Island.

If the landsmanshaftn were so important to the execution of this central cultural and ritual activity, how do we explain the inability of the New York kehillah and other formal

organizations to acknowledge this importance? Why were
the landsmanshaftn largely absent from the great census of
Jewish organizations conducted by the kehillah after World
War I? The fact is that *active* membership of the landsmanshaftn represented only a small fraction of the total immigrant population, and only a small proportion of the former
residents of any particular shtetl. Many persons who were
members of various societies only became "involved" with
their organization at the critical moment when a grave had
to be dug. Precisely because the landsmanshaftn controlled
the single most indispensable communal activity of the immigrant population—the cemeterles—they had the ability at
extreme moments to muster support far exceeding their actual numbers. In essence, the landsmanshaftn formed an
impermeable "underground" of immigrant culture and immigrant identity whose links extended back to the most vital
roots of East European life.

But if the older sections of the cemeteries illustrate why
the landsmanshaftn were important, the newer sections tell
us why and when that importance came to an end. Just as
the headstones and inscriptions allow us to date the heyday
of the landsmanshaftn, so they also allow us to date their
decline. The latter period began sometime in the early
1930s, when the obvious manifestations of Old World culture in the cemeteries disappeared. From that time onward,
Old World traditions were maintained only in a haphazard
manner, reflecting some vague attempts by the next generation to preserve the memories of a bygone life and society
within a small corner of their own culture.

Part of the problem was the rapid pace of change in
American life. The same Yiddish newspapers that printed
thousands of copies and were sold on every street corner of
the Lower East Side in the 1920s were defunct by the 1950s.

Yiddish actors who headlined before packed houses throughout the metropolitan area after World War I were forced to tell their jokes in English in order to get an occasional booking in the smaller hotels in the Catskills after World War II. The continuity of immigrant culture, extending backward several centuries in the Old World, but appearing only sporadically thereafter in the New, began to disappear by the early 1930s. This culture was retained within the lives of many of the original immigrants and within the landsmanshaftn they organized, but only bits and pieces were transmitted to succeeding generations.

From the 1930s onward, the landsmanshaftn and their members would be fighting a losing battle. In the collision of cultures they would lose out to the inexorable pressures of social and economic change generated by a society that held no place for their Old World outlook. They would lose out to the automobile, to the suburbs, to television, to the mass market and mass culture. At the same time, their homeland would be obliterated by the Nazi program of mass murder. In previous chapters we have examined how the landsmanshaftn reacted to the New York City community in which they played a major role. Now we will examine their response to a society in which their role continually diminished and ultimately disappeared.

The Lower East Side at the turn of the century. (Photograph by Byron, The Byron Collection, Museum of the City of New York)

A lemonade vendor on Hester Street, 1898: one of a multitude of street-vendor entrepreneurs selling traditional goods in Old World fashion. (Photograph by Byron, The Byron Collection, Museum of the City of New York)

The streets were jammed with every sort of commerce and trade. Congestion was a normal part of everyday immigrant life. . . (Photograph by Byron, The Byron Collection, Museum of the City of New York)

. . . and death. The shtetl-like cemetery of Mt. Zion, with stones on top of stones. (Photograph by Ken Levinson)

Open spaces were unknown to the immigrants, who filled in this cemetery and then filled in the walkway. (Photograph by Ken Levinson)

But manicured lawns, shrubbery, and aesthetics are important to the American-born, and the Old World tradition disappears in Mt. Hebron. (Photograph by Ken Levinson)

VI

A Homeland Destroyed

Our hope to see our dear parents again has vanished. I remember that my father had a family in
the USA by the name of Lampart but we don't
know their address.
—A Holocaust survivor in Europe
writing to the JDC in 1946

ON APRIL 4, 1947, a group of landsleit from the Polish
shtetl of Hrubieszow held an emergency meeting in Academy Hall on Broadway and 14th Street.[1] They had come
together to discuss plans to form a relief committee that
would collect money and send it to relatives and friends in
the village. At the beginning of the meeting, the president
of the landsmanshaft read a letter he had just received from
one of the few remaining residents of the village. The letter
said:

"On September 16, 1939, our town was occupied by the
Hitlerite hordes, which started at once to persecute the Jews.
They began by converting the Synagogue into a stable for
horses. Their second act was to gather a larger part of the
Jewish men and drive them under SS escort in the direction
of the Soviet border. About 100 persons fell from the bullets
of the SS. Only a smaller part managed to come to the Soviet
side, and the balance, naked and barefoot, returned home.

"With the year 1942, a mass liquidation of the Hrubies-zow ghetto started, which was carried out in three 'actions' and 'expulsions.' Only a very small group survived in Soviet Russia or in German camps, and a couple of persons were hidden by the Poles. These experiences have left a deep mark on the minds and bodies of everyone. A predominant part of them is chronically ill with rheumatism, tuberculosis, and mental afflictions, unable to start a new life on the ruins of our past.

"The situation of the survived Jews from Hrubieszow is a very difficult one. They found themselves after liberation in a state of exhaustion and half naked. So far the larger part of them can sustain themselves only with the assistance from outside."

Not yet knowing the true extent of the catastrophe, inso-far as there had been virtually no contact between the villag-ers and their American landsleit for more than five years, the Hrubieszow Society collected more than $1,000, which it gave to the Joint Distribution Committee for immediate use in the shtetl. The society also asked the JDC to ascertain the extent of the physical suffering that had occurred during the war.

One month later, the society received the grimmest possi-ble news from overseas. The leader of the local council in Hrubieszow sent a letter thanking the society for its help, and added, "this assistance brought much good to our sur-viving brethren and sisters who returned after long difficult experiences in the bunkers, in the woods, in the partisan groups, concealment on the Aryan [Polish] side, or as repa-triates from Russia, deprived of their homes, clothing, food and all other basic necessities." In a village that had housed nearly 10,000 Jews before the war, and had supported a Hebrew school, a Yiddish theater, a network of sports teams, and three libraries, there were now only 88 Jews. An additional 216 former residents had been located in the towns of Szczecin, Rychbach, and Wroclaw, and several more had turned up in DP camps in Italy and Germany. The rest had all disappeared in the Nazi killing machine.

The Landsmanshaftn Respond Again

The news about the village of Hrubieszow that reached New York in May 1947 was reduplicated in hundreds and thousands of meetings of American Jews during that year, as the world woke up to face the calamitous tragedy of the Holocaust. The events in Hrubieszow were not exceptional; they were the norm. In six brief years, the Nazis managed to exterminate more than 6 million Jews and effectively brought Jewish life in Eastern Europe to an end. What persecution, pestilence, and privation had failed to do between 1880 and 1920, the Nazi butchers had accomplished in half a decade.[2] The intensity of the slaughter was matched only by its extent. Jews living in a region stretching from the English Channel to the Soviet heartland, a distance of more than 1,500 miles, were deported, shot, gassed, and slain. The worst slaughter occurred in the Pale, particularly Poland and the Russian Ukraine, where more than 4 million Jews succumbed to the Final Solution.[3] Not a single Jewish place of residence in these regions escaped a visit from the mobile killing squads of the SS or from military functionaries who loaded Jews on trains for deportation to camps. When the war ended, it was virtually impossible to gauge the full extent of the slaughter. But it was clear that the events of 1939–45 had resulted in a catastrophe unprecedented in the annals of East European anti-Semitism. The response of American Jews to the catastrophe was also unprecedented, in terms of both funds raised and energies expended in the effort to alleviate the suffering of the survivors. This effort involved raising money not only to feed, clothe, and shelter the masses of impoverished victims huddled in DP camps throughout Europe, but also to transport most of the survivors away from the scene of the carnage and resettle them in new and hospitable locales, most particularly in Palestine.

As we have seen, postwar relief of East European Jews was hardly a novel undertaking in the American Jewish community. But the relief efforts that followed World War I had a rationale much different from those which commenced after World War II. Both in the earlier period and during the interwar years, relief programs emphasized rebuilding and reconstituting Jewish communities in Eastern Europe, most having been damaged rather than destroyed. Relief teams from the JDC, HIAS, and other organizations were sent into the field not only to estimate the immediate costs of medical care, food, clothing, and shelter but also to implement long-term programs for the rebuilding of factories, workshops, libraries, synagogues, and schools. In the process, relief officials discovered that Jewish communities not only were still functioning but were often carrying on much as before. These communities were often destitute and damaged, but they remained active, energetic, and committed to surviving within their traditional milieu.

The situation in Eastern Europe after the Holocaust was entirely different. Except in rare instances, Jews who managed to escape the Nazi juggernaut were wholly unable to reconstitute their lives along the lines of their prewar existence. Too many people had been exterminated, too many villages and towns had been wiped off the map. When relief officials encountered Jews living in their own communities after the war, such survivors, like the residents of Hrubieszow, were usually a handful of refugees who had returned briefly to their ruined homes and represented only a tiny fraction of the prewar Jewish population. Those survivors who did not return to their villages were usually unable to crowd into the larger cities and scratch out a semblance of normal life, as had so many refugees in the years after World War I. Instead, the post–World War II survivors were languishing in DP camps throughout Europe, often hundreds of miles away from their former homes and completely out of touch with family and friends.

It was within this context that the landsmanshaftn played a vital role in the relief efforts following the Holocaust. After World War I the landsmanshaftn had managed to direct relief efforts to the shtetlach and towns of the Pale because they had kept in contact with relatives and friends who had not yet followed them to the New World. Now the American landsmanshaftn would again provide relief organizations with information about the identities and locations of survivors, even though the survivors were scattered throughout the war zone.

Ironically, the monetary contribution of the American landsmanshaftn to the post–World War II relief effort was much less significant than their financial contribution after World War I. Many of the smaller societies donated sums that appear insignificant relative to the enormity of the problem; it was not unusual for a society to donate $500 or less to help its beleaguered landsmen languishing in a DP camp or returning to a decimated village. The financial contributions of the landsmanshaftn were minimal in the context of the overall relief effort, reflecting the extent to which the societies had long since passed their heyday. This was largely because the Jewish community had evolved considerably into a middle-class population during the interwar period, and Jewish charities like the UJA, Hadassah, B'nai B'rith, and ORT were able to tap the enormous resources of Jewish professional and business groups to a degree unimaginable just twenty years previously. For example, the JDC, which collected over $50 million in the years 1918–24, raised the impressive total of $240 million during the years 1943–48.[4]

But money was not a crucial factor in gauging the importance of landsmanshaft relief efforts. The landsmanshaftn played a vital role in the postwar salvation of Holocaust victims because it was through the efforts of many hundreds of individual landsmanshaft groups in New York and elsewhere that the personal bonds which had connected American Jews to their families and friends in Europe before the war were resurrected. The landsmanshaftn served as intermediaries between the masses of Holocaust survivors and the bureaucracies of governments and relief organizations, which were overwhelmed by this pathetic and brutalized flood of humanity. The societies pushed, prodded, and provoked welfare, relief, and immigration officials into action, and when the official networks did not suffice, the societies made relief efforts on their own. Typical of the efforts of the landsmanshaftn were the activities of New York's Wishnovic landsmanshaft, a small society comprising no more than a few hundred Jews in Brooklyn and the Bronx.

On September 12, 1945, the JDC office in New York received a letter which read: "I, Nathan Wirch, president of the Wishnovic Bros. Benevolent Assn., would appreciate greatly any information we can obtain about the town of Wishnovic as we have raised a certain sum of money for the purpose of aiding our people in this town who have survived. Hoping that you will do something in this direction so we can help our Brothers and Sisters as quickly as possible." The following month, the society sent a check for $500 to the JDC, which in a letter of October 17 responded that it was "advising our Teheran office to secure information pertaining to the Wishnovic landsleit." A week later, the society informed the JDC that it had secured the addresses of two survivors of the village, who had written directly to relatives in New York. These names and addresses were furnished to the JDC with a request to take a portion of the $500 and spend it on relief packages for these two landsleit, who were now in Rowno and Odessa.[5]

The survivors who had written to their relatives from Rowno and Odessa were a few of the lucky ones. The village of Wishnovic, or Wisniewicze, was located in the southernmost portion of Volhynia, adjacent to the border of Galicia and directly in the path of the Nazi invasion of the Soviet Union. Southern Volhynia was also a region where many Jewish settlements either organized active resistance movements or managed to stage mass escapes, avoiding deportation to the death camps of Belzec and Chelmno. Consequently, the German campaign against the civilian (read: Jewish) population in this area was ferocious, with 140,000 Jews being murdered between May and December of 1942. This figure included more than 1,000 residents of Wisniewicze who were exterminated by a German SS column on August 30, 1942.

Nearly four years later, on March 18, 1946, the JDC warehouse in Tehran shipped twenty-two relief packages to the village, and one package each to the landsleit in Rowno and Odessa. The money donated by the society the previous October had purchased the following items for the remnants of the village population: 3 overcoats, 8 lbs. coffee, 1 lb.

vitamins, 2 lbs. jam, 4 lbs. soap, 4 lbs. sugar, 5 lbs. powdered milk, 1 lb. raisins, 14 pairs of shoes, 9 blankets, and 25 yds. of cloth for dresses and shirts. We have no information on the number of Jews who were still living in the village in 1946, but the JDC office in Tehran reported that the landsleit had welcomed the items with "great relief."

In April the Wishnovic landsmanshaft contacted the JDC again. The society provided the office with the names of three landsleit: Beyla Schatz, who supposedly was living in Salzburg with her two children (more than 1,000 miles from the village), and Froim and Jacob Jakira, who, it was thought, were in a DP camp in Slovakia. The two Jakiras were sought by their brother, Samuel Jakira, who lived on Morris Avenue in the Bronx and had just been elected president of the society. This information was immediately forwarded by the JDC to its field staff in Europe.

Two months passed before the JDC office received a communication from its representative in Prague: "Last week we were going to write to you that there was no one named Jakira registered among the Jews of Slovakia but we have since learned that Jacob Jakira and his wife are living in Gratz, Austria. Would you please notify Mr. Samuel Jakira that his brother is alive."

The New York JDC office sent a copy of this letter to Samuel Jakira, who now wrote personally to the JDC office in Gratz attempting to verify the information. He mailed off his letter on June 16 but did not receive a reply until September. The news he was waiting for did not come. Instead, the JDC office in Gratz stated: "We were surprised to learn that Prague had informed you that the above-named were living in Gra[t]z. The community here is very small and during our ten months stay we would certainly have met this couple had they been here. The probability is that they were at one time inmates of the Graz DP centre, which was closed in September, 1945. In such a case they probably left Austria for Italy."

The society did receive better news in January 1947, when it was informed by the JDC that Beyla Schatz and her two children had been located in a DP camp outside Turin, Italy. The JDC also sent the society a list of eighteen survivors from the village who were scattered throughout Poland but had responded to an ad placed in all local Polish newspapers inquiring as to their whereabouts. In response the society donated $250 to buy food and supplies for these people.

In all, the society was able to locate twenty-one former residents of the shtetl and to send relief parcels to them, as well as to a few survivors in the village itself. But the two brothers of Samuel Jakira were still among the missing. On April 14, 1947, Samuel Jakira of Morris Avenue in the Bronx booked his own passage on a ship to Europe and set out on a personal mission to rescue his brothers. The records do not indicate the results of his search.

An Overwhelming Task

After World War I, the landsmanshaftn had remained involved in European relief, although on a much reduced scale. The JDC continued to collect money and send it abroad, and many societies maintained close connections with native villages and landsleit in the Pale. A large part of their effort went into the establishment of free loan societies, called Gemiloth Chesed kassas, which dispensed interest-free loans to workers' cooperatives, businessmen, and individual residents. The activity of the kassas and their connection to

American landsleit were crucial to the rebuilding of the shtetlach, particularly in areas that had been the scene of many pogroms or of heavy fighting during and after World War I. In the village of Skala, for example, the entire Jewish population was forced to leave when Russian troops invaded the region in 1915. When the Jews returned the following year, they discovered that nearly all their homes and business establishments had been ransacked and looted by soldiers and Ukrainian peasants. The connection to America was a crucial factor in restoring the village to a semblance of its prewar normalcy: "Quite a large percentage of Jewish families having no means of support would certainly have approached starvation if not for the two types of assistance offered them: first, the interest-free loans from the funds of the 'Gemilot Hasadim' [the kassa], established by local businessmen. This loan society was founded through the generous contribution of former residents who had emigrated to the United States, Skala's 'landsmanshaft,' and through contributions from foundations in other countries. Second, parcels of clothing and money were sent to families by their relatives abroad."[6]

The JDC administered more than 450 kassas in Poland and Russia whose operating funds came mainly from landsmanshaftn in New York. An interesting commentary on the importance of the kassa is provided by a resident of the Polish shtetl of Kamieniec, who sent a letter to the JDC requesting more aid from the New York landsmen: "The town numbers 2,800 Jewish inhabitants. They are mainly traders and craftsmen, cobblers, locksmiths and seamstresses. The economic situation is bad. The Jewish trade is in danger for in the [outlying] villages new Christian shops are arising which supply the peasants with all commodities and enable them to do away with journeys into town."[7] The situation in Kamieniec underscored the precarious position of Jews in the Pale, many of whom were so isolated that their only source of help was a group of landsmen thousands of miles away. The residents of Szczerzec, another Polish shtetl, appealed to the JDC for financial assistance for their kassa in order to pay a heavy tax levied on the Jewish community to cover the costs of rebuilding the town after the pogrom.[8]

During the 1920s and 1930s, American efforts to provide relief for Jews in Eastern Europe were split between Zionist and non-Zionist camps. The Zionists worked primarily through the United Palestine Appeal, which raised more than $2.5 million during its first year of operation, in 1925. In 1929, the Jewish Agency (whose board included leading non-Zionists) was founded, and both groups competed with the JDC for American money to be sent abroad. The competitive activities of these three organizations ended in 1939, when the reality of Hitler forced them to consolidate under the umbrella of the United Jewish Appeal. The UJA comprised a number of different suborganizations, with the JDC continuing its role as the primary conduit for landsmanshaft relief efforts on the European continent.[9]

The landsmanshaftn were aided in their relief efforts after World War II by the diligent work of Norman Gilmovsky, who became head of the JDC landsmanshaft section in 1945. Gilmovsky was born in Warsaw in 1901, and despite a liberal background and progressive education, he had a special feel for the problems of shtetl Jews and could communicate with the officers of even the smallest societies. He came to the United States in 1923 and began working as a journalist and fundraiser for various organizations, including the Federation of Galician Jews. Later, on radio station WEVD in New York, he would conduct a Yiddish radio program aimed primarily at publicizing the plight of East European Jews. In 1939 he joined the JDC.

When Gilmovsky began to organize the landsmanshaft section of the JDC, he had to address two separate problems. First, it was imperative to make contact with as many landsleit and benevolent societies as possible, in order to develop the widest potential net of contacts and support for relief work. Having lived through the pogroms of the early 1920s and having been abandoned with his brother in an isolated shtetl near the Russian front, Gilmovsky was fully cognizant of the fact that only relatives and friends in America would be able to provide a link to the devastated survivors on the other side. Moreover, the landsmanshaft population in New York was becoming harder to find. Many societies had ceased functioning on a regular basis; some met only on special occasions, particularly funerals of members. Others had merged into larger, more formal organizations connected with synagogues and community centers.

During the World War II years, Gilmovsky set out to locate as many landsmanshaftn as possible in New York and around the United States. He visited synagogues and shuls, meeting halls and lodges; he placed advertisements in the Jewish press and sent out personal appeals to friends and associates in the Jewish community. His background in journalism proved of great importance during these endeavors, for he had come to know just about every social grouping within New York's Jewish population, as well as most of the prominent lay and religious leaders. By 1945, when the landsmanshaft section of the JDC was officially inaugurated, Gilmovsky had made contact with more than 3,000 societies, including over 1,500 independent landsmanshaftn. The members were somewhat older and the meeting places were often different, but otherwise the smaller societies had not changed their attitudes and practices to any great extent. Gilmovsky remembers having difficulty getting into meetings because he was a "stranger," and rarely did he make his appeal for support in any language except Yiddish.

The second major problem for Gilmovsky and his JDC colleagues involved creating guidelines for the collection and disbursement of relief funds abroad. The JDC had adopted a basic policy of refusing to accept "earmarked" donations—that is, funds donated for use by a particular individual or group. Instead, all moneys went into a single fund which the JDC officials would then dispense as best they could. In addition, the JDC attempted to control the flow of funds to Europe by establishing a network of field offices and warehouses throughout the war zone. Thus, money would be collected in America, transmitted to JDC offices overseas, and then spent on food, clothing, and other relief goods under the supervision of local JDC staff. This system was designed not only to prevent the misuse of funds but also to guarantee that relief supplies ended up in the hands of those who needed them the most. In addition, the JDC was forced to comply with wartime restrictions on currency, which prohibited individuals from simply sending large amounts of cash abroad without authority.

Many of these guidelines were waived for the work of the landsmanshaft section, in part because a landsmanshaft's chief motivation was to provide relief on a personal and individual basis. When a landsmanshaft made contact with the JDC, it was not simply because the society wanted to donate money for the general purpose of Jewish relief. Rather, as in the case of the Wishnovic landsmanshaft, it was the result of a personal appeal made on behalf of a survivor or by the survivor himself to his landsleit in America. Just as the landsmanshaftn acted as a conduit between various bureaucracies in America and overseas, so the JDC was often used as a conduit between a particular landsman-shaft in America and a particular survivor on the other side. An example of both these connections is provided by the Kolbuszower Society's efforts to save two Holocaust victims who contacted the group after the war.[10]

Kolbuszowa was a small village located along the Vistula River, 100 miles east of Cracow. In late November 1942, more than 2,500 of Kolbuszowa's Jewish residents were forced onto railroad cars and deported to the death camps at Treblinka and Belzec or sent to the Majdanek concentration camp. One of the deported families left their infant daughter in the care of a Polish woman who, in December 1948, wrote a letter to the president of the Kolbuszower Society in New York. (The letter was actually given to a JDC field worker in Poland, who forwarded it to Gilmovsky who in turn sent it on to the society.) The Polish woman, named Nowaczyn-ski, said she was ready to give up the child if the young girl's relatives would sign away the rights to some village property the child was heir to. The relatives were immediately con-tacted and signed the necessary papers. But at the same time, the society's president, David Saltz, asked Gilmovsky to verify the facts contained in the letter and to make sure the child was receiving adequate care.

Several months went by, and nothing was heard from overseas. Gilmovsky dispatched another letter to the War-saw JDC office but was told that the case was still under investigation. In February, the president of the society wrote to Mrs. Nowaczynski, telling her that the property deed had been expedited but requesting further information about the child. In March, Saltz contacted Gilmovsky and told him that he had received a letter from Poland saying that the girl was no longer with the Nowaczynski family but was supposedly in a Jewish institution under the care of the Jewish committee in Cracow. Gilmovsky sent another inquiry to Warsaw, and on April 10 the Warsaw office sent a cabled reply: "RE YOUR LET MARCH 12TH LANDSMANSHAFT KOLBUSZOWA CHILD REGINA TERESA PROPKER LIVING CHILDRENS HOME KRAKOW LETTER FOLLOWS."

The letter, which arrived on May 8, 1947, read: "The girl's parents perished in 1942 during the German occupation. Mrs. Nowaczynski took care of the child till autumn 1946. Then the girl was taken away from her foster mother and placed in Jewish surroundings at a Childrens Home in Krakow, where she is still living. Recently Mrs. Nowaczynski called at the Jewish Committee in Krakow and presented some papers and quittances in connection with the property transferred to her. The inheritance fees amount to the sum of zł. 50,000 and Mrs. Nowaczynski asks to [be] reimbursed these expenses involved and for the child's maintenance during the German occupation a sum of two thousand dollars. We wish to point out that the child when taken away from Mrs. Nowaczynski was in very bad condition: without any dresses, only wrapped in a rug, besides the girl was bruised, nervous and frightful. She has recovered completely and is now under good care." Attached to the letter was a small photo of a young girl sitting at a table in the children's home.

Clearly, the interest and involvement of the Kolbuszower Society made a difference in the life of this young survivor. The society was not so fortunate in its efforts to help another victim. On December 18, 1946, the society president notified the JDC office in New York that a member had received a letter from his cousin, Joseph Korn, who was ill with tuberculosis in a hospital in Cracow. Korn had a wife and twelve-year-old son who were in dire need of support.

The hospital in Cracow was not organized to deal with cases of TB, but Korn did not have the money to get himself into another institution.

The JDC sent an inquiry to Cracow, but in January the landsmanshaft received another letter from Korn stating that he had been transferred to a hospital in Vienna but still was not receiving adequate care. He was completely out of funds and pleaded for money to move to a TB sanitarium in Switzerland. On February 26 the landsmanshaft gave the JDC a check for $1,400 to pay for moving Korn to the Swiss hospital. A month later, Saltz appeared at the JDC office totally distraught. He had received another letter from Korn, who reported that no money had yet arrived. Saltz begged the JDC staff to send another inquiry to Vienna and to expedite the payment of funds. On April 17 the Vienna office sent a cable to New York stating that Joseph Korn had left the Vienna hospital more than one year ago and had been transported to Switzerland at JDC expense. Consequently, the $1,400 would be refunded to the New York office to be given back to the Kolbuszower landsmanshaft. Gilmovsky called Saltz and asked him to come down to the office in order to apprise him of the information he had received from abroad. But the next day, when Saltz appeared, another cable arrived from Vienna which said that the previous day's communication had been in error and that the Vienna office was still unable to locate Joseph Korn.

On May 13, Saltz received another letter from his landsman Joseph Korn, who complained that he had not received the money, was still in the hospital in Vienna, and was "desperate" for help. Saltz called the JDC office, and a week later followed up his call with a letter that read: "We keep getting frantic letters and cables from Joseph Korn in Vienna, asking that someone please give him attention before he dies. Won't you please make an effort to speed this matter up?" Finally, on June 20, the JDC office in Vienna contacted New York with the report that it had located Joseph Korn and was prepared to expedite his travel to Switzerland. On July 22, Joseph Korn left Vienna for Switzerland, about seven months after his landsleit in New York had first brought his case to the attention of the JDC staff. But matters had not moved fast enough. Joseph Korn died on the train between Vienna and the Swiss border. The society had saved one victim, but the Holocaust had claimed yet another.

The activities of the Kolbuszower Society were typical of the relief efforts mounted by the landsmanshaftn in New York and throughout America. In the years 1945–47, more than a thousand independent societies sent money and relief parcels to survivors of their native villages throughout postwar Europe. Even more important, they went to great lengths to track down individual survivors and bring their suffering to the attention of officials of the JDC and other relief organizations. Bureaucracies moved slowly, communications broke down, offices were understaffed, and the misery of the Holocaust was compounded by the delay or indifference of welfare officials. Without the efforts of the landsmanshaftn, thousands of survivors like the little orphan, Regina Propker, would have languished unaided in DP camps, orphanages, hospitals, villages, and towns.

A survivor in a DP camp in Ulm described the situation in a letter to the Sassower landsmanshaft: "Who knows how long we shall be compelled to stay here in the camp? We would like to be equal to all other human beings to work and earn a livelihood and live decently. It isn't easy for me to ask you for assistance because a young person should be able to make a living for himself. But, unfortunately, we are in a camp. I shall end my letter now. I and my brother, Burak, send our greetings to the Sassower Landsmanshaft Shmuel Leib and Burak."[11]

These were the types of problems that money alone could not solve. They required the personal intervention and concern of family and friends, intangible factors that were sometimes more important than tangible forms of relief. Sometimes the problem involved simply letting an individual know that people on the other side knew about him and were doing whatever they could to help things along. The psychic bonds created between the landsmanshaftn and their landsleit who had survived the Holocaust were sometimes the crucial factor in allowing the survivors to make it through the post-Holocaust trauma of readjustment.

A case in point involves the Drobiner landsmanshaft's efforts to help a landsman after the war.[12] On February 19, 1947, the president of the Drobiner Society, Joseph Klapman, contacted the JDC office to say that he had received a letter from a landsman, Abraham Frankiel, who was in a DP camp in Stuttgart. "This man was in the Polish Army and has lost a leg," said Klapman. "He came back to Drobin, but had to leave, because he found no Jews there. Although he is a cripple he managed to get into Germany and now he seeks our help. You can realize his position." Klapman asked the JDC to make the necessary inquiries about Frankiel's condition and to let the society know what it could do.

On July 17, five months after Gilmovsky had written to the JDC office in Germany, a communication was received indicating that Frankiel needed money for an artificial leg. One week later, Klapman informed the JDC that the society had agreed to pay the medical expenses. For the next two months, letters and cables flew back and forth between Stuttgart and New York. Frankiel was informed that the society would pay the cost of an artificial leg, but he was proving to be a difficult patient. He rejected several artificial limbs after they were fitted, complained about the quality of the medical attention he was receiving, and finally asked to be moved to another camp where he might receive better treatment. At one point a social worker interviewed Frankiel and reported to the JDC that "the man has clearly suffered during the last few years and his mind has been affected. He believes that nobody here wants to help him and makes all kinds of unrealistic demands. He has been told that he must undergo further surgery in order to be fitted with a proper device but he doesn't trust any of the doctors. I want you to know that he is in constant contact with his landsman-shaft in America and feels he can ask them for help."

At the critical moment, the landsmanshaft connection provided the vital link. The Drobiner landsmanshaft donated money to purchase a wheelchair for the unfortunate Mr. Frankiel, and the case was closed. What this episode illustrates is that for many Holocaust survivors, the landsmanshaft was their only link to the world and represented the sole source of psychic sustenance in a situation they felt was beyond their control. The landsmanshaftn were also the only groups that could truly understand the needs of many survivors insofar as their members still maintained Old World attitudes and perceptions.

The ability to perceive the true needs of the shtetl survivors was a crucial factor in the help provided by the Makower Society to its native village in Poland.[13] The village of Makow was located less than 50 miles from the Treblinka death camp in eastern Poland, and most of its Jewish population was deported to the camp in November and December 1942. Almost all those who were not sent to Treblinka ended up in Auschwitz or in a mass grave in the village itself. On May 3, 1946, the JDC received a $500 check from the Makower landsmanshaft to send relief packages to the ten surviving Jews in the village, and on June 14, honey, cooking fat, cocoa, clothing, and shoes were dispatched from the Tehran warehouse for distribution in the settlement. The Makower Society also asked the JDC to ascertain the whereabouts of any other landsleit who had survived the camps, and in July the JDC office in Warsaw sent a list of 184 other survivors scattered throughout Poland. This dispersed group plus the ten Jews in the village were all that remained of the more than 6,000 Jews who had lived in Makow prior to the Nazi occupation. Upon receiving this sad news, the society immediately donated another $500 to these survivors, but its most important charitable work remained to be done.

On August 9 the JDC office in New York received a communication from the field office in Warsaw. A staff member had been approached by a Jewish resident of Makow who asked him to get in touch with the landsmanshaft in New York. The survivors in Makow had succeeded in locating the remains of Jews who had been murdered in the village. They wanted to exhume the bodies from the mass grave and bury them in the Jewish cemetery, but they did not have enough money to pay the workmen needed to accomplish this task. Unfortunately, this kind of request, according to the JDC office in Warsaw, fell outside the relief guidelines, but a final decision to waive the guidelines could be made in New York.

Within a week the society put together $250, which was immediately sent to Makow. In September the JDC office in New York received a letter from the Makow survivors, which it forwarded to the landsmanshaft. The letter described the heartrending efforts of a small group of survivors to restore to decency the remains of their family members, who were no doubt related as well to the landsleit in New York: "At 3 o'clock in the night, despite a heavy rainfall, work was begun. Five workmen came to work. A whole layer of earth had to be removed before traces of the bodies were found. Unfortunately, only traces were left. Recognition was quite impossible. Bodies were extracted, put in cases and transferred to the devastated Jewish cemetery and the important ceremony was finished, the cases with the bodies were lowered into the grave that had been dug, simultaneously the traditional Kaddish was said." One can only imagine the grief and anguish that must have accompanied the reading of this letter at the next Makower Society meeting.

Another landsmanshaft effort involved the Jews of Radomsko, also in Poland.[14] During the spring of 1942, the Jewish residents of the village, along with Jews from Ujazd and Szydlowiec, escaped and hid in the dense forestlands to the south of the settlement. But by the end of October, the combination of winter cold and lack of food forced them to come out and give themselves up. The Germans promised safe-conduct to an urban ghetto for these 6,000 Jews, but on January 10, 1943, they were loaded on trains, deported to Treblinka, and gassed to death.

In December 1946, the president of the Radomsker landsmanshaft in New York notified the JDC that he had received a letter from a resident of Radomsko, Mrs. Marie Chutkiewicz, who advised them that in 1942 she had taken in a one-month-old boy, the son of a tailor in the village whose name was Winciarski. She had raised the child throughout the war years but now requested aid from the landsleit in America because she could no longer afford to keep him. She also knew of another Jewish child who had remained behind in the village with a Polish family named Krazniewski and was now six years old.

On January 9, 1947, the JDC office in Warsaw notified the New York office that it was dispatching a staff member to Radomsko to verify the letter the Radomsker Society had received. More than ten months passed, however, before a full report reached New York. In the interim, the officers of the Radomsker Society made numerous calls to the JDC in an effort to ascertain the whereabouts of the two children, but to no avail. Then, on November 14, an official dispatch from the Warsaw office arrived:

> Family name: Dzienciarski, Edward
> Date and place of birth: 8:11:42
> Parents names: Unknown
>> At present we are to communicate that the child Winczarski, whose real name is Dzienczarski [sic] has been redeemed with our help from his guardian and is now living at a Zionist Children's home.
>> Concerning the second child, the 6 year old girl, name unknown, our investigations were without result until now. We are doing everything and as soon as we shall find some trace of her, we shall not fail to inform you.

In February 1948 the JDC office in Prague succeeded in locating the little girl—alive, well, and happy—in the home of her foster parents, Mr. and Mrs. Krazniewski. The report from Prague went on to say that the Polish parents were very attached to her and did not want to give her up, but that negotiations would proceed. The society was also sent two photographs of a little blond girl, smiling, as she was held in the arms of a man in front of his house. Evidently the Radomsker Society decided there was no reason to continue efforts on behalf of the girl; its final communication with the

JDC was in the form of a check for $350 to pay the cost of keeping the young boy in the Zionist home.

Members of the First Romaner Sick Benevolent Association responded to the slaughter of their landsleit in the Rumanian shtetl of Roman by holding a fundraising meeting on December 17, 1946, in the Central Plaza on East 7th Street.[15] The announcement of the meeting, sent to all members, read as follows:

"At this meeting we will discuss the post-war relief money, how to send it to Roman and nearby cities.

"Please come to this meeting, it is very urgent. We are about ready to send the money we have collected to be distributed to our relatives in Roman and nearby cities. If you have some of your relatives and they need help, come to the meeting and give us their names and addresses, so that we can send them the help they need."

Three days later, the JDC received a check for $1,000 from the society, along with a list of landsleit and a request to furnish the society with names of survivors still in the village. The society also forwarded to the JDC a letter it had received from the residents of Roman, who had formed a seven-member relief committee headed by the chief rabbi, Dr. M. Frankel. The committee asked the JDC to distribute the money according to the request of the Roman relief committee, which wanted funds to rebuild the Jewish hospital and Hebrew school and also needed money for general relief.

On January 10, 1947, the committee in Roman wrote a letter to the society thanking it for the funds:

"You were well protected by the Almighty to be spared of the horrid slaughter and the catastrophic misery which the wind of Antisemitism has brought with fire upon us.

"Here too, as in all other European countries, we suffer;

there is not one home which has been spared suffering because of a loss of a member of the family.

"And even here, in this little town whence you came, whence the sun has followed you with blessing, we were slaughtered, beaten, tortured, and placed in railway cars, locked up, and transported to camps, travelling for weeks without water, without food, and without light through cold, rain, wind and snow.

"A few of us returned to find sorrow in our once beautiful homes. Our goods thrown out, destroyed, our families in the streets without the right to the most necessary things in life."

Over the next four months, the Romaner society collected an additional $2,650 for the village. Each donation brought an immediate reply from the landsleit in Roman and a specific report on how the money was spent. The head of the relief committee in Roman during this period was the brother of the society's secretary in New York. At one point, brother wrote to brother to say that money from American landsleit had saved two families from having to go into the street to beg for alms. "These people were so moved," wrote the Roman brother, "that they wept and could not find words of thanks."

The Romaner Society was fortunate in being able to locate and identify a number of landsleit who had actually returned to their village. But this was not always the case. Often landsmanshaftn contacted the JDC with requests to find out about the survivors of a certain village, only to be told that there were no survivors to be found. When this happened, the JDC would undertake the long and tedious task of checking registration lists in DP camps, contacting field offices, placing notices in local papers, and combing its own archives for pertinent information, a process that could take months or even years. For example, on January 28, 1945, the United Alstadter Relief Fund sent a check for $500 to the JDC to be distributed to survivors from the village of Sambor. On December 27, 1945, however, the check was returned to the society because the JDC had been unable to locate survivors to whom the money could be sent.[16]

The United Bros. of Tomasov Society was somewhat more fortunate in its efforts to help the landsleit, inasmuch as the JDC was able to report that about 80 Jews were still in the village of Tomasov at the end of 1946.[17] But the report went on to say: "Tomasov had about 1300 Jewish inhabitants before the war from which only 500 are left. These 500 are scattered all over the world." Searching for the survivors, the JDC managed after five months to come up with a list of 228 names from various DP camps. Sometime later, another 126 landsleit turned up in the U.S.-occupied zone of Germany. Having quickly formed themselves into a chevra, they wrote to the Tomasov Society in New York for aid. No doubt the American society had also begun as a chevra when the early immigrants from the village first came to New York. History was repeating itself, although the circumstances were tragically different.

Not only did the landsmanshaftn face the problem of locating dispersed landsleit, but when they made contact, they had to cope with the disastrous physical and psychological consequences to the refugees of deportation, forced labor, and near starvation. The Solkolker landsmanshaft made contact with the JDC in 1946 to determine the fate of their landsleit from the village of Solkolka.[18] The society had good reason to be fearful. On November 2, 1942, the Nazis had conducted what one historian has called "one of the most carefully organized and intensive round-ups of the war" in the region around Bialystok, which included the village. By the time the deportations were concluded, more than 8,000 Jews from the settlement had been put on trains and sent to Treblinka and Auschwitz. In fact, more Jews were taken from Solkolka than from any village in the entire region. Following the society's request, the JDC was able to locate only 15 survivors from the village. The list sent to the society read as follows:

Abruczewski, Meier—tanner
Badasz, Feigel—very sick person confined to bed
Bialostocka, Adin & husband who works in a factory and
    earns very little. They were supposed to leave for Australia
    but have no money for transportation.
Barowicz, Tarria & husband—an aged couple. The husband
    works but earns very little.
Klucz, Semion & wife—he works in a factory.
Kotler, Isak
Kotler, Benjamin—had been arrested.
Kubina, Helen—husband works but earnings are very
    meager
Kuboviska, Chaja & husband—an aged couple
Kuszes, Michael—in a TB sanitarium. He is bedridden and
    his circumstances are very hard.

To people in such dire conditions, contact with landsleit in America constituted perhaps their only basis for hope, for psychic support, and for regaining some semblance of normal life. In November 1946 the Belzer landsmanshaft received from two DP camps in Europe the following communications, which had been given to a field representative of the JDC and forwarded to the main JDC office in New York.[19] The first appeal read:

To the Galician landsmanshaftn from Belz—
    I am the son [of] Aron Icek the tin smith and the grandson

of Sjyja the coppersmith. My wife and I are the sole survivors of our family. Please help us with food packages, as we are in very precarious circumstances. We are both natives of Belz and we always lived there.

P.S. My wife is the daughter of Esther who used to live near the cemetery. My wife's name is Liba.

SZIJA ZAKTER.

The second appeal to the Belzer landsmanshaft said:

To the Galician landsmanshaftn from Belz:

We are two sisters here in the Ziegenhain camp, the only survivors of our large family. We are the daughters of Av-runcio the cap maker and the grand daughters of Rywka, daughter of the coppersmith.

We are destitute and we have no relatives or friends who could help us in our dire need.

ITA AND PESIA SCHAFF.

The factor that most hampered Holocaust relief efforts was that the Jewish survivors were so widely dispersed. It was not uncommon for former residents of a particular shtetl to find themselves completely separated from friends and relatives, in wholly unfamiliar surroundings. Of 194 survivors of the village of Makow, for example, only 10 had returned to the village; the remainder were in Cracow, Warsaw, Friedland, Lubawa, Kladzko, Rychbach, Szczecin, and Lodz. These survivors were more fortunate than most, since they were all within an area of only a few hundred square miles. But it was not unusual for survivors from a Polish or Ukrainan shtetl to show up in Germany, Italy, Scandinavia, or France. Unable to return to their native village, they would send a communication to landsleit in America, who, in turn, would then make contact with the regional JDC office closest to the village. The JDC would then undertake to find other survivors from the same settlement by checking registers of inmates in DP camps, hospital lists, and orphanages and by placing ads in local newspapers. Frequently, the American landsleit would know the whereabouts of survivors long before individual Holocaust victims had any idea that any fellow villagers were still alive. An inmate in a DP camp might discover a landsman in the same camp only after first contacting the landsleit in America, who would then notify him that a fellow villager was interned there.

Just as the relief efforts of the landsmanshaftn brought together victims of the Holocaust in Europe, so their campaigns often resulted in the temporary reuniting of landsleit in America. The dispersion of Jews throughout New York City after 1920 had been paralleled by the dispersion of the immigrant population throughout the United States. By 1940 there were sizable Jewish populations in California, Chicago, Boston, and Philadelphia, as well as Jewish communities in virtually every other state and large city. The landsmanshaftn had attempted to maintain some degree of contact with kin who moved away from New York, but except in the largest societies, the contacts were maintained on a family and personal rather than organizational basis. After World War II, most of the New York landsmanshaftn were simply too small, too poor, and too insular to organize beyond the boundaries of the old neighborhood. By this time, many societies were operating primarily to maintain their cemeteries, a function that had little relevance to the lives of Jews who had left New York; this was also a great irony since most of the landsmanshaftn had begun as burial societies and would resume this basic function on the eve of their demise.

In the effort to rescue Holocaust survivors, however, the energies of the New York landsmanshaftn alone could not suffice. In some instances, landsleit who had moved away from New York were even more active than their brethren who had remained behind in Williamsburg, Brownsville, and the Bronx, as is evident, for example, in relief efforts on behalf of the remnants of the Lithuanian village of Glubokie.[20] Before the war the Jewish population of the settlement numbered nearly 10,000. But Glubokie was located within the Vilna region, a great "killing ground" of the Nazi SS. In September 1941 the Nazis swept through the zone, murdering more than 50,000 Jews. The Nazis were especially brutal when they reached Glubokie because on September 26 several hundred young men and women from the neighboring village of Swieciany had escaped from the roundup and run all the way to Glubokie, where they were caught and shot. Their pursuers then made sure that the residents of Glubokie would not be spared. When the war was over, the 10,000 former residents of Glubokie had been reduced to fewer than 200 survivors.

In June 1945 the Gluboker Benevolent Society held a meeting to discuss postwar relief for the settlement but could not decide on a plan of action. The leaders of the society then held several conferences with the JDC staff in New York, but matters remained unresolved. Then, in January 1946, the JDC office received a visit from Rabbi Solomon Bogin of Des Moines, Iowa, who was also a Glubokie landsman. He proposed to organize a relief effort throughout the United States, and the JDC arranged for him to place an ad in the *Forward* stating that all inquiries on behalf of Glubokie landsleit should be directed to him in Des Moines. In addition, the JDC cabled its field office in Vilna with instructions to have the surviving landsleit in Glubokie inform Rabbi Bogin of the names of survivors and the types of aid they required.

In February, Rabbi Bogin traveled to Chicago and met

with that city's Glubokie landsleit. Shortly thereafter, he sent to the JDC a check for $400 from the Chicago group, which called itself the Mothers Fraternal Club (although the president was a man), along with a check for $102 from the landsleit in Des Moines. Over the next several months, donations for Glubokie relief came into Bogin from all over the country. A couple in Barberton, Ohio, sent $10; another check for $10 was received from Akron; an attorney in Philadelphia sent $10, and an accountant in Buffalo donated $25. In April two landsleit families in St. Joseph, Mo., sent a check for $50, and a $304 check was sent to the JDC by a group of Glubokie landsleit in Los Angeles. All together, the JDC received nearly $1,000 for the relief of Glubokie, but the files do not indicate any contributions received from landsleit in New York.

On the other hand, an attempt by the JDC to enlist the resources of landsmanshaftn and Jewish benevolent associations throughout the United States did not necessarily result in increased cohesion or cooperation within or between specific landsmanshaft groups. Confederations of immigrants such as the United Bessarabian Jews, the Federation of Galician Jews, the Federation of Rumanian Jews, and the Federation of Ukrainian Jews did not represent even a large minority of the landsmanshaftn from their particular region. If anything, the groups belonging to these federations consisted primarily of fraternal lodges and community associations that had long since shed their specific landsmanshaft affiliation. A program distributed at a fundraiser for the Federation of Galician Jews listed more than thirty sponsoring organizations, of which only six were independent landsmanshaftn.[21]

In many instances, landsleit from a particular region refused to pool their resources, instead donating small sums of money from individuals or small groups to be sent to particular individuals on the other side. When the JDC would publish the list of village survivors in the *Forward,* the office in New York would receive a number of small contributions from the relatives of persons whose names had appeared, with instructions that the money be sent directly to those individuals and not to the village as a whole. Such individual contributions were received from thousands of Jewish families around the country, and the list of contributors for any given village might include Jews living in more than twenty different states. In every case, the JDC would acknowledge the contribution but take pains to point out that it was prohibited from making relief payments to specific individuals abroad. The donor, if he wished, could attempt to send money or goods directly to a survivor, but the JDC was in no position to expedite this type of arrangement.

It is impossible to calculate the extent of the "private" relief provided by American Jews in response to requests from their landsleit in the war zone, but it must have been considerable. However, we can get some inkling of the magnitude of these unofficial efforts because the landsmanshaftn played a vital role in this activity as well. JDC records indicate that many Holocaust survivors did not know the address of a specific relative in America but did have some vague knowledge that a group from the village had at one time or another emigrated to the other side. Consequently, JDC staff workers in DP camps and hospitals were often given letters addressed by refugees simply to the "landsleit of such-and-such" village. These messages would be forwarded to the JDC office in New York, where Gilmovsky and his staff would attempt to transmit them to the proper landsmanshaft. If the request for help fell within the guidelines of the JDC, a meeting would be arranged between JDC staff and representatives of the landsmanshaft to discuss means of organizing a general relief fund. But if the request did not fall within the purview of JDC (and United States government) regulations, then that particular landsmanshaft would have to go it alone.

Typical of the latter case is a letter that arrived at the New York JDC office in December 1949, written by a refugee in Israel to the members of the Gritzer landsmanshaft: "The writer of this letter is Shloime Feivish's son. My mother's name was Chana Gromen. She was the sister of Srolke and Chaim Shovel and my name is Berel Naftal. Dear Friends, I can tell you that I am in Eretz [Israel] one year and I am still unable to do anything. There are many unemployed in the country. I have a great request to make of the Gritzer landsleit. By trade I am a chauffeur. Would it be possible for the Gritzer landsleit to help me out with an [illegible word] that my wife and I should be able to make a living. I believe that in a very short time I would be in a position to repay the money which the machine would cost you. I would like to ask one other thing. My wife's father left Gritzer in the 18th year for America. His name is Chaim Ring. He was born in Vloczyv. In 1936 a letter came from Srul Flachit's father who demanded of me a picture. Please understand our situation. We beg you to inform him of what I write to you. We thank you in advance."[22]

The president of the Gritzer Society was located by Gilmovsky and came down to the JDC office to pick the letter up. We do not know how the writer's landsleit in New York responded to his plea (the JDC would have been unable to fulfill it). But such letters arrived at the JDC office on a daily basis. The JDC also was instrumental in contacting the landsmanshaftn for an even more critical postwar relief task over which the agency had little or no control. When refugees applied for visas to enter the United States, they were required to list on the application the name of an American citizen who would serve as their "sponsor" and guarantee their support when they arrived from abroad. The JDC received thousands of inquiries from immigration officials attempting to process the applications of persons whose only means of identification was their family name and place of birth. A young girl, for example, applied for a visa and stated that she had relatives in the United States who, like herself, had been born in the shtetl of Bobruisk. A copy of the application was forwarded to the JDC office in New York with the following notation: "We think that this village was in the Ukraine. Can you verify if such a landsmanshaft exists and establish contact?"

The Ties Are Broken

The landsmanshaft relief campaign after World War I and the rescue effort following World War II were in many ways similar. Jews who had been victims of pogroms or Nazi terror would establish contact with landsleit in America, who, in turn, would try to respond through official channels or work to solve the problem through personal contact. After World War I, communications from village councils to their American landsleit became the basic source of information for all American Jews regarding the situation in Eastern Europe. After World War II, messages from individual survivors to their American landsleit were a critical means of identifying displaced persons and orphans and of reuniting village residents who had been dispersed throughout the war zone. After both wars, the importance of the landsman-

shaft response was measurable not so much in terms of
money (although the societies' donations following World
War I constituted a significant portion of the JDC fundraising effort), but in terms of their continued contact with the
landsleit in the Pale, and in the societies' ability to utilize
such contact at times when other methods of reaching the
survivors had or might have failed.

Despite these similarities, there was a crucial difference
between the two landsmanshaft campaigns. To a large extent, the landsmanshaftn conducted their own relief effort
after World War I, often deliberately avoiding formal agencies such as the JDC. The societies had the numbers, the
resources, and the constant, intense contact with their native
villages to sustain a widespread relief effort on their own.
The membership of most societies then consisted primarily
of immigrants who had left their native village less than ten
years before. After World War II, on the other hand, the
private landsmanshaft relief efforts were not so evident.
This time the JDC did not develop its relief campaign in the
wake of—or in competition with—landsmanshaft activity,
as had occurred in 1920. Instead, it was the initial effort of
the JDC that provoked many of the landsmanshaftn to respond to the situation in the years after 1945. There were
still many occasions when individual societies made efforts
to help their landsleit, avoiding any real contact with official
relief campaigns; but this happened on a much smaller scale
than earlier relief efforts following the pogroms.

There were several reasons why the landsmanshaftn went
their own way after World War I but worked for the most
part within the official relief framework after the Holocaust.
For one thing, the situation in Eastern Europe following the
two world wars was entirely different. In 1919, thousands
of landsmanshaft delegates had returned to native villages

with money and other forms of assistance. This was impossible after World War II, especially within the zone now controlled by the Red Army. Moreover, after the Holocaust, many of the villages no longer existed, and if a shtetl was still standing, there probably were no Jews alive who were willing or able to return to it. The rationale for the kind of direct relief provided by the landsmanshaftn after World War I disappeared in the flames of the Holocaust.

Even though the issue is somewhat tangential, the landsmanshaft relief effort after World War II cannot be discussed apart from an evaluation of the overall Jewish-American relief campaign during the war, an issue that has generated extensive controversy down to the present day. In brief, there are two schools of thought on the matter. One position holds that the Jewish establishment, still consisting mainly of the German-Jewish elite, made only halfhearted efforts to enlist government support, for fear of jeopardizing the political alliance with the Roosevelt administration and the New Deal.[23] Although information about the Holocaust had been made public by 1943, representatives of official Jewish organizations and their friends in the administration (for example, Treasury Secretary Henry Morgenthau) never applied maximum pressure for measures to prevent further killings, such as bombing the death camps. The contrary position holds that Jewish-American leaders went to great lengths to alter Roosevelt's policy of noninterference with the Nazi genocide program but were thwarted by their inability to generate strong support from the American population as a whole.[24]

Instead of marshaling an indictment of one position or the other, we must acknowledge a larger historical issue. The decade of the 1940s was a critical period in the evolution of the Jewish-American community. Until the 1930s, American Jews were divided into two distinct groups: the old-line, German-Jewish elite on the one hand, and the East European immigrant masses on the other. The cleavage between these two groups in terms of social status, economic power, political influence, and—most important—degree of assimilation was obvious and profound. During the 1930s, the overwhelming majority of East European Jews alive in America had been born in the Old World, while nearly the entire German-Jewish population could trace its American-born lineage back at least several generations.

If we skip ahead to the 1950s, we discover a wholly different situation. By then, a majority of Jews of Eastern European parentage had been born in the United States, and three or four decades of social mobility had endowed them with a degree of economic power and political influence that was rapidly eclipsing the traditional status of the German-Jewish community.[25] As the following chapter will demonstrate, the descendants of East European immigrants had succeeded completely in divorcing themselves from the culture of their forebears. The decade of the 1940s marked the transition period for both groups: the German Jews were losing their traditional preeminence, but the East European population had yet to achieve its full measure of social and economic success. In essence, neither group had the power to confront the Holocaust directly.

Given these circumstances, the landsmanshaftn had nowhere to turn. They had always been anathema to the German Jews, and vice versa. Their own descendants did not yet have the social or political power to respond to the needs of their overseas landsleit. But most important, the landsmanshaftn who came to the major relief agencies for help in 1945 were far weaker than the societies that had avoided contact with the JDC in 1919. The truth is that the landsmanshaftn could no longer generate the resources or the energy to mount their own relief efforts. Many societies had already ceased functioning or had been reduced to only a handful of stalwarts; reestablishing contact among their far-flung American landsleit was a difficult and sometimes impossible task. The landsmanshaft population was no longer concentrated in inner-city neighborhoods, facilitating close personal contact among society members, nor did the Yiddish press command a readership sufficient to make it a vehicle for mass communication among those of East European Jewish descent. The destructive effects of the Holocaust could not have been ameliorated by a landsmanshaft campaign in America because the landsmanshaftn too were on the verge of destruction.

VII
The Old and the New

Unless we muster in a great many new members,
and by new members we mean young members,
our outlook for the next 25 year period cannot be
what it should.
—Comment in the 1937 Jubilee Journal
of the Bershad Benevolent Society

THE ENERGY of the landsmanshaft effort to rescue the victims of the Holocaust could not obscure the fact that by the end of World War II, the societies were already in the twilight of their existence. The JDC and the UJA would continue to solicit funds from the landsmanshaftn for the creation and building of Israel, and many societies responded with continuous streams of money and support for the new Jewish state; indeed, the fundraising campaign provoked by the 1967 war would bring an outpouring of assistance from the landsmanshaft sector. Nonetheless, an era in the history of American Jewry was clearly drawing to a close.

There were many symptoms of the decline of the landsmanshaftn, but the most obvious was the advancing age of the members. When Rontch surveyed the societies in 1938, he discovered that only 15 percent of the landsmanshaft membership in New York was American-born. Gilmovsky's recollections of the landsmanshaftn after World War II parallel Rontch's earlier findings in this regard. Overwhelmingly, the landsmanshaft members and officers who dealt with Gilmovsky and his staff at the JDC had been born on the other side. In fact, most of the correspondence between the JDC and the landsmanshaftn in America was carried on in Yiddish or another East European tongue.

The landsmanshaftn were formed during the period of mass immigration, 1880 to 1920; and even though the societies had attracted a few new members from the first American-born generation and were able to augment their ranks slightly through the inclusion of Holocaust survivors who immigrated between 1945 and 1948, the societies remained composed overwhelmingly of persons who had come to New York around the time of World War I. This means that by 1950 the societies consisted almost exclusively of middle-aged or elderly members, whose ability to continue their traditional habits and activities were increasingly constrained by the limitations of health and advancing years.

The inexorable passage of time and its effects on the size of the landsleit societies reveal themselves dramatically if one walks through any of the thousands of landsmanshaft cemeteries in New York. Let us, for example, pay a brief visit to the cemetery of the Brestowitzer Independent Society, a landsmanshaft first organized in 1907, which purchased a cemetery in Cypress Hills in 1915. Each row has twelve graves. There are now ten complete rows of graves in the small cemetery, and the eleventh is almost filled in, which means that the society has buried 129 of its members in this place. The earliest funeral occurred in 1918, three years after the cemetery was purchased, although another grave in the first row belongs to an individual who died in 1912 but was later reburied with the landsleit at Cypress Hills. The entire

A Brotherhood of Memory

first row of 12 graves was filled in by 1929. The second and
nearly the entire third row—a total of 22 places—were filled
in during the 1930s. (Although we do not know how many
Brestowitzer landsleit were buried elsewhere, we can assume the Cypress Hills cemetery contains a representative
sample.) A total of 37 society members were buried between
1940 and 1949, however, and 51 members were interred
between 1950 and 1959. Thus, of the 122 adult members of
the Brestowitzer landsmanshaft who died between 1920
and 1960, 88, or more than 70 percent, passed away during
the last two decades. On average, fewer than two members
of the society died each year prior to 1940, but more than
four members a year died over the next twenty years.

The cemetery of the United Tarnopoler Relief Society in
Beth David was not the society's original burial ground, but
even though it was opened later than the Brestowitzer cemetery in Cypress Hills, it tells a similar story. United Tarnopoler was organized in 1896, and the Beth David cemetery received its first burial in 1929. In this cemetery, each
row contains 14 graves, and four rows were filled up before
1940. However, eight additional rows were filled by the
1960s, with two additional rows just about completed since
1970. The United Tarnopoler brethren buried 61 of their
own between 1929 and 1953, and 135 members from the
mid-1950s to 1982.

The increasing incidence of death among landsmanshaft
members would not have foreshadowed the end of the societies had the losses been counterbalanced by the absorption
of new members into the ranks. While it is true that some
landsmanshaft cemeteries do contain many graves of
American-born members, these people rarely were active
participants in the society to which they belonged. If they
joined, it was simply because the annual dues were a cheap

means of purchasing cemetery plots for themselves, their wives, and their children. But most of them never came to meetings, never were involved in landsmanshaft activities, and never thought of the society as having any relevance or importance to their lives. The cultural gap between the original and the American-born members is reflected in the fact that prior to the 1950s most of the inscriptions on headstones were in Hebrew (and a few in Yiddish), more recent headstones are nearly all in English.

The inability of the societies to extend beyond the lifetimes of their original members is most clearly reflected in the decline in the number of societies from one decade to the next. In 1920 there were perhaps 3,000 independent landsmanshaft societies in New York (the actual total, as we have seen, may have been several thousand more). By 1938, Rontch estimated that fewer than 2,000 independent societies were still functioning; the number may have held at close to 2,000 through the early 1950s, given the upsurge in landsmanshaft activity associated with the Holocaust and the founding of the State of Israel. However, when the JDC launched another landsmanshaft campaign during the period of the 1967 war, it was able to locate only 1,200 independent societies, many of which had long ago stopped meeting on a regular basis. By 1980, JDC officials put the number of societies at fewer than 1,000, and assume that perhaps only 400–500 continue to meet and maintain some degree of regular contact between members. Indeed, JDC staff believe that this last number will probably dwindle to less than 100 by the end of the 1980s.

Unable to attract active new members, the landsmanshaftn also proved incapable of dealing with certain crucial problems that reflected changes in the society around them. In earlier chapters we have seen how vitally important the landsmanshaftn were at critical moments of the immigrant experience. They responded immediately to the trauma of migration and resettlement in a strange new land. They were a dynamic and active part of the effort to counteract the terror of the pogroms. They performed heroically when faced with the destruction of the Holocaust and the challenge of Israel. But their success in dealing with all these problems underscored the extent to which they had not really altered their Old World perspectives. Their personal and collective ties to the Old World were not matched by ties to the New, and thus they were severely limited in the extent to which they could respond to the problems of American society.

The most serious problem the landsmanshaftn collectively faced was the Great Depression. One might imagine that societies organized primarily to provide benevolence and charity would be in the forefront of the struggle to overcome the misery and privation of the Depression years. The landsmanshaftn all had sick funds, loan funds, and benevolent funds intended to alleviate poverty and suffering, which no doubt intensified during the decade of the 1930s. The members of the landsmanshaftn were drawn from the lower socioeconomic strata of the Jewish community, and many were either unemployed or experienced a clear decline in living standards during the Depression years.

In fact, the charitable and benevolent activities of the landsmanshaftn as a whole declined during the Depression. Many of the smaller societies that had been founded during the early part of the immigration era either faded into functionless entities or became "paper" organizations whose sole responsibility was maintenance of the cemetery plot. Many other groups collapsed completely, as their membership became secularized, assimilated, or indifferent to the whole landsmanshaft idea. Among those societies that remained in operation, the Depression proved a social calamity too great for their meager resources.

Examining the financial records of landsmanshaftn during the 1930s, one finds several significant trends. Generally speaking, the rate of absenteeism and nonpayment of dues increased, the number of suspensions for nonpayment of dues also went up (although many societies relaxed their rules), and the amount of money dispensed by landsmanshaftn through their benevolent and sick funds declined. Each landsmanshaft rarely granted benevolent payments to anyone except a full-fledged member of that particular society. Failure to pay dues resulted in suspension or expulsion from the organization and, accordingly, the loss of privileges, particularly the privilege to apply for a loan or provident fund payment. Consequently, those members most in need of benevolence and relief were often ineligible to claim it, since they had already withdrawn from the society's activities and fallen behind in their dues. At the same time, the drop in membership and the members' increasing inability to keep up regular dues payments resulted in an overall decline in the economic health of the landsmanshaftn.

As their financial resources dwindled, the landsmanshaftn began cutting back on expenses. Most societies retained the practice of making endowment payments to the survivors of deceased members, because the money was considered absolutely essential to ameliorate the immediate financial crisis that often occurred when an adult wage earner passed away; moreover, the endowment payment was a means of covering both the expense of the funeral and the later erection of a headstone at the grave site. The sick and loan funds, however, were not so sacrosanct. As the Depression wore on, loan and sick payments became smaller or ceased altogether. For example, the Progress Mutual Aid Society made sick payments to an average of three or four members each week in 1932 and 1933, but by the summer of 1934 the society rarely dispensed any sick funds at all. When a member named Simon Malta applied for a loan after being laid off from his job in April 1934, the Ways and Means Committee, which had previously handled such requests in routine fashion, referred this request to the entire membership of the society, which, in typical fashion, buried the issue in debate. The Strelisker Young Men's Benevolent Association dispensed regular sick payments from 1932 until 1935, but thereafter made only an occasional payment to members certified as being "chronical ill."

The exclusive nature of landsmanshaft membership necessarily limited the degree to which the societies could render assistance during the Depression, but this was not the case with other Jewish charitable organizations. Charities such as the Federation of Jewish Philanthropies were much better equipped, both financially and organizationally, to deal with the problems of poverty and unemployment, especially because they widened their relief efforts to include counseling and vocational training. The landsmanshaftn could never compete on that level. But even the fundraising and relief efforts of the major Jewish charities were hampered by the overall decline in resources and money within the Jewish community. Consequently, it was the federal government, through its New Deal and Social Security programs, which stepped into the breach. There is no doubt that many of the people who came to the landsmanshaftn for help in the 1920s would later, when circumstances required it, turn to government agencies for assistance. This had the effect of reducing the landsmanshaft appeal even further and of narrowing its potential field of members and adherents.

The Depression was perhaps the most obvious social phenomenon to which the landsmanshaftn were unable to respond, but there were other, more subtle social developments that likewise undercut the societies' importance. Not all these developments were negative. To the contrary, some of them reflected the social and economic advances made by American-born Jews, trends the landsmanshaft population for the most part did not experience nor could truly comprehend.

Upward and Outward

The first and most dramatic change was in the geography of Jewish settlement in New York over the course of the last sixty-year period during which the original members of the landsmanshaftn went from being young immigrants to elderly retirees.[1] In 1910 the city contained 1.2 million Jews out of a total city population of just over 5 million. Of the Jewish residents in the city, just about half lived on the Lower East Side, with the remainder located primarily in Brooklyn and the Bronx. Most of the Jewish population was of Eastern European background, as the German-Jewish elite rapidly became a small minority within the Jewish population as a whole.

By 1920 the city's Jewish population had grown to 1.6 million, reflecting the last great wave of immigrants who poured out of Eastern Europe to escape the pogroms. But this newer immigrant population was not drawn to or did not long remain on the Lower East Side. Although Delancey and Rivington streets were still considered to be the spiritual center of Jewish immigrant life in New York, the Lower East Side now contained only one-fourth of the city's Jewish residents, and the Jewish population of Brooklyn now was nearly as large as that of Manhattan.

At the beginning of the 1920s more than 75 percent of all the Jews in New York lived in four areas: the Lower East Side, the South Bronx, and Brownsville and Williamsburg in Brooklyn. The development of Jewish neighborhoods in Brooklyn and the Bronx had meant for the most part an increase in the size of ghettos in the outlying boroughs. The Jewish neighborhood clustered around Pitkin Avenue in Brownsville had a deserved reputation for more poverty, sweatshops, pushcarts, and congested tenements than the Lower East Side. The great needle trades strike in 1910 was as bitterly fought in the streets and factories of Brownsville as in the Jewish neighborhoods of Manhattan.

The landsmanshaftn originated within the compact social, economic, and geographic contours of these four immigrant neighborhoods. The smaller societies, which started mostly as chevras, usually enlisted their membership from within an area of several blocks. This was particularly true of the orthodox chevras, whose members had to walk to shul on the Sabbath. Even the larger societies, which had members in different boroughs and met at a central point in Manhattan, consisted almost entirely of residents of the four ghetto neighborhoods. For example, a membership census of the Kolbuszower Young Men's Benevolent Society in 1919 shows 70 members living in Brownsville and Williamsburg, 35 living in the Hunt's Point and Morrisania sections of the South Bronx, and 92 still living on the Lower East Side.[2] Thus, members of a society were in close proximity to other members, rendering landsman activities inseparable from the normal routine of daily life. When members moved to Brooklyn or the Bronx, coming "home" to Delancey Street or Second Avenue on the Lower East Side each Sunday was an accepted part of that normal routine.

The 1920s saw the initial breakdown of the old ghetto neighborhoods and the gradual dispersal of the Jewish population into other areas of the city. True, the old neighborhoods retained their basic ghetto character and, if anything, became more ghettoized over time. But the pattern of Jewish settlement in New York after 1920 not only resulted in the growth of new Jewish neighborhoods but also reflected an evident rise in living standards and in the socioeconomic mobility of the non-ghetto population. In 1925, a Jewish social worker remarked that "the young married people are going to outlying districts of the Bronx and Brooklyn, and their standards of living are higher than those of their parents."[3] From 1920 through the 1930s, Jews moved in large numbers out of the ghettos and into areas that had previously been the bastions of the Irish and WASP middle class. These neighborhoods did not become ghettos, as had happened in Brownsville and Williamsburg, but instead developed into enclaves of a new Jewish middle class. The 1920s brought the spread of Jewish populations down Flatbush Avenue to Sheepshead Bay and Canarsie in Brooklyn, and westward in the Bronx to the Grand Concourse and outward to Pelham Parkway and Fordham Road. From 1920 to 1929 the Jewish population increased by 250 percent in Flatbush, rose by more than 400 percent along the Grand Concourse, and registered an increase of more than 700 percent on Pelham Parkway.

The Depression and the war years slowed the pace of geographic dispersion somewhat, but the city's Jewish population continued to increase. By the end of World War II there were nearly 2 million Jews living in New York; while the total figure had been augmented somewhat by the post-Holocaust arrivals, most of this increase reflected the coming of age of the first generation of American-born Jews. Unlike their parents, they were educated and assimilated, and they were fully prepared to enter the economic and social main-stream of American life. Once the constraints of the wartime economy were lifted, they entered the mainstream by leaps and bounds, and the pace of economic, social, and geographic mobility accelerated to an extent previously un-imaginable. The "new frontier" for Jewish residents lay to the east, in the borough of Queens, and Jews began crossing the border between Brooklyn and Queens in ever greater numbers.

In 1923 there were only 50,000 Jews in Queens, repre-senting less than 3 percent of New York's total Jewish popu-lation. By 1950 the borough contained 200,000 Jews, and that figure jumped to 450,000 by 1957. The population that moved into Queens changed from apartments to private homes and substituted the automobile for the subway. In-creasingly, these Jews held white-collar jobs, and they were more secular and more financially secure than their parents. They no longer read the Yiddish press, they no longer re-turned to the Lower East Side on Sundays, and they cer-tainly had little concern for maintaining the vestiges of an Old World way of life. Not only was the Lower East Side abandoned as a center of Jewish life, but the other inner-city ghettos—Brownsville, Williamsburg, Morrisania—were also being left behind. Of course, these older neighborhoods were not emptied of residents. Some Jews remained, to be joined by the next waves of poor migrants to the city—first the blacks, who arrived in large numbers during the 1930s and 1940s, then the Hispanics, who crowded into the Lower East Side and the Bronx beginning in the 1950s.

The geography of landsmanshaft membership paralleled the overall pattern of Jewish residence in New York until the end of World War II. In 1939 the membership of the Lubowisker Young Men's Benevolent Society included 139 from Brooklyn, 64 from the Bronx, 80 from the Lower East Side, and 3 "pioneers" who had made the great move to Queens.[4] When the First Independent Storonitzer Bukowiner Sick and Benevolent Society gathered for its forty-third anniversary (and "victory") banquet in 1946, there were 69 members living in Brooklyn and 60 from the Bronx, but only 8 members still residing on the Lower East Side; nonetheless, the banquet was held in a hall on East 5th Street on the Lower East Side. In 1953, however, this same society celebrated its fiftieth jubilee not on East 5th Street but at the Hotel Diplomat on 43rd Street in midtown Manhattan. By this time the number of members from the Lower East Side had dwindled to 5, but there were now 12 members living in Queens.[5]

The landsmanshaftn, at least in their original form, could not survive the effects of this geographical dispersion. The early societies operated by word of mouth and sustained themselves through their members' continuous personal contact. Lillian Schlaff, now in her nineties, recalls that her society adopted the unusual practice of dispensing small amounts of charity to any needy family in the neighborhood, whether those in need were members of the society or not. A member of the society would describe at a meeting the particular circumstances of the potential recipients, and the members would then vote on the request to provide relief. "There was no problem doing it this way," recalls Mrs. Schlaff, "because we all lived within a few blocks of each other in the Bronx, and we knew everyone in the neighborhood." This intense degree of intimate social contact simply could not be sustained as

Jews moved from inner-city neighborhoods to the outlying boroughs and then to the suburbs. The societies would continue to exist in form, but their substance would gradually wither away. If we examine the changing distribution of Jewish settlement over the three and one-half decades following the end of the Great Migration, the geographic factors that heavily influenced the decline of the landsmanshaftn become quite clear.[6]

	Percentage of Jews in New York City	
	1923	1957
Manhattan	37	16
Bronx	20	24
Brooklyn	40	40
Queens	3	20

The continuous dispersion accelerated in the period after 1955, as Jews continued to move up the socioeconomic ladder and farther away from the older inner-city neighborhoods. The Jewish population of New York hit its peak around 1955 and then began to drop off. In 1960 the city held 1,750,000 Jews; the figure fell to 1,250,000 in 1970 and to just over 1 million by 1980. The decrease in New York's Jewish population reflected primarily the movement of Jews to the neighboring suburban counties. By 1980, Nassau and Suffolk counties together contained more than 400,000 Jewish residents, and more Jews lived in Westchester County (123,000) than had stayed in the Bronx.[7] If the landsmanshaftn encountered difficulties maintaining their traditional cohesiveness when their membership moved to outlying boroughs, they would play virtually no role in suburban Jewish life.

The landsmanshaft population not only became smaller as a proportion of New York Jews; it also became poorer, at least in relative terms. By the mid-1950s the geographic division between inner-city Jews and those of the outer boroughs and suburbs reflected clear differences in wealth and social status. In 1957 the median income of Queens Jews was more than twice that of Jewish residents of Manhattan or the South Bronx, despite the fact that Manhattan still contained vestiges of the old and wealthy German-Jewish elite.[8] A comparison of income figures between the inner-city ghettos and the suburban Jewish communities at that time would show an even greater disparity. Not only were the landsmanshaftn unable to compete with government welfare programs and with such Jewish welfare agencies as the Federation of Jewish Philanthropies, but they did not even have enough money to maintain their own modest endeavors.

In 1951, for example, the members of the First Przemysler Sick Benefit Society held a series of meetings to revise provisions of its constitution regarding the dispensation of benevolent funds. Under the new bylaws, the society declared that, henceforth, "no new members admitted under this [new] amendment shall be entitled to receive any sick benefits of any kind nor endowment on either his or his wife's death but only burial and grave in Beth David Cemetery."[9] Organized in 1889, the society had for the next sixty-two years paid weekly sick benefits of $10 to any qualified member, as well as a lump-sum payment of $100 (or $50 to the spouse) at the time of death. But as small as these payments might appear to the modern reader, the society could no longer afford to make them after 1951.

The decline in the size of the landsmanshaft population was also the result of the wholesale movement of immigrants out of the city when they reached their retirement years. Although many immigrant Jews were too poor ever to leave their tiny apartments in the inner-city ghettos, many others had managed to save enough money once again to abandon their traditional environment in search of a more hospitable place to live. Many elderly Jews moved to the Sunbelt, a shift in population that became clearly evident by the end of the 1950s. In particular, immigrant Jews moved down to Miami and other points along Florida's east coast, and little enclaves like Miami's South Beach soon exhibited much the same character as the inner-city neighborhoods of Brooklyn and the Bronx.[10]

In the late 1960s or early 1970s a visitor to South Beach might have thought he was walking along Morris Avenue in the Bronx. South Beach was a 230-acre neighborhood at the southern tip of Miami Beach, and it was home at any one time to between 5,000 and 10,000 transplanted New York immigrant Jews. The main commercial streets, Collins and Washington avenues, were lined with small retail shops whose proprietors, like the residents around them, came from inner-city neighborhoods in New York. The year-round residents, who all lived within three or four blocks of the commercial district, went shopping in the morning and spent the afternoons sitting and *schmoozing* (talking) in Flamingo Park. Many food shops sold only kosher products, and the *Daily Forward* easily outsold the *Miami Herald* on the corner newsstands. South Beach was the only neighborhood in America outside of New York where the counterman in every coffee shop still knew how to mix a proper egg cream, and it was the only place outside of Brooklyn and the Bronx where trucks made morning deliveries of seltzer in glass bottles, exchanging full bottles for the empties that had held the previous day's order. In fact, the company that delivered the seltzer was also a transplant from New York, its owner having moved his filling machines and trucks down to a Miami warehouse in 1958 when he realized that his clientele was now more numerous in Miami than in the old neighborhoods of the Bronx.

The immigrant Jews who came to South Beach brought everything with them from the old neighborhood except their landsmanshaft. In some instances, a few transplanted members of a particular society would get together on a casual basis, and they might even send a small donation back to the organization in New York for the annual fundraising party of the UJA. But they were unable to reconstruct their societies in the new neighborhood because their psychic roots were still back in New York, as were the cemeteries where they wished to be buried. They had children and grandchildren up north; they were in contact with friends and relatives who had not yet moved down; and when they died, their remains would be flown back for burial in the society's cemetery in Brooklyn or Queens.

South Beach began to die out as a Jewish immigrant enclave in the late 1970s, for much the same reasons that the inner-city neighborhoods in Brooklyn and the Bronx had disappeared as centers of immigrant life. For one thing, the original generation of immigrants was almost extinct. Those who were still alive represented only an infinitesimal proportion of those who had come to America sixty, seventy, or eighty years earlier. More important, by the late 1970s, the Jews who were retiring and moving to Florida were no longer Old World immigrants but American-born Jews reared in middle-class neighborhoods. They had more money than their parents had, and they were not comfortable settling into the small rent-controlled apartment or bungalow-type hotels that formed the bulk of residential housing in South Beach. Instead of recreating the inner-city neighborhoods of the previous generation, they recreated the suburbs of New York in the hundreds of condominium "villages" that sprawled along the coast from North Miami to West Palm Beach. They brought not only their suburban habitats to southern Florida but also their shopping malls and their automobiles. When possible, they even moved their aged parents out of the South Beach ghetto and installed them in condominiums as well. But South Beach did not actually experience any loss of population. For in place of the poor, elderly Jews came the Cubans and other Hispanic minorities, who quickly spilled over into South Beach from their section on the other side of Fifth Street, transforming yet another Jewish neighborhood into a minority ghetto.

Tradition Versus Change

Just as the first generation of American-born Jews refused to stay behind in the old neighborhoods, so they also gravitated away from the traditional occupations and business activities that had supported their parents during their working years. Landsmanshaft Jews, as we have seen, moved quickly into the retail trades, becoming petty shopkeepers in Jewish neighborhoods and utilizing their landsmanshaft contacts to further their enterprises. They also took over certain parts of the garment trade, but they were not so active in wholesaling, and few became professionals. To the extent that the children of landsmanshaft members became shopkeepers, they usually owned larger, more prosperous retail establishments in middle-class shopping districts or suburban malls. Such enterprises bore little resemblance to the small "ma and pa" grocery stores or fruit markets of the inner-city ghetto; indeed, they were often franchise operations of national chains. For that matter, the predominance of landsmanshaft Jews in certain aspects of the retail food trade, such as fruits and vegetables, disappeared entirely once the Jewish population began to move away from the inner cities. The involvement of the landsmanshaft population in the garment industry also began to disappear, as the total number of Jews engaged in the production of apparel dwindled. It is not possible to collect figures on the exact number of Jews enrolled in the various garment unions, but it is safe to say that a work force that was mainly Jewish before World War II had a majority of non-Jewish members (largely blacks and Hispanics) within a decade after the war.[11]

The failure of landsmanshaft Jews to bring their children into business or the workplace with them—as happened often among other ethnic groups, such as the Italians or Greeks—did not necessarily reflect any conscious desire to force the next generation to find more viable forms of vocational commitment. The desire of landsmanshaft Jews to push their children into education no doubt foreclosed the possibility that these children would then turn around and come back to work in the family store. But a much more important factor in the lack of generation succession in landsmanshaft business was the change in the city's economy that took place while the children of the landsmanshaft population were coming of age. In 1920, retailing, wholesaling, petty manufacture, and apparel accounted for more than 75 percent of all the jobs available to the New York work force, a figure that was probably not much different from what it had been at the turn of the century. By 1950, however, the composition of the work force had undergone a dramatic change. New York was no longer a blue-collar or gray-collar town, and the typical New Yorker now worked in an insurance office, a bank, or some other service industry. Employment in the city continued to rise until the mid-1960s, but jobs now required education, training, and office skills, vocational attributes that certainly did not exist within the immigrant milieu. To the extent that immigrants did become professionals, such as accountants and bookkeepers, they were employed mostly in other immigrant firms and rarely were qualified to deal with anything but the most petty level of business.

The transformation of neighborhoods, the geographical dispersion of Jews, and the modernization of the city's economy formed the material basis for the disappearance of the landsmanshaftn in New York. Indeed, these changes affected the basic existence and attitudes of every immigrant population that had first settled in urban American ghettos at the end of the nineteenth century. But these changes do not tell the whole story. They do not fully explain why the original immigrants were unable to attract their children into the societies and organizations that had played such an important role in their survival and in their ability to underwrite, through hard work and sacrifice, the socioeconomic mobility of succeeding generations. It is not enough to say that American-born Jews refused to get involved in immigrant organizations because they were no longer immigrants. What needs to be examined is not just how and why the life-styles of the children differed from those of their parents. The real problem is to define how those different life-styles produced different attitudes toward life and toward the means by which each generation coped with life's challenges. For what really spelled the demise of the landsmanshaftn were the attitudinal differences—indeed, cleavages—that developed between generations. These differences were not just a function of neighborhood and employment but reflected the fundamental transformation of an urban society that had ceased to be an enclave and refuge for East European Jews.

Not surprisingly, this cleavage in attitudes first emerged within a religious context, as American-born Jews began moving into the mainstream and abandoned the traditional religious beliefs and attitudes of their immigrant parents. As we have seen, most of the early landsmanshaftn had a clear religious component. Often they were adjuncts to the small orthodox shuls that sprang up on the Lower East Side, and they functioned primarily as religious burial societies, much as such chevras had functioned in the shtetl. Even in the latter part of the immigration period, when there was a noticeable tendency toward secularization within the landsmanshaftn, the attitudes of the members remained tied to Old World orthodoxy. Women either were not allowed to join or, if admitted, were given a clearly subordinate role in society affairs. Even the more progressive, secularized societies had strict rules governing the Jewishness of their members. Marrying outside the faith was prohibited, and burial in the society cemetery was restricted to natural-born Jews, not converts. In addition, most societies tried to enforce rules requiring the maintenance of a landsleit connection. Membership in most societies was open only to those who could prove that they or their relatives had actually come from the particular shtetl or region that gave its name to the society. And even when this rule was relaxed in later years to accommodate younger persons born and married in America (as well as to keep open the possibility of attracting new members), the narrow provinciality of the landsleit connection remained strong.

American-born Jews and their children were unwilling

and unable to maintain this traditional set of attitudes. As orthodox religious belief and affiliation eroded, the social perceptions and activities that had accompanied religious orthodoxy began to erode as well. The clearest example of this change, which began to occur as early as 1920, was the shift from the chevra to the Jewish center as the basic institution of religious belief.[12] The small chevras or shuls had dominated immigrant neighborhoods, if only because there were so many of them. Nearly every block on the Lower East Side, Brownsville, and Williamsburg had its own little shul, the congregation consisting of just enough male members to form the ritual minyan for morning worship. The shul was not only a direct throwback to the shtetl but also represented a personal bond among its members, who lived and worked together in the New World (as in the Old) along the same block or within walking distance of each other.

When Jews began moving out of the ghettos and into middle-class neighborhoods like the Grand Concourse and Flatbush, the storefront chevra gave way to the neighborhood synagogue-center. This institution, in its organization, affiliation, and size, more closely reflected the needs of what was becoming a dispersed middle-class population. The shul was orthodox, the center conservative or even reform. The social activities of the shul focused on a very narrow range of immediate concerns, all within the context of traditional religious belief; the Jewish center, on the other hand, widened its scope to include virtually every type of social and educational activity, religiously oriented or not. With the development of middle-class neighborhoods in the 1920s, synagogue-center construction occurred on a scale never previously witnessed, and nearly all these institutions embodied the ideals of a population that looked outward to the wider society rather than inward to the narrow range of immigrant experience. The Brooklyn Jewish Center on Eastern Parkway consisted of a synagogue, an auditorium, a gymnasium, and a swimming pool, earning it and other centers like it the epithet of "a pool with a school and a shul." The building cost more than $1 million to construct, this at a time when most ghetto chevras were still meeting in the rabbi's cramped tenement apartment.

The transition from chevra to synagogue-center coincided with the emergence of the conservative and reform movements and the consequent decline of orthodox belief. English-language prayers and sermons were introduced into the service; men and women sat together rather than apart, as in orthodox shuls; and Friday night services began to replace the all-day Saturday devotions that were typical of orthodox chevra activity. Even the minyan, the gathering of ten males for daily prayer, became less frequent in conservative synagogues and disappeared altogether in reform congregations.

Even more pronounced than the changes in religious doctrine and devotion were the changes that occurred within the social context of middle-class Jewish life through their conservative and reform movements. The larger synagogue-centers proceeded to develop literally every type of social activity, from the men's club and sisterhood to senior citizens' groups and preschool facilities. Every center had an active program of religious education, with afternoon classes, a Sunday school, and evening sessions for adults. As Deborah Dash Moore has observed, the synagogue-center was an attempt to retain an ethnic identity while reconciling it to an Americanization of Jewish life. Perhaps the key factor in this regard was the emphasis on the religious rather than the social history of Jewish life. Children of American-born Jews spent hours learning the history of the prophets and the ancient tribes of Israel, but they were never exposed to Yiddish and could more easily locate Palestine on a map than point out the region in the Pale where their grandparents were born.

As the social activities of the synagogue-center widened, its religious aspect diminished in importance. The synagogue-centers provided all the social activities that had been offered by the landsmanshaftn, but on a much wider scale that embraced all members of the community. The centers ran card games, bingo, and Las Vegas nights, and provided space for bar mitzvah parties, weddings, and other family affairs. They elevated women to a status nearly equal to that of men, while orienting all activities toward the family. The landsmanshaftn not only could not compete with the synagogue-centers for younger members; they could not even conceive of the situation in competitive terms.

Is Life Here Any Better?

The synagogue-center versus the chevra might be the most salient example of the cleavage in attitudes between the landsmanshaft members and their descendants, but there are other examples as well. Public education had not existed in the shtetl, nor in the Old World was secular education often an alternative to the cheder and the yeshiva. In New York, on the other hand, the school system was viewed as a vehicle for transmitting American attitudes and for turning immigrants of all ethnic backgrounds into Americans. Largely in response to the massive European migration, the number of public schools and the size of the teaching staff increased enormously during the early decades of the twentieth century.[13] In the years 1924 to 1929 alone, the Board of Education built 130 new schools, and the number of public school teachers nearly doubled between 1903 and 1925.

More than any other ethnic group, Jews entered the school system and remained within it as teachers and administrators. Although most Jewish neighborhoods still contained a wide assortment of institutions for religious education, both independent of and attached to synagogues, these were always considered as adjuncts to the public school system. In the 1930s only 2 percent of Jewish school-age children were being educated full-time in Jewish schools, the lowest percentage of parochial education of any New York ethnic group. As the number of Jewish students increased, so did the number of Jewish teachers. By 1940 more than 50 percent of all teachers entering the system were Jewish, and by the mid-1960s, Jews comprised more than two-thirds of the system's 55,000-member instructional staff.

Although the public school curriculum was clearly designed to eradicate the social and cultural vestiges of immigrant Jewishness, some attempts were made to retain an element of traditional beliefs and language. For a brief period during the 1920s there was a movement to allow the teaching of Yiddish in the public schools, but American-born Jewish teachers quickly shifted their energies to trying to convince the Irish-dominated Board of Education to permit the teaching of Hebrew. Yiddish was considered both culturally and politically un-American, while Hebrew was associated with a more progressive, enlightened, and secular attitude toward Jewish affairs. In 1931 the board finally agreed to adopt Hebrew as an elective subject on the high school level, and this decision, in effect, drove any hint of Yiddishness out of the system forever.

As well as fostering the abandonment of the immigrant

language, the schools also consciously promoted ideas about social progress and assimilation. The high school curriculum increasingly became a means of preparing students for entrance to secular colleges, institutions that had traditionally been the bastions of the WASP upper class. American-born Jews who began entering City College, NYU, and Columbia in the 1930s, and who gained admittance to these schools in increasing numbers thereafter, soon realized that the disparity in outlook between themselves and their immigrant parents had become irrevocable. Norman Podhoretz said that while attending his first classes at Columbia, he "discovered, and really for the first time, that there were more things in heaven and earth than were dreamt of in the philosophy of Brownsville."[14] The atmosphere of a secular college, with its emphasis on liberal arts, technical training, and professionalization, irreparably drew American-born Jews away from the ghetto, away from the immigrants, and most of all, away from the landsmanshaftn.

While the cultural effects of public education no doubt produced strains between the East European immigrants and their children, this does not seem to have influenced the parents to attempt to stop their children from becoming educated. On the contrary, Jewish immigrants made great sacrifices to afford the luxury of education for their children, even though they knew these efforts would ultimately result in their children's abandoning a traditional way of life. But many of these same immigrants remained steadfast within the culture and network of the landsmanshaftn. "I don't remember ever going to the [society] meetings," recalls the son of a landsmanshaft member now in his fifties, "although I'm sure that I was taken to a few. But I do remember being left at home on Sunday and being told to spend the day studying, even though I was usually in the balcony of

Loew's on Fordham Road within five minutes after my parents left the house."

Like the synagogue-centers, the public school system fit the needs of American-born Jews but was irrelevant to the requirements of their parents. The parents who belonged to landsmanshaftn were clearly aware of this dichotomy. "I went to college because it was the natural thing to do," remembers an American-born Jew who is today the chief partner in a large accounting firm in Manhattan. "My father used to brag about 'his son the college student' at meetings of the society, but I'm sure he never knew exactly what I was studying in school."

The educational and social gains of American-born Jews opened generational cleavages that left parents and children speaking different languages, literally as well as figuratively. For the immigrants, money—even very small sums of money—was a constant worry. During 1951 the United Rozaner Relief Society membership spent six entire meetings haggling over whether to take $200 out of the treasury to erect a new cemetery gate, or assess each member a $4 "tax" in order to raise the necessary funds.[15] That same year, the members of the First Przemysler Sick Benefit Association argued at great length over whether to raise the annual dues by $5 per annum but finally decided to leave the dues payment what it had always been.[16] The members of the First Probuzna Sick Benevolent Society could not make up their collective mind in 1959 as to whether to purchase and donate a wheelchair to an old-age home where several of the members had become permanent residents.[17]

One could easily imagine a debate over increasing the annual dues by several dollars becoming a major issue in 1905. After all, men and women worked all week in sweatshops for $10, and 25 cents could buy an entire meal. But to argue over such trifling sums in the 1950s reflected the maintenance of a particular attitude that no longer had any objective basis. The landsmanshaft members would never truly enter the middle class, but most of them were economically secure (at least marginally) by the 1950s and 1960s. If nothing else, they could depend for financial support on their children, whose incomes and living standards had risen enormously over the previous several decades. While the older generation argued at meetings about spending $50, their children were buying houses that cost $50,000. Landsmanshaft members who sat at meetings on Sunday and ate boiled chicken for $5 a plate could not comprehend that their children were home asleep after having spent $100 the night before on "dinner and a show."

"I don't remember my parents ever having money," says the daughter of immigrants who came to New York in 1919, "but we were never really poor. My father had a small grocery store in the Bronx, and we ate all our meals in the back. When we needed furniture, we bought something used from a landsman. My parents never went to a bank because all their money was put into the register in the morning and taken home at night. They didn't need anything because they never left the store." This brief anecdote not only says something about money but also says a great deal about the different style of life that money later came to represent. The stories that landsleit tell about the early years of settlement revolve around a life of simple and continuous routines, in work as well as social relations. Survival meant the maintenance of these routines, and great care was taken to preserve them. Having money was not necessarily a key to survival, because survival was predicated on the maintenance of a life in which money played a very limited role. At the same time, seeking money implied risk taking and the disruption of routine, both of which were to be avoided at all costs.

On the other hand, the children and grandchildren of the landsmanshaftn were brought up in a society that venerated the search for money and the acquisition of material goods that money could buy. Although many American-born Jews were constrained in their pursuit of money by the attitudes of their parents, who pressured them into foregoing the entrepreneurial route in favor of a more "secure," modest professional livelihood, they nonetheless saw palpable evidence of *other* people around them making money all the time. But this was not the case with the landsmanshaftn. The societies were extremely homogeneous in socioeconomic terms, and the aspirations and accomplishments that sufficed for one member usually sufficed for all. The fact that many landsmanshaft members used the landsleit network to secure a living meant that, by and large, occupations and earnings remained fairly constant from one decade to the next. One society, whose members operated small fruit markets during the 1920s and 1930s, did not have a single professional member in the 1950s. Several of the landsleit had "made it" by dint of becoming petty wholesalers in the fruit business, but they sold almost entirely to other members of the same society who were still operating little stores. The great "success" of the society was one member who actually became a fruit and vegetable buyer for a small grocery chain in the late 1950s. He was probably the only member of his landsmanshaft who wore a tie and sport jacket to work every day and sat behind a desk.

These archaic attitudes about money, reflecting a genuine fear of the risks of success, largely disappeared when landsleit sat down at a meeting and talked about their children. Often going to the other extreme, they would promote their

245

own naive version of their children's financial accomplishments and engage in long and sustained competition over whose son or son-in-law had made it to the top. If one's child was a doctor or a lawyer, this was an immediate, unquestionable source of pride, but it was the more subtle nuances of his or her material success that were viewed with awe and delight. One aged landsman returned from a visit to his children's condominium to regale his fellow members about the amenities and luxuries in the apartment in West Palm Beach. When asked to describe the most unique feature of this deluxe residence, he puffed up his chest, spread his arms out for emphasis, and replied: "When they brought me back from the airport in the car, they stopped in front of the garage, pressed a button in the glove compartment, and the door opened by itself!" This man, like most of the landsleit, was suspected of stretching the truth somewhat when he bragged about the accomplishments of his children. But notwithstanding the fact that the condominium was located 1,200 miles south of New York, and therefore the exactitude of his story could never be verified, how could he have made up such a thing? Bragging rights about the children were clearly his, at least for the duration of that particular meeting.

The original members of the landsmanshaftn were never able to comprehend the materialism and mobility of modern life in America. Unlike their children, whose professional and business careers allowed them to separate home from work and move out of the ghettos with ease, the immigrants remained tied to their little shops and stores in the neighborhoods where they lived. When the neighborhood deteriorated, they found another marginal area like Bensonhurst, Kew Gardens, or South Beach, where they reestablished their basic livelihoods and domestic relationships. Rather than confronting their own inability to take advantage of the possibilities offered by America, they simply ignored the opportunities for themselves while accepting them uncritically for their children.

Over the course of their lives, these immigrants had reduced the problem of survival to a series of simple routines, and they were not prepared to alter those routines regardless of what the consequences might be. Most of them started their lives in the absolute poverty of the shtetl and ended their lives in the relative poverty of an inner-city ghetto. They clung tenaciously to their little apartments, little shops, and little landsmanshaftn as the world changed around them, just as their parents had clung tenaciously to their little shtetlach while the world changed around them. But as the world changed outside the shtetl, it ultimately devoured and destroyed the Jewish community of the Pale. Life in America might change at an even faster pace, but the minimal security it provided the immigrants was far greater than anything they had ever been offered before.

VIII

The Beautiful Young Women of Boyerke

Just as the members of the Boyerker Benevolent Society devoted so much time and effort to preserving the memory of Boyerker and their beloved families and friends, so their wives also dedicated themselves to the preservation of this sacred memory.
—Statement by the Boyerker Ladies' Auxiliary in the 1969 Anniversary Journal

MARY SAVETSKY, Fannie Savetsky, Molly Sukernek, and Helen Feldberg arrived in New York in 1923. Mary, Molly, and Helen were born in the little shtetl of Boyerke in the Russian Ukraine, while Fannie came from a nearby settlement. They all arrived in New York in the full bloom of youth, Mary the oldest at twenty-nine, Fannie the youngest at nineteen. They had all escaped from the Pale during the pogroms that followed World War I, and their last memories of their homeland were of death, destruction, isolation, and fear. None of them would ever see their villages again. In fact, only Mary and Fannie would ever leave New York, accompanying their retired husbands who moved to Miami Beach. The only people from the villages the four young women would ever meet in America were those other venturesome young people who fled the pogroms either just before or along with them.

They came to New York not knowing a word of the English language and not knowing anything about America except that other landsleit had made the journey before them. All of them would be met at the pier by these landsleit, and would be taken to the homes of landsleit in order to settle in. Fannie and Mary ended up in Brooklyn; Helen settled first with a sister in Harlem, then moved to the Bronx; and Molly got on a train with her husband and traveled to Buffalo, where she would remain for seven years until she, too, moved to the Bronx.

The friends and relatives who met each of them at the dock in New York harbor would form the basic social network in which these four women would exist for the remainder of their lives. Not a day would pass during the next sixty years when each of these four women would not make contact with one another or with any of the other men and women who had come to pierside to greet them when the long journey from Eastern Europe came to an end. These four women would live through the births of their children, their grandchildren, and their great-grandchildren, as well as the deaths of all their husbands, but the fundamental bonds created in the Pale would remain unbroken to the end. This is the story of how they managed to maintain those bonds, and of the choices they made and did not make along the way.

Mary Savetsky, the oldest of the four women, was born to Jacob and Rachel Krupnick in 1894. She was one of nine children, and her father was the one who supervised the ritual slaughter of animals in the town. As the *shochet*, or ritual slaughterer, he was regarded as a man of great piety and learning, and in fact was descended from a long line of *shochtim* in the region. But he had an aversion to killing, and spent most of his life going around the village performing "good deeds"—in particular, collecting food to be distributed to poor people for their Sabbath dinners. He was also regarded as a man who "knew from nothing" about business, and was therefore an easy mark for people who would borrow money from him without ever paying it back.

To supplement the meager family income, Mary's mother operated near their home a small dry-goods store, where most of the children were employed at various times. She was the daughter-in-law of a rich merchant family in the city, and through this connection was often able to secure luxury goods for sale in her shop. Mary remembers selling caviar and halvah from the Caucasus as well as fruit from the orchard areas around the Black Sea. She also remembers that her mother, who could read both Yiddish and Russian, received from Odessa a weekly newspaper which she read out loud to the other women and then circulated around the town.

In 1919, Mary married Joseph Savetsky. He had served in the Russian army during the war, and upon returning to the village he went to work for his father. Joseph came from a much richer family than Mary. His father was an agent for several great landlords in the region, owned and operated a mill, and traded in timber, beet sugar, and grains. His wealth therefore allowed him to travel outside the Pale. Joseph remembers as a small boy accompanying his father to a large city and catching a glimpse of the tsarist Minister Stolypin as the official drove by in his carriage. The family owned two houses—one out in the countryside, near the farms which the elder Savetsky managed, the other a larger residence in

Boyerke. Before going into the army, Joseph had been educated in a gymnasium, where he mastered Russian and an intensive curriculum of scientific subjects.

The young Savetskys were married in traditional fashion in the open air. They stood beneath the wedding canopy, or *chupah,* which was held up by four young male friends. Each man held the canopy with one hand and in his other hand clenched a rifle. The wedding took place at a time when the Ukraine was already being devastated by pogroms, and the residents of Boyerke knew that at any moment the terror might descend on their village.

In fact, the first pogrom hit Boyerke in April 1917, during the Easter season, always a time of tension between Jews and gentiles in the region. Sometime during Easter week a group of armed peasants marched into the middle of the shtetl, chased the Jews into their houses, and then went from house to house looking for the most pious males, who were easily identified with their long beards. They herded a group of bearded men, including Mary's father, into a lake near the settlement and shot them. Mary remembers running down to the lake and, as she caught sight of her father's lifeless body floating on the water, hearing a peasant yell at her, "Where is your God now?" From that day on, Mary, though remaining a Jew, lost all faith in religion.

The village of Boyerke was just one of thousands of settlements that felt the fury of the pogroms in 1919. At one point, news reached the village that a pogrom was taking place in a neighboring settlement where many families, including the Savetskys, had relatives. Joseph's father left the village one night and made a heroic trip through bandit-infested hills to rescue his cousin's children, who had been orphaned in a pogrom. One of these children, Max Savetsky, would become Joseph's lifelong friend, and the woman he married in America, Fannie, would similarly become Mary Savetsky's lifelong friend.

In 1919 a much more vicious pogrom took place in Boyerke. Some of the younger villagers were able to escape by running out of the settlement with the Cossack band hot on their heels. Joseph and Mary had previously escaped to Kiev and attempted to return to Boyerke by jumping on a freight train. Joseph jumped aboard, but Mary slipped and was saved only because Joseph was able to hold her arm from inside the train as she dangled on the outside of the car. Later that night, having been forced to leave the train, they wandered, alone and helpless, through unknown territory, just managing to duck out of the way of Red Army patrols who were "recruiting" all able-bodied men into the ranks. The next morning, Joseph found some tattered women's clothing in an abandoned house, and they were able to walk past several army checkpoints with him disguised as a peasant woman!

Joseph and Mary never returned to Boyerke, but made it to a neighboring village where they consoled the few survivors. They were told that shops had been wrecked, the synagogue burned, and not a single family had escaped the massacre without the loss of loved ones. In all, the pogrom had claimed the lives of more than 120 men, women, and children, including 21 persons in the home of Joseph's father alone. Three days later, the survivors threw their belongings on wagons, and like the pioneers of the Old West, set out on their journey. When the wagon train arrived several weeks later at the outskirts of Kiev, they were met by some fellow villagers who had already come to the city and had established makeshift residences. The people from Boyerke remained in Kiev for about a month, living off relief packages provided by HIAS, supplemented by food that some of the men who had found jobs in Kiev were able to bring home at night.

Over the next several months, many of the younger people in Kiev began to leave. Some went to Odessa in the hope of securing visas for travel to America; others were able to move to Rumania, and still others simply disappeared to other regions of the Pale. Mary was now pregnant, and a decision had to be made concerning the future. The couple had applied for visas to America, but they were told the waiting period might last for several years. One night a group of younger men got together and decided to form a convoy for the trip through the Pale. They had learned that Jews were living more securely in Rumania, that jobs were available in towns close to the Rumanian border, and that they might receive visas more quickly if they somehow could get out of Russia. Mary said good-bye to her mother and her brothers and sisters, who were planning to return to the village. She packed up several bags of belongings and in a parcel of clothes carefully hid several hundred rubles and her mother's jewels. These had been given her to pay for the passage to America if and when the visas were finally secured.

Late one night, Mary, her husband, and a small group of friends from the village left the refugee camp and set out for the town of Kishinev just across the Russian border. It was now wintertime, and she remembers the wind howling around her ears as they set off on the road. Joseph and several of the other men had made an arrangement with some local peasants to guide the group to the border and bypass towns where Cossacks were lying in wait for small groups of refugee Jews. The small band of refugees pooled their money and gave nearly all of it to these local peasants as payment for taking them through hostile territory.

The trip through the Ukraine lasted several weeks. The party traveled by night and spent the daylight hours hiding in the woods or huddled together in barns. Many nights they would set out along a road or over a field, only to retreat when one of their guides learned that Cossacks had been seen in the area ahead. Several times the refugees had to circle back, returning to sleep in the same grove of trees they had slept in the night before. Mary remembers many years later going to see Western movies in New York and thinking that she had experienced the same fear and uncertainty as the pioneers had felt when they were crossing the Great Plains.

Finally the group reached the banks of the Dnestr River, which flowed down to Kishinev. The river was frozen, and the plan was made to cross it at night. For nearly a week the refugees sat in the woods lining the river, within view of Rumania on the other side. Each night a group of men would set out to reconnoiter the border but would return because they felt the area was unsafe. One night they were visited by a band of local peasants who said they would guide the Jews across the river and into Rumanian territory, but the Jews would have to pay money to bribe the Russian border guards before they could all set out. The refugees pooled their dwindling money and gave it to the leader of the peasant band, but their guides then vanished into the night and never returned.

The next night the Jews decided to try to cross the river by themselves. They waited until it was completely dark and no sound could be heard on either side. Then they set out across the ice, stumbling, freezing, running, expecting at any moment to be caught by a border patrol that would send them back or perhaps even shoot them on sight. Somehow they made it to the other side of the river, but they had gotten lost on the way, and suddenly they stood facing a high cliff. Mary began climbing up the cliff but slipped on the ice and fell all the way back down. The group abandoned the effort, and with daylight fast approaching, the refugees ran back across the river to the safety of the trees.

The next evening a landsman from the village walked into their camp. He and several friends had managed to cross the Dnestr at a point several miles farther south, and he had returned to guide the group along this new route. Hoping against hope, they waited for the moon to rise and then set out again. Several hours later, after running and scrambling through woods and over ice, they sat exhausted but happy on the far side of the river. They had finally left the Ukraine and the murderous bandits behind, but they had left their families behind as well.

Several days later, Mary and Joseph were standing in an immigrant reception center outside of Kishinev. It was now May 1921, more than a year since they had left the shtetl of Boyerke. They applied for visas and then waited for permission to emigrate to America. During this time, they lived on the outskirts of the city, in a portion of an abandoned barn that had been turned into a barracks for refugees. Mary Savetsky gave birth to her daughter in this barn in July, and Joseph began working every day in the pharmacy of a large hospital in Kishinev. He was paid only a small salary, but he could take food home from the commissary for his wife and infant child. The family lived in these circumstances for a year, then moved to Bucharest, and waited another year until they received permission to go to America. Every day Joseph would stop off at the immigration office to ask whether their visas had been expedited. Finally, in April 1923, they were informed that the necessary documentation had arrived and that they could book passage on the next boat.

Mary would rather forget the trip to America. She had managed to save most of the jewelry she had been given before leaving Russia, and when the jewels were pawned there was enough money to buy second-class passage. Thus the young family, contrary to the experience of many immigrants, did not come to New York in steerage. In fact, they had a private room and could eat all their meals in the luxury of the second-class dining room. But Mary got extremely seasick on the first day of the trip, and she spent the next three weeks lying in her cabin. Joseph, on the other hand, quickly got accustomed to shipboard life and never forgot the thrill of the journey. Many years later, when his oldest grandchild was preparing to go to Europe as part of his college "junior year abroad" program, he told the young man that he had seen everything the young student was about to see. "The boat first went to Constantinople, then to Alexandria, where I took a tour of the pyramids. Then it anchored near Athens, and I took a tour of the Parthenon. The next week we stopped at Rome, and I got off again to see the Colosseum and the other old ruins. I was an immigrant in America, but I was a tourist before I got there."

The ship carrying the Savetskys sailed into New York harbor on Labor Day, 1923. Most of the immigrants were removed and put on a small ferry that took them to Ellis Island. But Joseph, Mary, and their daughter Jean, having traveled as second-class passengers, walked down the gangplank on the pier in Brooklyn. They were met at dockside by a large group of relatives and friends, including Joseph's brother Nathan, who had arrived several months before, and Mary's cousin Frank, who had been one of the earliest to leave the village and would later be one of the first to earn enough money to buy a car. The group celebrated the family's arrival on the pier, and then everyone loaded onto the elevated. But they did not go directly to an apartment. Instead, the new immigrants were taken to Coney Island, where they spent the day reminiscing about the trip, talking about life in America, going on the rides in Steeplechase Park, and spending money on the boardwalk. Only by the end of the day did the festivities that surrounded their arrival qualify them as being "tired and poor."

Mary was the last of the four women to arrive in New York. Molly Sukernek, her husband Harry, and their infant daughter had left the village with the Savetskys, but the Sukerneks had encountered even greater difficulties in getting to the border, and they had spent some time in a Russian jail. But because their visas had been approved more quickly, they had already arrived and settled in Buffalo, where Harry's uncle had given him a job in a small factory that salvaged iron goods. Fannie had arrived at the end of 1922 and was now living in Brooklyn. She had met Joseph Savetsky's cousin Max and would soon become his wife. Helen Feldberg, whose maiden name was Cohen, had also just arrived in New York and was boarding in her sister's apartment in Harlem. All in all, nearly everyone from Boyerke who had set out for America had actually arrived, and a few more would complete the journey at the end of 1923. Most of them were young people in their twenties and thirties, married a short time and with one or two infant children. A few of the younger generation had brought their parents with them or managed to get their parents to America shortly after they themselves were settled. There were also a few landsleit, like Joseph Savetsky's uncle Motl, who had come to New York before the war. The men were all literate, as were most of the women. Many had been trained in a skill or trade, and the several years spent waiting for visas had given them some exposure to the outside world. Mary had a good friend from the neighboring village of Tareshka, Celia Feldberg, who remembers attending the ballet and opera in Kiev.

Despite their youth, energy, and good health, the landsleit

of Boyerke were, in the main, penniless refugees. They did not speak a word of English, and as the men were soon to discover, their skills and training had little meaning in New York. They were totally unprepared for the anonymity and pace of life in this great city. But they did have each other: by the time the Great Migration came to an end, nearly sixty persons from the village or surrounding shtetlach were living in the New World. The personal connections within this group formed the "safety net" upon which all of them would depend for the remainder of their lives.

Within a few years after their arrival, Mary Savetsky, Fannie Savetsky, and Helen Feldberg were all living with their husbands in the Bronx. Helen had married Dave Feldberg, whose younger brother Hymie had also come to New York, along with their sister Celia and their parents. With the exception of Max Savetsky, who got a job in a shop salvaging iron goods, and Dave Feldberg, who went to work in a shop in the garment district, all the men were employed in little fruit and vegetable markets in the Jewish ghetto of the South Bronx. They all lived within walking distance of their stores (sometimes in the backs of the stores), and they all lived within walking distance of each other. The women would meet daily, and none of them had a telephone because the only people they might call were the same people they saw every day.

The routine of their lives rarely varied. The stores opened early in the morning and closed late at night, operating on Saturday and often Sunday as well as all weekdays. The men moved from job to job and store to store, always working for landsleit or for proprietors who hired them on the recommendation of a landsman. They lived in small walk-up apartments, sharing a common toilet in the hall and sometimes also sharing a common refrigerator or stove in the hallway. They did not own cars, but they traveled through the city with ease on the subway, going to Lewisohn Stadium in Harlem for open-air concerts or making a Sunday expedition down to the Lower East Side. Their socializing had an intimate, continuous flavor, and in 1923, the year the last immigrants arrived from Boyerke, they established a landsmanshaft called the Boyerker Benevolent Society.

Nobody alive today remembers the actual formation of the society. Of the four women and their husbands, only Max Savetsky was present at the first meeting; David Feldberg joined the organization shortly thereafter. Joseph Savetsky considered the landsmanshaft concept a little too conservative for his more modern taste, and Harry Sukernek was still living in Buffalo. But even though Joseph and Mary Savetsky were not founding members of the society, their refusal to join in no way altered their social relations with the other landsleit. The patterns of work, recreation, and socializing were already fully intertwined with those of society members, so that Joseph and Mary Savetsky were, in effect, members of the society without actually joining.

The society began to meet in a rented room in Harlem, then moved down to Second Avenue, on the Lower East Side. The meetings were held once a month, and they were lively and festive affairs. From the beginning, the Boyerker Society eschewed ritual and secrecy. Meetings were open to both men and women, although only men could serve as officers and conduct the society's business affairs. The women took a more active role in social activities, including preparing the herring and potatoes that remained the standard fare at all society meetings for the next forty years. Secular in outlook, the society never had any connection with a religious institution. Parties were held to celebrate

Jewish holidays, such as Purim and Chanukah, but this was more a reflection of Old World habits than any direct attempt to maintain a religious faith.

By the end of the 1920s, the landsleit of Boyerke had managed to secure a toehold in the New World. Joseph Savetsky and Dave Feldberg were no longer working in other people's stores but had managed to open small fruit and vegetable stores of their own. Likewise, Max Savetsky, having gone into business for himself, was running a salvage operation and junkyard in the Bronx. The incomes of these three families had become somewhat more secure, but their living standards had not improved to any great degree. Joseph and Mary's store, which was located on Allerton Avenue, had fruit piled on top of wooden crates, which were placed against the walls; a partition separated their store from that of a butcher who shared the space. Every morning Joseph would get up at 4 A.M., travel down to the Washington Street market at the southern end of Manhattan (where the World Trade Center now stands) and order fruit to be delivered in the Bronx later that day. He would return to the store and open it by 8 A.M. There he would be joined by Mary, who, having sent her daughter off to school, would cook him breakfast in the back. They would work side by side in the store for the remainder of the day. After lunch, Joseph would take a nap on empty potato sacks spread out on the floor in the rear; Mary left in the late afternoon when her daughter returned home from school. In the evening, after dinner, they would walk in the neighborhood or stop in to say hello to landsleit who lived in the same apartment building or nearby. They rarely closed the store for a day, they never took vacations, and they never had free time except for several hours in the evening until Joseph, who had to get up at 4 A.M., went to bed at 8 or 9 P.M. All the Boyerke landsleit lived this way, but nobody remembers these years as particularly difficult or the conditions of life as especially onerous. They still kept contact with family back in the village, but the news from abroad convinced them they had made the right choice. After the pogrom period was over, the survivors had returned to Boyerke, but work was scarce and the settlement was barely able to maintain itself. Other relatives and friends had begun to leave, some to go away to school, others to seek work in larger cities and towns. Increasingly, the village was populated only by those of the older generation who had been too weak or too frail to consider attempting to survive in the outside world.

Not that Mary Savetsky, Fannie Savetsky, Helen Feldberg, or Molly Sukernek had much contact with the outside world in America. Their lives for the most part were enclosed within the small circle of friends and relations who had come with them from the Pale. The men learned to speak, read, and write enough English to carry on their business affairs, but the women remained totally within the Yiddish orbit. Often their use and understanding of English came by way of their children, who were quickly becoming Americanized in the public schools. The immigrant women worked side by side with their husbands, shopped in stores owned by landsleit and friends, and socialized only among themselves. An excursion out of the neighborhood usually meant a trip to the Lower East Side, perhaps to see a Yiddish movie or to attend the Yiddish theater. They read only Yiddish newspapers and yiddish books, and they avoided, as much as possible, any contact with persons, groups, or institutions that represented the American way of life.

In 1930, the economy of the South Bronx, like that of nearly every other part of the country, deteriorated. Shops closed, workers were laid off, money disappeared. Harry Sukernek's uncle in Buffalo lost his business, and Harry,

Molly, and their daughter moved back to the Bronx. In fact, they moved in briefly with Joseph and Mary Savetsky, whose second child had been born in 1929. The families lived in the same apartment house near Pelham Parkway, and over the next several years were tenants in a number of the same apartment buildings in the neighborhood. Helen and David Feldberg also lived in a number of different apartments during the Depression years, and sometimes shared space with other landsleit. The frequency of the moves resulted from the fact that landlords would offer several months' free occupancy, known as a "concession," in order to keep their buildings filled. When the grace period ended and money was not available to pay the rent, the family would find another landlord who was willing to make a similar concession in the hope that he might later be able to collect rent on the apartment.

Neither the Sukerneks, the two Savetsky families, nor the Feldbergs ever applied to the government for assistance during the 1930s, nor did they have any contact with the major Jewish relief organizations. Had they applied, they certainly would have qualified for aid. But welfare was never seen as a viable option; these people were too proud to admit real poverty, and making such an application would have meant coming into contact with agency bureaucrats and state officials. All their Old World habits, instincts, and experiences warned them to distrust government agencies and officials, and these were attitudes that even the Depression could not break. Instead, they relied even more heavily upon their own circle of landsleit for relief and support. Several families would jam into an apartment designed to hold only one; men who could find work would tell their friends of job openings for others; women shared clothing and sometimes even food. Although they were politically aware, none of the men became active unionists or got deeply involved with political movements designed to improve working conditions. Joseph Savetsky's brother Nathan was a member of the floor-finishers' union and worked both on WPA projects and on the Communist party's construction of the Cooperative Apartments in the Bronx; another landsleit had a cousin who briefly held an office in the Amalgamated Clothing Workers Union. But the petty entrepreneurship that had characterized the careers of Joseph Savetsky, Max Savetsky, Dave Feldberg, and Harry Sukernek in the years before 1930 carried over into the Depression years. The only difference was that the level of entrepreneurship became much more petty.

Mary Savetsky remembers the Depression years too well. At the end of every day they had food, but there were many evenings when they went to bed not sure where the next day's food would come from. "We never had any money," she says, "we just never bought anything at all. The kids always had something to eat, but there were many meals when if Joe ate I had to go without. The Depression was bad, but we lived through worse in the village." Most of the small storeowners who made up the ranks of the Boyerker Society got through the Depression years by living minimally, extending credit to their customers, and operating on a barter basis when cash was not available. At one point, in 1933, things got so slow that Joe Savetsky went to work briefly in a larger store, but he soon was back as the proprietor of a small stand across the street from his apartment house. In the summer of 1934, despite the Depression, Mary, Molly (or Malkie as she was called), and Molly's mother took the kids away to the Catskills for the summer. They rented one room in an old house on the grounds of a bungalow colony, and just as they had earlier in the Bronx, seven people shared a communal toilet and stove. Until their husbands retired from business, this was the only summer vacation the women ever took. The men could not allow themselves the same luxury. They would come up to the mountains on Sunday morning, and return to the city the same night.

As a means of warding off the material and psychological effects of the Depression, the landsmanshaft network was crucial to the lives of all these families. That network was strengthened considerably in 1933, when the women got together and formed an auxiliary, which they called the Boyerker Heimishe Ugent, or Beautiful Young Women of Boyerke. The name was actually chosen by Joe Savetsky's sister-in-law and Mary's first cousin, Pessie Savetsky (who had married Joe's brother Nathan), to distinguish the organization from the many other landsmanshaft auxiliaries that simply gave themselves the same name as the men's organization. From the beginning, the women operated in independent fashion, arranging their own meetings, keeping their own list of members, holding their own social affairs, and choosing a separate slate of officers. They lacked only one element of independence from the men's society, and that was money. Initially the society had a single bank account, and even though separate books were kept for the two organizations, the women's assets remained firmly under the men's control. This situation would later change abruptly, as we shall see.

Even with the addition of the ladies, the Boyerker Society remained a fairly small organization. The society had four main family groupings, and nearly everyone else was related to or close friends of the members of these four branches. The Kruglack family was headed by Benjamin and Sara Kruglack, one of the oldest couples to leave the shtetl and come to America. They were both in their late fifties when they arrived, but they would live on for nearly thirty years in their adopted country. They had three children, Hyman, Lillian, and the youngest sister Elaine. Hyman was married to Celia Feldberg, the sister of David, Paul, and Hyman Feldberg. David Feldberg was married to Helen Cohen, whose mother was the sister of the wife of Hymie Bell. Joe and Hymie Bell had come to New York several years before the rest of the landsleit, and their sister was Molly Sukernek. Finally, Max Savetsky's father was the first cousin of Joe Savetsky's father. These four families—Kruglack, Feldberg, Bell, and Savetsky—together accounted for twenty members of the society.

By the beginning of World War II, the society had begun to move into middle age. Only a few older immigrants, such as the parents of Hyman Kruglack, had come to New York in the 1920s, and that generation had all now passed away. The remaining European-born landsleit were in their late forties or early fifties, and with a few exceptions, they were all still alive. All had married other Jewish immigrants, none had gotten divorced, and nearly all of them still lived in the Bronx. But the war and its aftermath brought change, and slowly but surely this homogeneous, close-knit group began to unravel.

Molly and Harry Sukernek would continue to live on or near Pelham Parkway until Harry died in 1963. Several years later, Molly went to live with her daughter and son-in-law in Queens. Helen and David Feldberg would continue to live in the Bronx for the remainder of their lives. However, in 1949, Max and Fannie Savetsky moved out of the Bronx and down to Lakewood, New Jersey, where Max bought himself a chicken farm. Just before the war, Joe Savetsky's brother Nathan had bought a farm in Lakewood; in rapid succession, four other landsleit families followed

Family Groups in the Boyerker Society

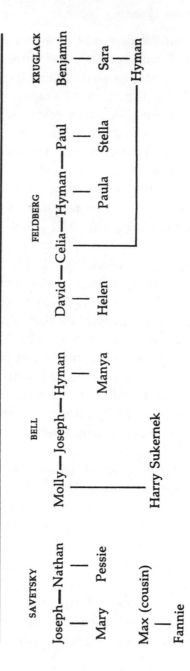

SAVETSKY

Joseph—Nathan
|
Mary   Pessie

Max (cousin)
|
Fannie

Harry Sukernek

BELL

Molly—Joseph—Hyman
|
Manya

FELDBERG

David—Celia—Hyman—Paul
| | |
Helen   Paula   Stella

KRUGLACK

Benjamin
|
Sara
|
Hyman

him down. In fact, for a brief period after Nathan moved to Lakewood, Joe abandoned the fruit and vegetable business and sold door-to-door the eggs from Nathan's farm. Just before the war, Mary and Joe Savetsky set out for new frontiers as well. Joe Bell had opened a small store on the beach in Far Rockaway, Queens, and he persuaded Joe and Mary to set up a fruit store on a nearby block. Far Rockaway was booming; the subway was extended out to the beach, which was fast becoming popular among inner-city Jews as a place to rent summer bungalows and go for weekends. For a few years, Joe and Mary lived in the Bronx, kept a store in Rockaway for the summer, and then returned and rented space on Morris Avenue in the fall. In 1949, however, they moved out of the Bronx entirely and established themselves year-round in Queens.

Several years before this move, Joe Savetsky had finally dropped his resistance and joined the landsmanshaft. He was getting older, he no longer lived in the old neighborhood in the Bronx, and the monthly meetings on Second Avenue were a good opportunity to stay in touch with the old crowd. The society itself was changing as well. The members met as always, but a certain spontaneity was beginning to disappear. The monthly meetings drew a much smaller crowd than previously, and most of the members who had formerly attended on a regular basis now only appeared for special occasions, such as funerals, the annual memorial meeting, the installation of officers in January, or the large Chanukah party at the end of the year. The society continued to charge nominal dues for membership and still assessed each member one dollar to pay for burial expenses when someone died. But the sick fund (which had never dispensed much money anyway) was disbanded, and contributions were now solicited on behalf of the UJA.

Despite these changes, certain basic landsleit traditions and activities remained. The society continued to conduct its meetings entirely in Yiddish and to keep minutes of the meetings in Yiddish as well. The slate of officers elected each year by acclamation still included separate hospitalers for the Bronx and Brooklyn, who were responsible for administrating the sick fund even though it was now defunct. The meetings were as raucous as ever, and the members argued tenaciously and sometimes bitterly over the smallest problems. Most important, as with nearly every other landsmanshaft, the American-born children often joined at the behest of their parents, but they never put in an appearance at meetings or other society functions.

One great breakthrough occurred after the war, however, and in later years it became the stuff of legend within the Boyerker Society. Again in keeping with landsmanshaft custom, the issue was money. Modest as dues were, the society's expenditures were even more modest, and by the end of the war the society's treasury contained several thousand dollars. Not a single member of the society could boast such a large sum in his own bank account, for most of the families probably had never earned more than $3,000 in a single year. The women, who had been contributing money from their own social affairs since the formation of the auxiliary in 1933, decided to ask the men to allow them to establish a separate bank account, a request that provoked a series of extremely lengthy and bitter wrangles. Finally, the women could stand the obstructionist tactics of their husbands no longer. They had spent their lives supporting their men, both within and outside the landsmanshaft, but the question of separate bank accounts had become a matter of principle that transcended everyday affairs. In June 1948, after a series of inconclusive negotiating sessions with the

Boyerker Benevolent Society, the women of the Boyerker Heimishe Ugent took the unprecedented step of hiring a lawyer, who obtained a court injunction requiring the officers of the Boyerker Society to show cause why the women should not be allowed to control their own funds.

The court order was given to Helen Feldberg to serve on the men. But Helen's husband was at that time and had been for many years the financial secretary of the men's organization. Undaunted, Helen came home from the ladies' emergency meeting to find Dave at the corner barbershop getting his weekly haircut and shave. Drawing herself up to her full height of slightly less than five feet tall, Helen marched into the shop and dropped the court order in her husband's lap.

The men quickly capitulated, and the women were finally free to run their own financial operations. But even beyond this short-term victory for the women, the affair had profound long-term consequences for both the Boyerker Benevolent Society and the Boyerker Heimishe Ugent. Dave Feldberg officially remained the financial secretary of the men's organization until his death in 1978. But even though the financial reports for the Boyerker Society were always issued in David's name, it was Helen who actually kept the books and did the accounting for both organizations. In later years, when the two organizations effected a de facto merger for lack of members, the women were already prepared to step in and take over for the men.

The lack of new members began to be felt in the 1950s, a decade marked by the first deaths among the younger immigrant generation and by the continuing geographic dispersion of their children. The first American-born generation was now out of college and well on its way into business and the professions. Few of these Jews spoke Yiddish (none of them could read or write it), hardly any lived in the inner city, and not one was interested in the society's affairs. When one Boyerker's son who was born in 1928 was asked why he never got involved in the society, he gave a typical answer: "I just knew it wasn't for me." This man, like his peers, would have had great difficulty relating to the landsmanshaft milieu. After college he served in the army, went to graduate school in California, and never came back to New York to live.

With the exception of Ida Post's son, who married Ida Goldberg's daughter, not a single member of the first American-born generation married another person whose parents were members of the society. In fact, several children married non-Jews, and several others got divorced. None of the American-born descendants went into business with his parents, and even though many of the children grew up and went all the way through college together, hardly any retained those close associations in later life. Most joined the society to please their parents but came to a meeting only if a parent was installed as an officer, or attended a funeral only if a parent or relative had passed away. None of the American-born children spoke Yiddish as a first or even a second language, even though their parents spoke nothing but Yiddish in the home. When a child got married or when a grandchild was bar-mitzvahed, the Boyerker members turned out in full force. But these were never considered society functions as such, and the society had no role in planning them or carrying them out. When a grandson of a member had his bar mitzvah in a fancy catering place on Long Island, that hall was a far cry in every respect from the room the society rented for its affairs on Second Avenue.

By the end of the 1960s, the society and its members had passed into old age. Molly Sukernek was a widow. Helen Feldberg's husband was feeble and infirm. Fannie and Mary Savetsky were preparing to move with their husbands to year-round residences in Miami Beach. Joe Savetsky had first gone out to Rockaway to run a fruit store when he was in his early forties and the area was a thriving seaside resort. But now Joe and Mary were in their seventies, and the Jews had long since stopped coming out to Rockaway Beach. Jews had even stopped going to the Catskills in great numbers, the younger generation preferring to send the kids away to summer camp while renting beach houses for themselves on Cape Cod and on the shore of Long Island Sound. Like the inner-city neighborhoods from which Jews had fled twenty years earlier, Far Rockaway had become a black ghetto and a "dumping ground" for welfare recipients. The breezy blocks of summer bungalows had been razed, and in their place stood miles of grim housing projects built by the city for the nonwhite poor. Fannie and Max Savetsky were also in their seventies and could no longer run a farm. They lacked the strength and the energy, and the farm lacked profits, since the chicken and egg trade was beginning to succumb to the muscle of large, impersonal agribusinesses. Helen and Dave Feldberg still lived in the Bronx, but Dave rarely left the apartment, and Helen spent most of her time sitting in her daughter's office on Fordham Road. Molly Sukernek continued to live with her daughter and son-in-law, but the addition of two children and the search for more space had taken them out of Flushing and into a larger home on the border between Nassau and Queens.

On January 18, 1969, the Boyerker Society held a forty-fifth anniversary dinner at the Picadilly Hotel in Manhattan. It was the largest and fanciest social event in the entire history of the organization. The society still had 160 family memberships on its rolls, and more than 200 persons turned out for the gala, including nearly all the original members who still lived in New York. For the first (and perhaps the only) time, the room was filled with children and grandchildren of the original members, many of whom were themselves now entering or passing through middle age.

Like all important society functions, the party became an occasion to raise funds for Israel and the UJA. Earlier fundraising campaigns by the organization had built a kindergarten in the kibbutz of Baraket, and now money was needed to complete the construction of a Boyerker-sponsored medical clinic in the village of Even-Sapir. The society had been hooked into the UJA fundraising network since the 1940s, but very few of the original members had ever gone to Israel to view firsthand the results of their charitable work. After the meal was consumed, the speeches and announcements began. In time-honored fashion, they ran on at great length. Every officer and every past officer in attendance was given the honor of standing up and addressing the group. But on this occasion, for the first time in anyone's memory, many of the speeches were given in English, and those who spoke Yiddish first apologized to members of the younger generation for forcing them to sit through an address they would not really understand.

Following the 1969 celebration, another important change began to occur within the ranks of the society. Until that time, the Boyerker Benevolent Society and the Boyerker Heimishe Ugent were still separate organizations, with separate membership lists and separate bank accounts. They also maintained separate slates of officers, although by the mid-1970s they had dispensed entirely with the practice of electing officers and now merely appointed anyone who was still willing to serve. The men's organization no longer had a hospitaler, the last such person having passed away in 1975. Although the two organizations were still separate de jure, they had become, de facto, a single entity. David Feldberg was still the financial secretary for the men, but as noted earlier, Helen kept both sets of books. Yona Sokol had become president of the men's group, and although he presided over the meetings, his wife Esther provided a large measure of support. The few members who attended on a regular basis met as one group and discussed issues in common.

The organization had managed to maintain a fairly stable membership over the years, insofar as the deaths of the original members had been compensated for by children and grandchildren who joined when they were asked. But the society made no effort to bring the younger generation into its activities in any sustained manner, nor would this have been possible. The factors that had kept these people together in a cohesive social unit for sixty years were the same factors that drove their children away. The Boyerker Society, like most of the smaller landsmanshaftn, consisted almost entirely of persons who were always marginal, socially and economically, to the society in which they lived. Most of the members had become petty entrepreneurs by the 1930s, and they would remain petty entrepreneurs until the end of their lives. They ran their little stores in marginal neighborhoods which, over time, turned into black or Hispanic ghettos. They never had the money or the enterprise to "crack" a middle-class neighborhood, and when they moved from one declining section of the inner city they usually ended up in another that would shortly go downhill. Having been unable or unwilling to assimilate, these landsmanshaft Jews were never in a position to alter the basic social formulas they had clung to since the beginning.

Their children were in a position to take a different path. The simple fact that they had been educated in New York presented them with opportunities their parents never had. Not that the second or even the third generation of Boyerkers produced millionaire entrepreneurs. To the contrary, most of the children moved right into the professional middle class, as managers, accountants, attorneys, and educators —the typical escape routes of the first generation of American-born Jews. In the main, their parents encouraged this escape, or at least they did not actively try to prevent it. The children of the original members of Boyerker, men and women alike, all went to school and few, if any, were held back from educational opportunity because they had to join mom and pop in the store. To the extent that a generation gap existed, it was handled by both generations with ease. The older generation made few demands on the children, and the children felt little pressure to conform.

One suspects that the lack of conflict between the generations resulted primarily from the attitudes of the immigrants themselves. If the original Boyerker made no significant effort to bring their children into the society, then they did not really attempt to pass on their immigrant culture to their descendants. Why was this the case? The usual answer is that Jewish immigrants were aware that their cultural values, if transmitted to their children, would inhibit the next generation from assimilating and achieving a measure of social and economic security and success. Or, to put it in more positive fashion, the immigrants "pushed" their children into the mainstream to give them a measure of economic mobility that the Boyerkers themselves would never possess. But this answer assumes that the immigrants who formed such landsmanshaftn were in a position to judge the requirements and demands of a society they hardly knew at all.

The real question posed by the social dichotomy between the landsmen and their children lies in the motives for the formation of the landsmanshaftn themselves. The fact is that while the societies represented a continuation of the Old World, they soon came to represent something else as well. By the time the original members of the Boyerker

Society had become parents and had to face the question of how to raise their children, they no longer possessed the Old World base as a point of reference. Their relatives either had been murdered or displaced by the pogroms or, with any luck, had been rescued and brought over from the other side. The world of the shtetl, the origins of the landsmanshaftn, would soon entirely cease to exist. The societies in America had begun as an outgrowth of the Old World, and now they served the needs of Old World immigrants who were living somewhere else.

The disappearance of the shtetl had profound psychological consequences for the immigrants from the Pale. For one thing, the events of 1919–22 reinforced their fears and suspicions of the outside world and made them, if anything, more careful and deliberate in their choices, expectations, and goals. But the destruction of the Pale also had the effect of removing a considerable burden from the lives of these immigrants, a burden and a responsibility that continue to be imposed on other ethnic populations in America who still retain a European homeland to which they might at some point return. The tenacity of ethnic culture among Greeks and Italians is partially explained by the fact that these communities are continuously bolstered by the arrival of new immigrants. It is also explained by the desire of Greeks and Italians in America to maintain a bridge back to the cultural attitudes and traditions of their respective regions, facilitating their return. To the extent that many ethnic groups consciously create barriers to prevent the complete assimilation of their children, this is done with one eye on America but with the other looking back to the traditional society from where they came. The Jews who formed the landsmanshaftn were not capable of sustaining this dual vision. If they remained in their societies, it was because they had made a decision about assimilation and acculturation that suited themselves. But the Boyerker Society could never truly replace the little shtetl located either east or west of Kiev. That world had come to an end, and neither the Boyerker landsleit nor their children would ever return to it.

Joe Savetsky died in Miami Beach in 1977, but the funeral was held in New York. Fittingly, the service took place at the Gramercy Funeral Home on Second Avenue, just one block away from the old meeting hall, now boarded up, where the society had met for many years. The funeral director was Abe Nagel, whose father Isidore had first become the society's undertaker in 1928. When Abe inherited the business from his father in 1950, he inherited the Boyerker Society as well. Every notice the society sent to its members contained a little message at the bottom of the page, reading "In case of emergency, call I. Nagel." Joe Savetsky was buried in the first grave of the ninth row of male members, alongside the path that separated the men from the women. His wife, as was the custom, will eventually be buried among the ladies on the other side.

Dave Feldberg died in 1978 but was buried in the back of the cemetery in a double grave, of which the other half was reserved for Helen. (In order to raise money to purchase the cemetery, eight original members had been allowed to buy double plots in the back, the only instance when men and women could be buried side by side in the cemetery.) A year after the Feldberg funeral, Max Savetsky passed away, and he too was buried in the back in a double grave. He had been one of the society's earliest presidents, which explained the special burial status accorded him. All four women—Mary, Fannie, Helen, Molly—had outlived their husbands, although Molly, dying in 1978, predeceased the husbands of two of her close friends.

When a member of the society died and was buried in Beth David, it was incumbent upon the officers of the Boyerker Benevolent Society to send a delegation to attend the funeral in an official capacity as representatives of the organization. Sometimes a member would die who had not been active, and family and friends whom nobody had ever seen before would come to the cemetery. But the crowd of mourners always included three or four elderly men who stood somberly apart from the rest, conferred in hushed tones with Nagel, and waited around until everyone else had departed to make sure that the grave was filled up just right.

At the funeral of Max Savetsky, this delegation did not appear. Both the president and the vice-president were too old to come to the cemetery, and the secretary was recuperating from a minor stroke he had suffered while spending the winter in Miami Beach. As Max Savetsky's family arrived at the cemetery and the coffin was unloaded from the hearse, three women led by Helen Feldberg got out of a car and began talking earnestly to Nagel. They were the officers of the Boyerker Heimishe Ugent, and they were now in charge of these important arrangements. When the funeral service was over and the coffin had been lowered into the grave, Helen stood by to make sure that everything was finished up in proper fashion. She then walked over to Fannie Savetsky, now a widow, who was receiving condolences from her family and friends. "It's all done now," she said to the group, "and it's time to leave." She joined the two other officers, Ida Goldberg and Esther Sokol, who had accompanied her on this official mission, and they began to walk back to their car. But as she was getting into the vehicle, Helen paused, turned around slightly, and said with a note of quiet satisfaction, "We are the men now."

Appendix:
The Ethnicity Debate

WHILE this book is primarily an attempt to capture the personal drama and emotions of a particular part of the immigrant population, it cannot avoid touching on complex intellectual issues, of which the question of ethnicity is perhaps the most serious. The seriousness of the issue is underscored by the extensive literature on the topic, most of it dealing with various aspects of assimilation and acculturation.

The ethnicity debate—that is, the debate over the extent to which immigrants assimilated into American culture—was first sparked by the writings of the sociologist Robert Park, whose best-known work is *Race and Culture* (Glencoe: Free Press, 1950). In this work and others, Park posited the notion of a gradual loss of immigrant culture and ethnic identity that paralleled the absorption of immigrants into the American mainstream, a process he examined with reference to trends of ethnic intermarriage and linguistic usage. Park and his followers became known, rightly or wrongly, as the champions of the "melting pot" theory of American culture, although they never attached to their ideas the moral approbation that characterized the exhortations of earlier assimilationist writers during the Great Migration.

The assimilationist or "melting pot" school was at least partially rejected by other scholars who, while acknowledging the tendencies toward cultural homogenization in American society, nevertheless asserted the strength of ethnic cultures in retaining large segments of the pre-migration way of life. Chief among the revisionists were Nathan Glazer and Daniel Moynihan, *Beyond the Melting Pot* (Cambridge, Mass.: MIT Press, 1970); Richard Gambino, *Blood of My Blood* (Garden City, N.Y.: Anchor, 1975); and Michael Novak, *The Rise of the Unmeltable Ethnics* (New York: Macmillan, 1971). A recent work that tries to strike a middle path between these two schools of thought is Stephen Steinberg's *The Ethnic Myth: Race, Ethnicity and Class in America* (Boston: Beacon Press, 1981).

Numerous scholarly monographs compare the experiences of specific ethnic groups. The reader might consult, among others, Josef Barton, *Peasants and Strangers: Italians, Rumanians and Slovaks in an American City, 1890–1950* (Cambridge, Mass.: Harvard University Press, 1975); John Bodnar, *Immigration and Industrialization: Ethnicity in an American Mill Town* (Pittsburgh: University of Pittsburgh Press, 1977); Bodnar's *Lives of Their Own: Blacks, Italians, and Poles in Pittsburgh* (Urbana: University of Illinois Press, 1982); and Ronald Bayor, *Neighbors in Conflict: The Irish, German, Jews, and Italians of New York City, 1929–1941* (Baltimore: Johns Hopkins University Press, 1978).

Studies of particular ethnic groups include Virginia Dominguez, *From Neighbor to Stranger: The Dilemma of Caribbean Peoples in the United States* (New Haven, Conn.: Yale University Press, 1975); Stanford Lyman, *Chinese Americans* (New York:

Random House, 1974); and Virginia Yans-McLaughlin, *Like the Fingers of a Hand: Italian-Americans in Buffalo* (Ithaca, N.Y.: Cornell University Press, 1976). A recent summary of ethnic literature is provided in Thomas Sowell, *Ethnic America: A History* (New York: Basic Books, 1981).

The issue that stands behind the "ethnicity debate" is the extent to which assimilation also promoted economic and social mobility. A work that directly links these phenomena is Thomas Kessner, *The Golden Door: Italian and Jewish Immigrant Mobility in New York City, 1880–1915* (New York: Oxford University Press, 1977). Summing up his research, Kessner argues that "mobility was both rapid and widespread even for immigrants who came from the peasant towns of southern Italy and the Russian Pale" (p. 165). Kessner's conclusions have recently been disputed by Sherry Gorelick, whose research on education and social mobility is cited in chapter 3. Unfortunately, Gorelick and Kessner both deal with the period of the Great Migration and do not extend their research into the contemporary period.

Several works exploring aspects of modern Jewish life should be mentioned. Roberta Strauss Feuerlicht's *The Fate of the Jews* (New York: Times Books, 1983) analyzes the political evolution of the Jewish community with reference both to domestic and foreign affairs. A penetrating analysis of the relationship between modernization and political attitudes among Jews is provided by C. Goldscheider and A. Zuckerman, *The Transformation of the Jews* (Chicago: University of Chicago Press, 1984), and a poignant memoir about growing up as an assimilated Jew can be found in Anne Roiphe, *Generation Without Memory: A Jewish Journey in Christian America* (Boston: Beacon Press, 1982).

While most of the scholarship on the ethnicity debate rests on solid empirical evidence, the judgments imposed on this evidence have reflected, in part, the social and political currents in American society at the time the literature was produced. So, for example, Park's work and the works of his followers reflected the optimism of the 1950s and of the postwar economic boom that had seemingly lifted all segments of American society into the middle class. On the other hand, the revisionist school took its cues from the political and social struggles of the 1960s, when many individuals and groups began to question (and protest against) the "American dream." Just as the 1970s and 1980s have witnessed a reaction against the political and social "excesses" of the 1960s, so the literature on ethnicity has moved back to a middle ground. Recent scholarship tends toward sober examination of specific issues and particular ethnic groups, rather than rendering all-encompassing judgments about society.

This is not to say that a new consensus has arisen among scholars about the history and role of ethnicity within American life. If anything, the ethnicity debate stands at a crossroads, reflecting the extent to which so many traditional social forces and institutions appear to be in temporary disarray. This is not surprising in view of the rapidity of change both in American society and in the basic viewpoints of ethnic scholarship. But it should serve as a warning to any enterprising scholar or reader who feels that he can render judgments in a definitive or timeless manner. If there has been one constant factor in American ethnic history, it is the volatility of the history itself.

Could the history of immigrant populations be otherwise? We look back at the Old World from where the immigrants came, and we see societies, in Oscar Handlin's words, "ponderously balanced in a solid equilibrium for centuries" (*The Uprooted*, 2nd ed. [Boston: Little Brown, 1973], p. 7).

Then we look ahead to America, and everything is in a state of rapid change. As we fix our sights on the contrast between cultures, a human dimension begins to disappear. We cannot fully grasp the vitality, the energy, and the sheer will to survive of the people who moved between such different worlds. So we create terms like "assimilation" and "mobility" to express these survival mechanisms, obscuring the strength and effort required to translate those phrases into human terms. Can ethnic scholars convey to their audience the depths of those experiences? This is the true task that lies ahead.

NOTES

Chapter I

1. YIVO Institute for Jewish Research, Landsmanshaft Archive (hereafter referred to as YIVO-Lands.), carton 901. The Landsmanshaftn Project at the YIVO Institute for Jewish Research, directed by Rosaline Schwartz, gathered materials from over 800 New York societies, and is the major repository for these materials in the United States.

The need to retain familiar cultural traditions as a defense against the traumas of American life was spelled out in a letter to the Yiddish newspaper *The Daily Forward* in 1909: "Sitting in a synagogue among landsleit and listening to the good cantor, I forgot my unhappy weekday life, the dirty shop, my boss, the bloodsucker, and my pale, sick wife and children. All of my America with its hurry up life is forgotten." From Isaac Metzker, ed., *A Bintel Brief* (New York: Behrman House, 1971), p. 101.

2. Particularly relevant on this point are the comments of a radical labor organizer and Yiddish poet, Sam Liptzin:

> Mr. Gaffen had been a butcher in the old country in Galicia. Here in America he was at first a presser, then he became a partner in a "corporation." He was the right man to be a boss in the sweatshop system. His shop was an immigration bureau. It was the first home for many a greenhorn "just off the boat." It was the first place to find your landsleit. Here the decision was made as to what trade an immigrant would follow. Naturally, it was the trade Mr. Gaffen suggested. If Mr. Gaffen happened to be short of an operator at the time, then the immigrant became an operator. If it was a presser that was lacking, then he became a presser.

From *Tales of a Tailor* (New York, 1965), p. 51.

3. See Appendix: The Ethnicity Debate.

4. From "The Town of the Little People," in *Selected Stories of Sholom Aleichem* (New York: Random House, 1966), p. 33.

5. M. Rischin, *The Promised City: New York's Jews, 1870–1914* (Cambridge, Mass.: Harvard University Press, 1962), p. 20.

6. Judah Shapiro, *The Friendly Society: A History of the Workmen's Circle* (New York: Media Judaica, 1970), p. 16. Further information on the demography of Jewish immigration is provided by Salo Baron, *Steeled by Adversity: Essays and Addresses on American Jewish Life* (Philadelphia: Jewish Publication Society of America, 1971), pp. 274–82.

7. The early settlement house movement is one of the multitude of subjects compellingly analyzed in Irving Howe, *World of Our Fathers* (New York: Harcourt Brace Jovanovich, 1976), pp. 90–94. This book, painstaking in detail and rich in content, remains the paradigm for studies of immigrant history in modern America.

Chapter II

1. The basic outlines of Jewish life in Eastern Europe are found in Salo Baron, *The Russian Jews under Tsars and Soviets* (New York: Macmillan, 1974). See also Celia

Notes

Heller, *On the Edge of Destruction: Jews of Poland between the Two World Wars* (New York: Schocken, 1980).

2. The philosopher Martin Buber spent a half century writing about Hasidic beliefs. Most of his basic ideas are summarized in *Hasidism and Modern Man* (New York: Horizon Press, 1958).

3. *Selected Stories of Sholom Aleichem*, p. 28.

4. William Hinton, *Fanshen: A Documentary of Revolution in a Chinese Village* (New York: Vintage, 1966); Oscar Lewis, *Five Families: Case Studies in the Culture of Poverty* (New York: Basic Books, 1959).

5. The section on Aisheshuk is taken from a soon-to-be published work by Ellen Livingston, *Tradition and Modern in the Shtetl: Aisheshuk, 1919–1939*. I wish to thank the author for generously allowing me to quote from this compelling and original work. For a poignant and heartrending view of shtetl life during the interwar period, see also Sheila Friedling, "Wedding in Izhbytze," *Midstream* (March 1984): 42–45.

6. Livingston, *Tradition and Modern in the Shtetl: Aisheshuk, 1919–1939*.

7. Ibid.

8. *Sefer Skala* (New York: Skala Benevolent Society, 1978). The *Sefer Skala* is one of several hundred *Yiskor* (memorial) books in the YIVO archives. These books were written and published by various societies to memorialize the events of the Holocaust. Excerpts from the YIVO collection have been translated and published by Jack Kugelmass and Jonathan Boyarin in *From a Ruined Garden: The Memorial Books of Polish Jewry* (New York: Schocken, 1983).

9. Irving Howe and Eliezer Greenberg, eds., *Voices from the Yiddish* (New York: Schocken, 1975), pp. 100–108.

10. *Selected Stories of Sholom Aleichem*, pp. 31–32.

11. See Donald Mackenzie Wallace, *Russia on the Eve of War and Revolution* (New York: Vintage, 1961).

12. Passages in Gorki's *My Childhood* portray the brutality and primitiveness of rural life in Russia prior to the revolution, and Trotsky devotes a long and incisive section to the backwardness of the rural sector in his *History of the Russian Revolution*. Trotsky's views were no doubt influenced by the anti-peasant mentality of the Bolshevik leadership, exemplified by the following joke, which made the rounds of the revolutionaries in 1920. According to the tale, Trotsky and Lenin decided to assess the morale of the Red Army on a firsthand basis during the civil war. Traveling through the front lines incognito, they came upon a group of peasants, identified as members of the Red Army by the red stars pinned to the sleeves of their homemade uniforms. Trotsky stepped forward and pointedly asked: "Comrades, what do you think of the Bolshevik leadership?" After a hasty conference, one of the group warily replied: "We like Trotsky but we don't trust that Lenin—he's a Jew!"

13. G. T. Robinson, *Rural Russia under the Old Regime* (Berkeley: University of California Press, 1967), p. 2.

14. The village of "San Lucás" does not actually exist. It is a composite of many peasant villages in Spain, derived from anthropological studies such as Julian Pitt-Rivers, *The People of the Sierra* (Chicago: University of Chicago Press, 1961), and David Gilmore, *The People of the Plain* (New York: Columbia University Press, 1980).

15. Diane and David Roskies, *The Shtetl Book* (New York: Ktav, 1979); Mark Zborowski and Elizabeth Herzog, *Life Is With People: The Culture of the Shtetl* (New York: Schocken, 1952).

16. For a general discussion of the rise of Zionism, see Walter Laqueur, *History of Zionism* (New York: Schocken, 1976), pp. 40–83, 270–331. The fundamental work on the intellectual beginnings of Russian dissidence remains Franco Venturi,

Roots of Revolution: A History of the Populist and Socialist Movements in Nineteenth Century Russia (New York: Knopf, 1960). For an analysis of Jewish socialism in pre-Bolshevik Russia, the reader should consult Jonathan Frankel, *Prophecy and Politics: Socialism, Nationalism and the Russian Jews, 1862–1917* (New York: Cambridge University Press, 1981). For specific discussion of Jews and the labor problem, see Henry Tobias, *The Jewish Bund in Russia from Its Origins to 1905* (Stanford, Calif.: Stanford University Press, 1972), and Ezra Mendelsohn, *Class Struggle in the Pale* (Cambridge, Eng.: Cambridge University Press, 1970).

17. Mendelsohn states that the shift from "traditional" to "radical" beliefs among Jewish workers was exemplified by the rise of union organizations, called *kassas*, which evolved out of local chevras (p. 44). The irony here is that after World War I, many New York landsmanshaftn, which also arose out of chevras, sent large amounts of money to support worker and village kassas in Eastern Europe.

18. Rischin, *Promised City*, p. 45.

19. The description of the pogroms is taken from Saul Friedman, *Pogromchik: The Assassination of Simon Petlura* (New York: Hart, 1976), pp. 1–26.

20. A rally in New York City in November 1919 attracted 500,000 persons, and similar demonstrations occurred in Paris, London, Buenos Aires, and other world capitals (ibid., p. 19). The efforts by landsmanshaftn to aid pogrom survivors are examined in Chapter 4.

Chapter III

1. Metzker, ed., *Bintel Brief*, p. 76.

2. Description of the city's economic development from Rischin, *Promised City*, pp. 3–12.

3. An overall synthesis of New York history has yet to be written, but for an analysis of the city's growth just prior to the Great Migration, the reader should consult David Hammack, *Power and Society: Greater New York at the Turn of the Century* (New York: Russell Sage, 1982).

4. There are no exact figures for the number of immigrants who came to New York, but the figures for immigration to America are indicative of trends in the city. The following table shows the number of Italian and Central and East European immigrants who came to America in selected years:

	Italian	Central/East Europe
1885	12,000	47,000
1890	52,000	102,000
1895	35,000	69,000
1900	100,000	210,000
1905	221,000	426,000
1910	215,000	469,000
1914	283,000	565,000
1921	222,000	200,000

SOURCE: *Historical Statistics of the United States* (Washington, D.C.: Government Printing Office, 1975)

Notes

5. For a graphic portrayal of Lower East Side life, see Howe, *World of Our Fathers*, pp. 67–168; Rischin, *Promised City*, pp. 76–94; and Ronald Sanders, *The Downtown Jews: Portraits of an Immigrant Generation* (New York: Harper, 1969).

6. The lack of municipal services for the poor is discussed in Robert Caro, *The Power Broker: Robert Moses and the Fall of New York* (New York: Vintage, 1975), p. 143.

7. Deborah Dash Moore, *At Home in America* (New York: Columbia University Press, 1981), p. 23.

8. A Landesman, *Brownsville: The Birth, Development and Passing of a Jewish Community* (New York: Bloch, 1969).

9. For a comparative analysis of how immigrants to America developed economic and commercial networks within their own communities, see Ivan Light, *Ethnic Enterprise in America: Business and Welfare Among Chinese, Japanese and Blacks* (Berkeley: University of California Press, 1973).

10. Sherry Gorelick, *City College and the Jewish Poor: Education in New York, 1880–1924* (New York: Schocken, 1982), p. 115. Gorelick argues that the ending of immigration after 1922 distorts all the statistics on social mobility because the overall pool of immigrants was no longer being replenished by new waves of semiskilled and laboring immigrants from abroad. She correctly points out that the degree of mobility has been exaggerated as a component of the "melting pot" ideology. But she does not compare the mobility of immigrants in America to their pre-migration experience. Moreover, were it possible to extend the statistics beyond the 1920s, the trends of socioeconomic mobility for Jewish immigrants and their descendants would become even more evident. By the 1950s the Jews were the one ethnic group in America that no longer had a significant representation within the working class. See W. Rubenstein, *The Left, the Right and the Jews* (New York: Universe Books, 1982), pp. 20–26.

11. Moore, *At Home in America*, p. 40.

12. The gradual divorce of work and home was common to all societies and populations that made the transition from preindustrial (rural) to industrial (urban) life. See Peter Laslett, *The World We Have Lost*, rev. ed. (New York: Scribner's, 1984).

13. I. Rontch, ed., *Di yidishe landsmanshaftn fun New York* (New York: Y. L. Peretz Shreiber Ferein, 1938). For an anthropological study of family lineages within immigrant associations, see William E. Mitchell, *Mishpokhe: A Study of New York City Jewish Family Clubs* (New York: Mouton, 1978). Mitchell's study was confined to "family clubs," which arose largely in opposition to the landsmanshaftn. Their membership consisted largely of American-born Jews. Such groups did not have the restrictive membership criteria of the Old World associations, and they reflected the breakdown of traditional social bonds and cultural attitudes among the original immigrant population.

14. Although estimates on the total number of landsmanshaftn vary widely, most authors follow Rontch's figures on the number of societies and the total size of landsmanshaftn membership. Rontch is also cited for the assertion that most societies were formed between 1903 and 1909. But Rontch based his conclusions on answers to a questionnaire sent to landsmanshaftn in 1938. By that time, many of the smaller societies had gone out of business or were impossible to locate. According to Isaac Levitats, "The Jewish Association in America," in *Essays on Jewish Life and Thought* (New York: Columbia University Press, 1959), p. 342, the United Jewish Appeal worked with 3,000 landsmanshaftn and 4,000 other benevolent associations in 1951. Privately, UJA officials have told this author that the pre–World War II figure for landsmanshaftn may have been as high as 6,000.

15. Abraham Cahan, *The Rise of David Levinsky* (New York: Harper, 1960), p. 378.
16. Metzker, *Bintel Brief,* p. 113.
17. *YIVO*-Lands., cart. 1021.

Chapter IV

1. On the history of overseas relief, see Joseph C. Hyman, *Twenty-five Years of American Aid to Jews Overseas* (New York: Jewish Publication Society of America, 1939), and Oscar Handlin, *A Continuing Task: The American Jewish Joint Distribution Committee, 1914–1964* (New York: Random House, 1964).
2. This section and the quotes therein are based on the private papers of Dr. Leff, generously lent to the author by David and Jonathan Leff.
3. Norman Gilmovsky, *My Life, My Destiny* (New York: Cornwall Books, 1984), p. 52.
4. Handlin, *Continuing Task,* pp. 48–49.
5. I. Rontch, "The Present State of the Landsmanschaften," *Jewish Social Science Quarterly,* 15, no. 4 (June 1939): 376.
6. Joint Distribution Committee Archive (hereinafter referred to as *JDC*), file 78.
7. Ibid.
8. Ibid.
9. Ibid.
10. Ibid.
11. Ibid.
12. Ibid.
13. Ibid., file 80a.
14. Ibid., file 81.
15. Ibid.
16. Ibid., file 80a.
17. Ibid., file 123.
18. Ibid., file 80a.
19. Ibid., file 79.
20. Ibid., file 81.
21. Ibid.
22. Ibid., file 123.

Chapter V

1. Arthur A. Goren, *New York Jews and the Quest for Community: The Kehillah Experiment, 1908–1922* (New York: Columbia University Press, 1970), p. 7.
2. See Eric Wolf, *Peasants* (Englewood Cliffs, N.J.: Prentice-Hall, 1966), for a survey of anthropological literature on rural regions worldwide. A recent update on the structure of peasant society is provided by James C. Scott, *The Moral Economy of the Peasant* (New Haven, Conn.: Yale University Press, 1979).
3. Goren, p. 49.
4. Ibid., p. 47.
5. *The Jewish Communal Register of New York City* (New York: Kehillah, 1918). The

Notes

various statistics on Jewish organizations presented in this chapter are drawn from this volume.

6. Ibid., p. 860.

7. Goren, p. 47.

8. Rischin, *Promised City*, p. 183.

9. The "suburbanization" of Jewish cemeteries culminated in 1934 with the opening of Mt. Ararat Cemetery in Suffolk County. From its beginnings, this cemetery refused to sell any plots to societies, instead offering plots to individuals or families only.

10. Gerard R. Wolfe, *The Synagogues of New York's Lower East Side* (New York: New York University Press, 1978).

Chapter VI

1. YIVO, JDC Archive (hereinafter cited as YIVO-JDC), carton 25, file 672.

2. The literature on the Holocaust is extensive, but the most comprehensive works still remain Lucy S. Dawidowicz, *The War Against the Jews, 1933–1945* (New York: Holt, Rinehart & Winston, 1975); Raul Hilberg, *The Destruction of the European Jews* (Chicago: Quadrangle, 1967); and Nora Levin, *The Holocaust* (New York: Schocken, 1973).

3. Aside from the letters and accounts of the massacres that are preserved in archival sources, much of the information on specific incidents during the Holocaust is taken from Martin Gilbert, *Atlas of the Holocaust* (London: Michael Joseph, 1982).

4. Handlin, *Continuing Task*, p. 49.

5. YIVO-JDC, cart. 38, file 984.

6. YIVO Landsmanshaft Archive (hereinafter cited as YIVO-Lands.), cart. 1039.

7. YIVO-JDC, cart. 5, file 159.

8. Ibid., cart. 11, file 416.

9. Joseph J. Schwartz and Beatrice I. Vulcan, "Overseas Aid," in *The American Jew: A Reappraisal*, edited by Oscar Janowsky (Philadelphia: Jewish Publication Society of America, 1964), pp. 289–90.

10. YIVO JDC, cart. 26, file 695.

11. Ibid., cart. 4, file 38.

12. Ibid., cart. 3, file 26.

13. Ibid., cart 18, file 516.

14. Ibid., cart. 22, file 704.

15. Ibid., cart. 18, file 532.

16. Ibid., cart. 2, file 34.

17. Ibid., cart. 3, file 821.

18. Ibid., cart. 28, file 717.

19. Ibid., cart. 3, file 40.

20. Ibid., cart. 24, file 658.

21. Ibid., cart. 42.

22. Ibid., cart. 24, file 666.

23. Melvin Urofsky, *We Are One! American Jewry and Israel* (Garden City, N.Y.: Doubleday, 1978). See also David S. Wyman, *The Abandonment of the Jews: America and the Holocaust, 1941–1945* (New York: Pantheon, 1984).

Notes

24. Lucy S. Dawidowicz, "American Jews and the Holocaust," *New York Times Magazine* (April 18, 1982).
25. Rubenstein, *The Left, the Right and the Jews,* pp. 24–26.

Chapter VII

1. Data on population and geographical dispersion from Moore, *At Home in America,* and C. Morris Horowitz and Lawrence J. Kaplan, *The Jewish Population of the New York Area, 1900–1975* (New York: Federation of Jewish Philanthropies, 1959).
2. YIVO-Lands., cart. 957.
3. Moore, *At Home in America,* pp. 23–24.
4. YIVO-Lands., cart. 827.
5. Ibid., cart. 901.
6. Data in the following table compiled from Horowitz and Kaplan, *The Jewish Population of the New York Area, 1900–1975,* pp. 22–25.
7. The 1980 population figures are from a survey conducted by the Federation of Jewish Philanthropies.
8. Horowitz and Kaplan, p. 82.
9. YIVO-Lands., cart. 932.
10. For a brief description of the South Beach community, see Ann Banks, "Miami Beach Tries to be Venice," *Mother Jones* (November 1976): 11–12.
11. The yearly report of the Amalgamated Clothing Workers Union, *Proceedings,* contained a breakdown of every ethnic group represented by the membership. As late as 1940, the list contained virtually every nationality within Eastern and Central Europe. The Amalgamated stopped publishing this list in 1948.
12. The section on Jewish centers is taken from Moore, *At Home in America,* pp. 123–47.
13. Ibid., pp. 95–98.
14. Norman Podhoretz, *Making It* (New York: Random House, 1967), pp. 42–43.
15. YIVO-Lands., cart. 926.
16. Ibid., cart. 937.
17. Ibid., cart. 814.

INDEX